SINISTER
SELF-DEFENSE
MASTER THE ART OF DEADLY SELF-DEFENSE

SAMMY FRANCO

Also by Sammy Franco

Engage With Rage
War Machine II
1001 Street Fighting Secrets: The Principles of Contemporary Fighting Arts
Combat Pressure Points
Cane Fighting
Double End Bag Training
The Heavy Bag Bible
The Widow Maker Compendium
Invincible: Mental Toughness Techniques for Peak Performance
Unleash Hell: A Step-by-Step Guide to Devastating Widow Maker Combinations
Feral Fighting: Advanced Widow Maker Fighting Techniques
The Widow Maker Program: Extreme Self-Defense for Deadly Force Situations
Savage Street Fighting: Tactical Savagery as a Last Resort
Heavy Bag Combinations
Heavy Bag Training
The Complete Body Opponent Bag Book
Stand and Deliver: A Street Warrior's Guide to Tactical Combat Stances
Maximum Damage: Hidden Secrets Behind Brutal Fighting Combinations
First Strike: End a Fight in Ten Seconds or Less
The Bigger They Are, The Harder They Fall
Self-Defense Tips and Tricks
Kubotan Power: Quick & Simple Steps to Mastering the Kubotan Keychain
Gun Safety: For Home Defense and Concealed Carry
Out of the Cage: A Guide to Beating a Mixed Martial Artist on the Street
Warrior Wisdom: Inspiring Ideas from the World's Greatest Warriors
War Machine: How to Transform Yourself Into a Vicious Street Fighter
When Seconds Count: Self-Defense for the Real World
Killer Instinct: Unarmed Combat for Street Survival
Street Lethal: Unarmed Urban Combat

Sinister Self-Defense: Master the Art of Deadly Self-Defense
Copyright © 2024 by Sammy Franco
ISBN: 978-1-941845-90-5
Printed in the United States of America
Visit online at: ContemporaryFightingArts.com

In a world of shadows, strength lies not in avoiding the darkness but in mastering it.

SINISTER SELF-DEFENSE

Contents

Disclaimer

The author, publisher, and distributors of Sinister Self-Defense expressly disclaim any and all liability or responsibility for any injuries, damages, or losses that may result from the practice, instruction, or application of the techniques and concepts contained within this book. By engaging with the material presented, you acknowledge and fully assume all risks and responsibilities for any outcomes, and agree that neither the author, publisher, distributors, nor contributors shall be held liable for any claims, damages, costs, or legal consequences arising from your use of the information provided.

It is your sole responsibility to research, understand, and comply with all applicable local, state, and federal laws concerning the use of self-defense tools and techniques. This book is intended solely for educational and informational purposes and should not be construed as legal or professional advice.

Before participating in any physical activities or exercises described in this book, consult with a qualified physician to ensure you are medically fit to do so. The techniques and training methods discussed are physically demanding and may not be suitable for individuals with pre-existing health conditions. This book is not intended to diagnose, treat, or manage any medical conditions or injuries.

About This Book

In a world where violent crime can strike without warning, the ability to defend yourself and your loved ones is not an option - it's a necessity. *Sinister Self-Defense* provides instruction on the most extreme and effective self-defense methodologies developed from my combat system, Contemporary Fighting Arts (CFA).

Unlike traditional martial arts or Mixed Martial Arts, which emphasize tradition, sport, and controlled environments, this book is about real-world survival. It equips you with the knowledge, skills, and mindset to confront life-threatening violence with overwhelming force and effectiveness.

The title *Sinister Self-Defense* was chosen to reflect the dark reality of life-and-death situations where self-defense is not merely survival but dominance. The word "sinister" embodies the extreme and unorthodox techniques in this book - methods designed to end violent confrontations swiftly and decisively. It also represents the significant shift in mindset necessary for this level of combat: a willingness to embrace tactics others might find uncomfortable or morally ambiguous, but which are essential when your life, or the life of a loved one, is at stake.

What sets *Sinister Self-Defense* apart is its focus on integrating extreme combat techniques into a fluid, cohesive fighting system. The goal is to teach the law-abiding citizen how to seamlessly transition between various fighting methods based on the level of threat, allowing you to scale your use-of-force as needed. Whether facing a minor confrontation or a deadly attack, this book equips you to respond with the appropriate level of force at each stage of the altercation.

Chapter One lays the foundation for the self-defense tactics and techniques in this book. Before mastering advanced fighting methodologies, you must understand the essentials:

stances, body weapons, combat attributes, footwork, target zones, ranges of unarmed combat, defensive skills, and mental toughness.

Chapter Two delves into the First Strike Principle—a decisive concept that often separates survival from defeat. This principle centers on one critical truth: in real combat, the first to strike gains a commanding advantage. Here, you'll master the mindset and tactics to act with precision and preemptively deliver a debilitating blow, neutralizing your attacker before they have the chance to respond.

Chapter Three covers Combat Pressure Points, a tactical escalation of force that combines pinpoint devastation with overwhelming effectiveness. While the First Strike method delivers powerful and overwhelming blows, Combat Pressure Points target specific areas of the body to incapacitate an assailant quickly, regardless of their size or strength, using minimal effort to end the confrontation.

Chapter Four introduces the Widow Maker Program, a revolutionary combat methodology that unleashes extreme force in response to imminent, life-threatening attacks. Brutal and unrelenting, this unorthodox fighting style does more than incapacitate; it instills deep psychological terror in the adversary, swiftly transforming the predator into prey.

Chapter Five focuses on Savage Street Fighting Tactics, a ferocious approach to real-world self-defense. In the chaotic and ruthless environment of the streets, there are no rules. This chapter teaches the most vicious and effective techniques for facing the direst self-defense situations.

The purpose of *Sinister Self-Defense* is to prepare you for the full spectrum of self-defense, from non-lethal situations to deadly criminal attacks. This is not a book for sport or competition; it addresses scenarios where extreme force may be necessary, but also offers non-lethal methods for situations that require less force. You will learn how to respond appropriately, whatever the level of danger.

When deadly force is involved, the stakes are even higher. Deadly force is any action that creates a substantial risk of death or serious bodily harm. As a law-abiding citizen, you may use deadly force only to counter an unlawful threat of deadly force. The techniques in this book are lethal and should only be used when you or a loved one is in immediate danger of death or serious injury.

Using deadly force must always be a last resort. All other means of avoiding violence should be exhausted before engaging in extreme physical retaliation. These techniques are not about dominance or ego; they are about survival in the face of an unlawful, immediate threat.

This book is also a skill-building tool, meant to be studied and practiced. As you read each chapter, take notes, underline key passages, and return to sections that resonate with you. Learning these deadly serious techniques is an ongoing process, and for best results, read the book cover to cover before using it as a reference guide.

Finally, the tactics and techniques in this book are dangerous and should only be used in life-threatening situations. With the power to save lives comes great responsibility. These methods are not to be taken lightly and must always be a last resort, used only when all attempts to avoid or defuse the confrontation have failed.

Finally, I urge you to "walk in peace." The goal of learning self-defense is not to seek violence, but to be prepared when it finds you. Be mindful of the power these techniques give you, and use them responsibly, always with the intent of protecting yourself and others from harm.

Sammy Franco
Founder & President
Contemporary Fighting Arts

SINISTER SELF-DEFENSE

INTRODUCTION
Contemporary Fighting Arts
The Evolution of Survival Combat

SINISTER SELF-DEFENSE

Exploring Contemporary Fighting Arts

Before you dive into this book, I'd like to introduce you to my unique system of fighting, Contemporary Fighting Arts (CFA). For those of you new to CFA, this introduction will give you a deeper understanding and appreciation of the material covered in this book. If you're already familiar with CFA, feel free to jump straight into Chapter One.

Contemporary Fighting Arts® (CFA) is a state-of-the-art combat system designed specifically for real-world self-defense. This practical and highly effective system is built to help individuals avoid, defuse, confront, and neutralize armed and unarmed assailants in deadly situations.

Unlike traditional martial arts such as karate, kung-fu, or mixed martial arts, CFA is the first offensive-based American martial art tailored for the brutal realities of street violence. It eliminates unnecessary techniques and rituals, focusing purely on the practicalities of street fighting.

Every CFA technique must meet three essential criteria: efficiency, effectiveness, and safety. Efficiency ensures that techniques achieve the combative objective swiftly and economically. Effectiveness guarantees that each technique produces the desired result. Safety means the methods employed minimize the risk and danger to you, the fighter.

CFA isn't about tournaments, competition, or performing forms (katas). There are no theatrical kicks or exotic moves. This system doesn't adhere to tradition for tradition's sake; it's a scientific and pragmatic approach designed to help you survive on the streets.

Over the years, CFA has been taught to individuals from all walks of life, including federal, state and local law enforcement personnel, security guards, military personnel, black belts, boxers, MMA fighters, and many others. CFA's appeal lies in its ability to teach people how to truly fight.

The Meaning Behind CFA's Name

Before discussing the three components that make up Contemporary Fighting Arts, it is important to understand how CFA acquired its unique name. To begin, the first word, "Contemporary," was selected because it refers to the system's modern, up-to-date orientation. Unlike traditional martial arts, CFA is specifically designed to meet the challenges of our modern world.

The second term, "Fighting," was chosen because it accurately describes the system's combat orientation. After all, why not just call it Contemporary Martial Arts? There are two reasons for this. First, the word "martial" conjures up images of traditional and impractical martial art forms that are antithetical to the system. Second, why dilute a perfectly functional name when the word "fighting" defines the system so succinctly? Contemporary Fighting Arts is about teaching people how to really fight.

Let's look at the last word, "Arts." In the subjective sense, "art" refers to the combat skills that are acquired through arduous study, practice, and observation. The bottom line is that effective street fighting skills will require consistent practice and attention. Take, for example, something as seemingly basic as an elbow strike, which will actually require hundreds of hours of practice to perfect.

The pluralization of the word "Art" reflects CFA's protean instruction. The various components of CFA's training (i.e., firearms training, stick fighting, ground fighting, natural body weapon mastery, and so on) have all truly earned their status as individual art forms and, as such, require years of study and practice to perfect. To acquire a greater understanding of CFA, here's an overview of the system's three vital components: the physical, the mental, and the spiritual.

The Physical Component

The physical component of CFA focuses on the physical development of a fighter, including physical fitness, weapon and technique mastery, and self-defense attributes.

Physical Fitness

If you are going to prevail in a combat situation, you must be physically fit. It's that simple. In fact, you will never master the tools and skills of combat unless you're in excellent physical shape. On the average, you will have to spend more than an hour a day to achieve maximum fitness.

In CFA physical fitness comprises the following three broad components: cardiorespiratory conditioning, muscular/skeletal conditioning, and proper body composition.

The cardiorespiratory system includes the heart, lungs, and circulatory system, which undergo tremendous stress during the course of a high-stakes self-defense situation. So you're going to have to run, jog, bike, swim, or skip rope to develop sound cardiorespiratory conditioning. Each aerobic workout should last a minimum of 30 minutes and be performed at least four times per week.

5

The second component of physical fitness is muscular/ skeletal conditioning. In the streets, the strong survive and the rest go to the morgue. To strengthen your bones and muscles to withstand the rigors of a real fight, your program must include progressive resistance (weight training) and calisthenics. You will also need a stretching program designed to loosen up every muscle group. You can't kick, punch, ground fight, or otherwise execute the necessary body mechanics if you're "tight" or inflexible. Stretching on a regular basis will also increase the muscles' range of motion, improve circulation, reduce the possibility of injury, and relieve daily stress.

The final component of physical fitness is proper body composition: simply, the ratio of fat to lean body tissue. Your diet and training regimen will affect your level or percentage of body fat significantly. A sensible and consistent exercise program accompanied by a healthy and balanced diet will facilitate proper body composition. Do not neglect this important aspect of physical fitness.

Weapon and Technique Mastery

You won't stand a chance against a vicious assailant if you don't master the techniques of fighting. In CFA, we teach our students both armed and unarmed methods of combat. Unarmed fighting requires that you master a complete arsenal of natural body weapons and techniques. In conjunction, you must also learn the various stances, hand positioning, footwork, body mechanics, defensive structure, locks, chokes, and various holds. Keep in mind that something as simple as a basic punch will actually require hundreds of hours to perfect.

Range proficiency is another important aspect of weapon and technique mastery. Briefly, range proficiency is the ability to fight effectively in all three ranges of unarmed fighting (kicking, punching and grappling).

CFA also teaches a myriad of chokes, locks, and holds that

can be used during a ground fight. While such grappling range submission techniques are not the most preferred methods of dealing with a ground fighting situation, they must be developed.

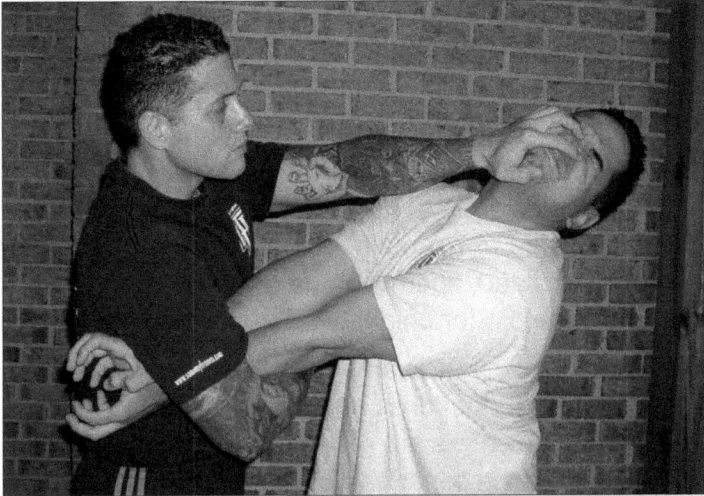

Defensive tools and skills are also taught. Our defensive structure is efficient and uncomplicated. It provides the fighter maximum protection while allowing complete freedom of choice for acquiring offensive control. Our defensive structure is based on distance, parrying, blocking, evading, mobility, and stance structure. Simplicity is always the key.

Students are also instructed in specific methods of armed fighting. For example, CFA provides instruction about firearms for personal and household protection. We provide specific guidelines for handgun purchasing, operation, nomenclature, proper caliber, shooting fundamentals, cleaning, and safe storage. Our firearm program also focuses on owner responsibility and the legal ramifications regarding the use of deadly force.

CFA's weapons program also consists of kubotans, knives, single and double stick, tactical canes, makeshift weaponry, the side-handle baton, and oleoresin capsicum (OC) spray.

Combat Attributes

Your offensive and defensive tools are useless unless they are used strategically. For any tool or technique to be effective in a real fight, it must be accompanied by specific attributes. Attributes are qualities that enhance a particular tool, technique, or maneuver. Some examples include speed, power, timing, coordination, accuracy, non-telegraphic movement, balance, and target orientation.

CFA also has a wide variety of training drills and methodologies designed to develop and sharpen these combat attributes. For example, our students learn to ground fight while blindfolded, spar with one arm tied down, and engage in combat under uniquely adverse conditions.

Reality is the key. For example, in class students participate in full-contact drills against fully padded assailants, and real weapon disarms are rehearsed and analyzed in a variety of dangerous scenarios. Students also train with a large variety of equipment, including heavy bags, double-end bags, uppercut bags, pummel bags, focus mitts, striking shields, mirrors, rattan sticks, training bats, kicking pads, knife drones, trigger-sensitive (mock) guns, full-body armor, and numerous environmental props.

There are more than two hundred unique training methodologies used in Contemporary Fighting Arts. Each one is scientifically designed to prepare students for the hard-core realities of real world combat. There are also three specific training methodologies used to develop and sharpen the fundamental attributes and skills of armed and unarmed fighting, including proficiency training, conditioning training, and street training.

Proficiency training can be used for both armed and unarmed skills. When conducted properly, proficiency training develops speed, power, accuracy, non-telegraphic movement, balance, and general psychomotor skill. The training objective is to sharpen one specific body weapon, maneuver, or technique at a time by executing it over and over for a prescribed number of repetitions. Each time the technique or maneuver is executed with "clean" form at various speeds. Movements are also performed with the eyes closed to develop a kinesthetic "feel" for the action. Proficiency training can be accomplished through the use of various types of equipment, including the heavy bag, double-end bag, focus mitts, training knives, real and mock pistols, striking shields, shin and knee guards, foam and plastic bats, mannequin heads, and so on.

Conditioning training develops endurance, fluidity, rhythm, distancing, timing, speed, footwork, and balance. In most cases, this type of training requires the student to deliver a variety of fighting combinations for three- or four-minute rounds separated by 30-second breaks. Like proficiency training, this type of training can also be performed at various speeds. A good workout consists of at least five rounds. Conditioning training can be performed on the bags with full-contact sparring gear, rubber training knives, focus mitts, kicking shields, and shin guards, or against imaginary assailants in shadow fighting.

Conditioning training is not necessarily limited to just three-

or four-minute rounds. For example, CFA's ground fighting training can last as long as 30 minutes. The bottom line is that it all depends on what you are training for.

Street training is the final preparation for the real thing. Since many violent altercations are explosive, lasting an average of 20 seconds, you must prepare for this possible scenario. This means delivering explosive and powerful compound attacks with vicious intent for approximately 20 seconds, resting one minute, and then repeating the process.

Street training prepares you for the stress and immediate fatigue of a real fight. It also develops speed, power, explosiveness, target selection and recognition, timing, footwork, pacing, and breath control. You should practice this methodology in different lighting, on different terrains, and in different environmental settings. You can use different types of training equipment as well. For example, you can prepare yourself for multiple assailants by having your training partners attack you with from a variety of angles, ranges, and target postures.

When all is said and done, the physical component creates a fighter who is physically fit and armed with an arsenal of techniques that can be deployed with destructive results.

The Mental Component

The mental component of CFA focuses on the cerebral aspects of a fighter, developing killer instinct, strategic/tactical awareness, analysis and integration skills, philosophy, and cognitive skills.

The Killer Instinct

Deep within each of us is a cold and deadly primal power known as the "killer instinct." The killer instinct is a vicious combat mentality that surges to your consciousness and turns you into a fierce fighter who is free of fear, anger, and apprehension. If you want to survive the horrifying dynamics of real criminal violence, you must cultivate and utilize this instinctive killer mentality.

Visualization and crisis rehearsal are just two techniques used to develop, refine, and channel this extraordinary source of strength and energy so that it can be used to its full potential.

Strategic/Tactical Awareness

Strategy is the bedrock of preparedness. In CFA, there are three categories of strategic awareness that will diminish the likelihood of criminal victimization. They are criminal awareness, situational awareness, and self-awareness.

When developed, these essential skills prepare you to assess a wide variety of threats instantaneously and accurately. Once you've made a proper threat assessment, you will be able to choose one of the following five self-defense options: comply, escape, de-escalate, assert, or fight back.

CFA also teaches students to assess a variety of other important factors, including the assailant's demeanor, intent, range, positioning and weapon capability, as well as such environmental issues as escape routes, barriers, terrain, and makeshift weaponry. In addition to assessment skills, CFA also teaches students how to enhance perception and observation skills.

Analysis and Integration Skills

The analytical process is intricately linked to understanding how to defend yourself in any threatening situation. If you want to be the best, every aspect of fighting and personal protection must be dissected. Every strategy, tactic, movement, and concept must be broken down to its atomic parts. The three planes (physical, mental, spiritual) of self-defense must be unified scientifically through arduous practice and constant exploration.

CFA's most advanced practitioners have sound insight and understanding of a wide range of sciences and disciplines. They include human anatomy, kinesiology, criminal justice, sociology, kinesics, proxemics, combat physics, emergency medicine, crisis management, histrionics, police and military science, the psychology of aggression, and the role of archetypes.

Analytical exercises are also a regular part of CFA training. For example, we conduct problem-solving sessions involving particular assailants attacking in defined environments. We move hypothetical attackers through various ranges to provide insight into tactical solutions. We scrutinize different methods of attack for their general utility in combat. We also discuss the legal ramifications of self-defense on a frequent basis.

In addition to problem-solving sessions, students are slowly exposed to concepts of integration and modification. Oral and written examinations are given to measure intellectual accomplishment. Unlike other systems, CFA does not use colored belts or sashes to identify the student's level of proficiency.

Philosophy

Philosophical resolution is essential to a fighter's mental confidence and clarity. Anyone learning the art of combat must find the ultimate answers to questions concerning the use of violence in defense of himself or others.

To advance to the highest levels of combat awareness, you must find clear answers to such provocative questions as: Could you take the life of another? What are your fears? Why are you interested in studying Contemporary Fighting Arts? Why are you reading this book? And what is good, and what is evil? If you haven't begun the quest to formulate these important questions and answers, then take a break. It's time to figure out just why you want to know the laws and rules of combat.

Cognitive Combat Skills

Cognitive combat exercises are also important for improving one's fighting skills. CFA uses visualization and crisis rehearsal scenarios to improve general body mechanics, tools and techniques, and maneuvers, as well as tactic selection. Mental clarity, concentration, and emotional control are also developed to enhance one's ability to call upon the controlled killer instinct.

The Spiritual Component

There are many tough fighters out there. In fact, they reside in every town in every country. However, most are nothing more than brutes lacking self-mastery. And self-mastery is what separates the true warrior from the eternal novice.

I am not referring to religious precepts or beliefs when I speak of CFA's spiritual component. Unlike some martial arts, CFA does not merge religion into its spiritual aspect. Religion is a very personal and private matter and should never, be incorporated into any fighting system.

CFA's spiritual component is not something that is taught or studied. Rather, it is that which transcends the physical and mental aspects of being and reality. There is a deeper part of each of us that is a tremendous source of truth and accomplishment.

In CFA, the spiritual component is something that is slowly and progressively acquired. During the challenging quest of combat training, one begins to tap the higher qualities of human nature. Those elements of our being that inherently enable us to know right from wrong and good from evil. As we slowly develop this aspect of our total self, we begin to strengthen qualities profoundly important to the "truth." Such qualities are essential to your growth through the mastery of inner peace, the clarity of your vision, and your recognition of universal truths.

One of the goals of my system is to promote virtue and moral responsibility in people who have extreme capacities for physical and mental destructiveness. The spiritual component of fighting is truly the most difficult aspect of personal growth. Yet, unlike the physical component, where the practitioner's abilities will be limited to some degree by genetics and other natural factors, the spiritual component of combat offers unlimited potential for growth and development.

In the final analysis, CFA's spiritual component poses the greatest challenges for the student. It is an open-ended plane of unlimited advancement.

CHAPTER ONE
The Core Skills of Self-Defense

SINISTER SELF-DEFENSE

BUILDING YOUR COMBAT FOUNDATION

In the world of self-defense, mastering the fundamentals is akin to laying a strong foundation before building a fortress. Without a solid foundation, even the most basic techniques will crumble under pressure.

This chapter is designed to provide that critical foundation, covering the essential stances, offensive skills, and core principles that are the backbone of any effective combat system. Just as a house built on shaky ground cannot withstand a storm, a fighter lacking a mastery of the basics will falter when faced with real-world threats.

The techniques in this chapter lay the groundwork for everything else in the book. Ranges of combat, stances, and footwork provide the essential structure, mobility, and spatial awareness needed for effective fighting. Understanding targeting helps you identify and exploit vulnerable areas, while combat attributes like speed, timing, and power ensure that your movements are both efficient and effective. Defensive techniques are equally critical, enabling you to protect yourself while maintaining control of the encounter. Additionally, mental toughness plays a pivotal role, allowing you to stay composed under pressure, make quick decisions, and remain resilient in the face of adversity. These foundational elements - both physical and mental - are practical skills that will allow you to execute more advanced techniques with confidence and safety throughout the course of this book.

Think of these fundamentals as the roots of a tree. Without strong, deeply ingrained roots, the tree itself cannot grow strong or resilient. Similarly, mastering these core self-defense principles ensures that your more advanced combat skills will be grounded in solid, reliable tactics.

By focusing first on these essentials, you are not only preparing yourself for success in the heat of battle but also ensuring that your self-defense abilities will stand the test of time and adversity.

RANGES OF COMBAT

Before you can effectively apply the stances and techniques in the following chapters, it's crucial to grasp the concept of range or distancing. Range refers to the spatial relationship between you and your adversary, both before and during combat.

When evaluating your adversary, you must assess the strategic advantages and limitations of their range. For instance, are they close enough to land a punch, or are they positioned far enough to evade your strike?

In hand-to-hand combat, there are three primary ranges:

- **Kicking range**
- **Punching range**
- **Grappling range**

However, before delving into these specific fighting ranges, it's essential to first understand the Neutral zone.

THE NEUTRAL ZONE

The Neutral Zone is the distance at which neither you nor your assailant can strike or kick one another. The key advantage of this zone is that it creates space between you and the attacker, giving you valuable reaction time to defend yourself. In simple terms, it buys you time to respond effectively.

However, don't become complacent - certain situations or environments may not allow you the luxury of maintaining a neutral zone.

From a tactical standpoint, the neutral zone serves several key purposes:

- To safely assess a potential threat.
- To de-escalate a hostile individual.
- To assert yourself from a safe distance.
- To create an opportunity for strategic repositioning or retreat.
- To manage multiple potential threats.

KICKING RANGE

At Kicking Range, the distance between you and your opponent is too great to effectively use your hands, so you must rely on your legs to strike. Kicking from this range allows you to maintain a safer distance while still delivering powerful strikes. However, in real-world combat, it's essential to focus on low-line kicks, which target areas below the waist. This is because high kicks, while impressive in controlled sport settings, can leave you vulnerable to counterattacks and are less practical in unpredictable street combat situations.

Low-line kicks are aimed at vulnerable areas like the groin, thigh, knee joint, and shinbone, all of which can severely impair your adversary's ability to continue fighting. These targets are both effective and accessible, minimizing your own exposure to retaliation. Striking low also allows you to maintain balance and stability, giving you a better chance to recover quickly if the fight shifts to another range.

Effective low-line kicks include techniques such as:

• **Side Kick:** Targeting the shin or knee to cause injury as well as disrupt balance and inhibit mobility.

• **Push Kick:** A forceful kick to the thigh, knee or shin, designed to create distance or knock the opponent off balance.

• **Hook Kick:** Used to strike the side of the knee or thigh, aiming to destabilize or incapacitate the opponent.

• **Vertical Kick:** A straight upward kick, often aimed at the groin to incapacitate the adversary.

These kicks are practical, powerful, and efficient in real-world scenarios, allowing you to maintain control while minimizing the risk of exposure to counterattacks.

PUNCHING RANGE

Punching Range represents the mid-range of unarmed combat, where you are close enough to engage your adversary with hand strikes. At this distance, your hands and fists become your primary tools for both offense and defense.

This range allows for quick, direct strikes that can disrupt your opponent's balance, create openings, or inflict significant damage.

In real-world self-defense, punching range techniques must be quick, efficient, and effective, as they form the core of any successful compound attack. The key to dominating at this range is speed and precision - each strike should be delivered with purpose and minimal telegraphing to prevent your opponent from anticipating or countering your movements. This requires mastering both hand speed and accuracy, ensuring that each punch reaches its target with maximum impact and minimal waste of energy.

At punching range, your strikes should focus on key vulnerable target areas. However, your punches should be combined with proper body mechanics - utilizing your hips, shoulders, and legs to generate power. This makes your strikes not only faster but also far more devastating.

Incorporating punches into compound attacks is crucial at this range. Compound attacks involve combining various strikes in rapid succession, overwhelming your opponent with a barrage of hand techniques. These attacks should flow seamlessly, transitioning from one strike to the next to keep your adversary on the defensive, reducing his ability to retaliate.

Punching range techniques include:

• **Lead Straight:** Fast, precise strike delivered from the lead arm.

• **Rear Cross:** Powerful straight punch from the rear arm that disrupts your opponent's defense or knocks them out.

• **Hooks:** Circular punches targeting the side of the head or body, ideal for exploiting openings in your opponent's guard.

• **Uppercuts:** Punches that target the chin or solar plexus, perfect for close-quarters encounters.

Ultimately, mastery of punching range techniques gives you control over the fight's momentum. By delivering efficient, well-placed punches, you can disrupt your adversary's strategy and set yourself up for successful follow-up strikes or transitions into other ranges of combat.

GRAPPLING RANGE

The third and closest range of unarmed combat is the Grappling Range, also known as Close-Quarter Combat (CQC). At this distance, your opponent is far too close for you to effectively use kicks or most punching techniques. Instead, you rely on close-quarters techniques and strikes that are specifically designed to work in tight, confined spaces where you have limited movement.

In real-world confrontations, grappling distance is one of the most challenging ranges, as physical proximity to your assailant means that every second counts and every move can either secure your advantage or expose your vulnerabilities.

Grappling range allows you to employ strikes, submissions,

and holds that are impossible in kicking or punching ranges. It's not about distance-based attacks, but rather about controlling your opponent, gaining leverage, and delivering devastating strikes at point-blank range. Grappling range can be divided into two distinct planes of combat: the *vertical plane* and the *horizontal plane.*

Vertical Plane (Clinch Range)

In the vertical plane, often referred to as *clinch range*, you are standing upright but extremely close to your opponent. In this scenario, the primary weapons become elbows, knees, head butts, and other impact-based techniques.

Clinching allows you to control your opponent's movements by restricting his ability to deliver effective strikes, while also positioning yourself to land powerful blows. In the clinch, you can disrupt his balance, tie up his arms, and create openings for quick, brutal strikes. Techniques like knee strikes or elbows are devastating and can rapidly turn the tide of a fight.

Horizontal Plane (Ground Fighting)

The horizontal plane occurs when both you and your opponent have gone to the ground. At this level, the fight becomes even more intense and physical, as you work to dominate through grappling, submissions, and positional control. Whether it's through securing a dominant position like the full mount, or applying submission techniques such as chokeholds and joint locks, ground fighting is about timing and control. You must use your body weight, leverage, and knowledge of positioning to neutralize your opponent while simultaneously protecting yourself from counterattacks.

Mastering close-quarter combat (CQC) means being comfortable in both vertical and horizontal planes, knowing how to transition smoothly between them, and using your environment to your advantage.

Whether you are standing toe-to-toe with your adversary or grappling on the ground, understanding the dynamics of grappling range is essential for surviving and dominating real-world self-defense encounters.

STANCES

A skilled self-defense practitioner will never position themselves directly in front of their opponent. Whenever possible, he will aim to adopt a strategic stance or posture. The stance you assume dictates your ability to attack or defend, playing a critical role in determining the outcome of any self-defense encounter.

Stances are vital in combat as they minimize your exposure as a target, improve balance, enhance mobility, and significantly boost your striking power.

However, it's important to recognize that in some self-defense situations, you may not have the luxury of assuming a proper stance. Therefore, always be prepared to execute your offensive and defensive techniques without relying on a foundational structure. With that in mind, let's begin with the natural stance.

NATURAL STANCE

The *natural stance* is ideal when approached by someone who seems non-threatening but suspicious, like a stranger or passerby. Angle your body at 45 degrees, with feet shoulder-width apart and knees slightly bent. Keep your hands in front, moving casually—rubbing your hands or scratching your wrist—to protect your upper body without appearing aggressive. Stay relaxed but alert, avoiding tension in your shoulders, neck, and arms. This stance allows you to maintain readiness while appearing non-confrontational.

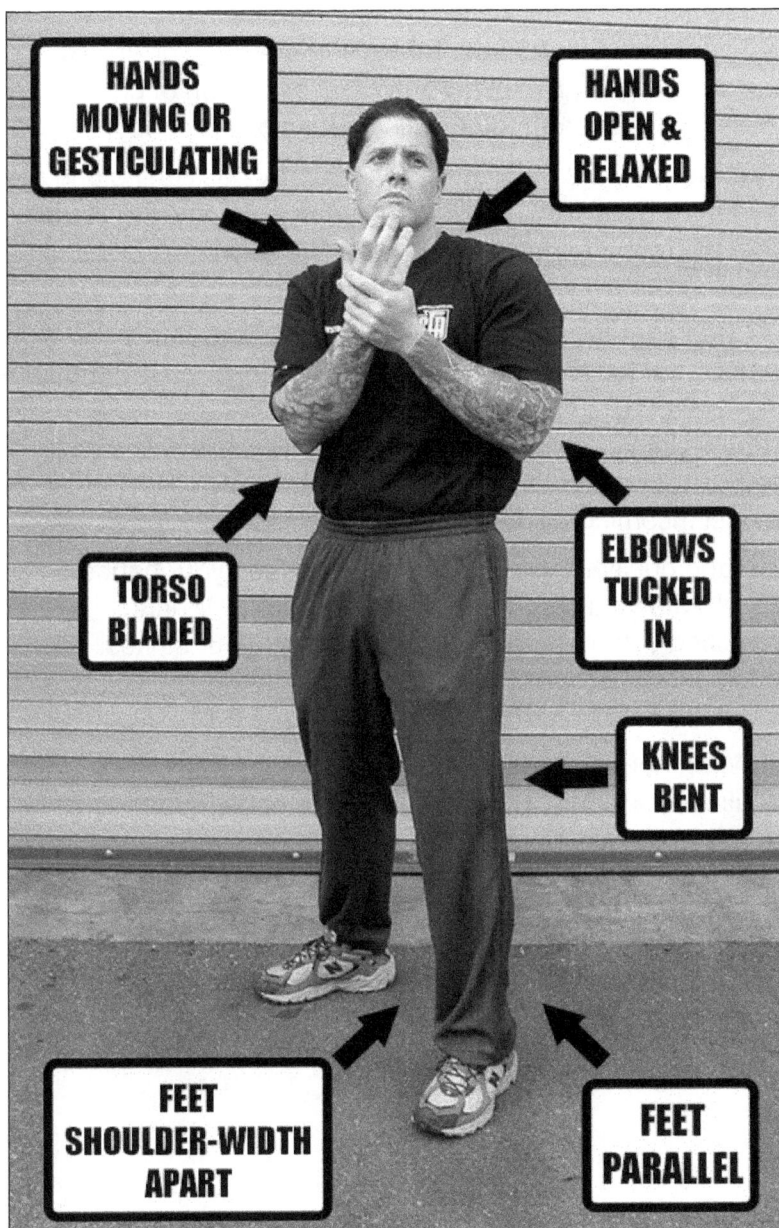

HANDS MOVING OR GESTICULATING

HANDS OPEN & RELAXED

TORSO BLADED

ELBOWS TUCKED IN

KNEES BENT

FEET SHOULDER-WIDTH APART

FEET PARALLEL

FIGHTING STANCE

The *fighting stance* is a strategic, aggressive posture designed to maximize your offensive potential while protecting your vital targets. It allows for optimal execution of compound attacks while safeguarding critical areas of your body.

To assume the fighting stance, start by positioning one side of your body forward, angling both your body and feet at 45 degrees from your assailant to minimize exposure to direct strikes (see photo on opposite page).

Keep your feet shoulder-width apart and slightly bend both knees. Your legs should act as power springs, enabling quick transitions through various ranges of combat. Aim for an even 50-50 weight distribution to maintain agility, allowing you to move in any direction while staying stable and ready to defend against incoming attacks.

Hand positioning is equally crucial. Keep your hands raised, with your lead hand in front of your rear hand, protecting your centerline while setting up your strikes. Your hands should be loosely fisted, fingers curled, and wrists straight to avoid tension and maintain speed.

When holding your guard, avoid tightening your neck, shoulders, or arms, and keep your chin angled down to reduce the risk of a strike to your chin or windpipe. This stance combines protection with readiness, ensuring you're prepared for both offensive and defensive maneuvers.

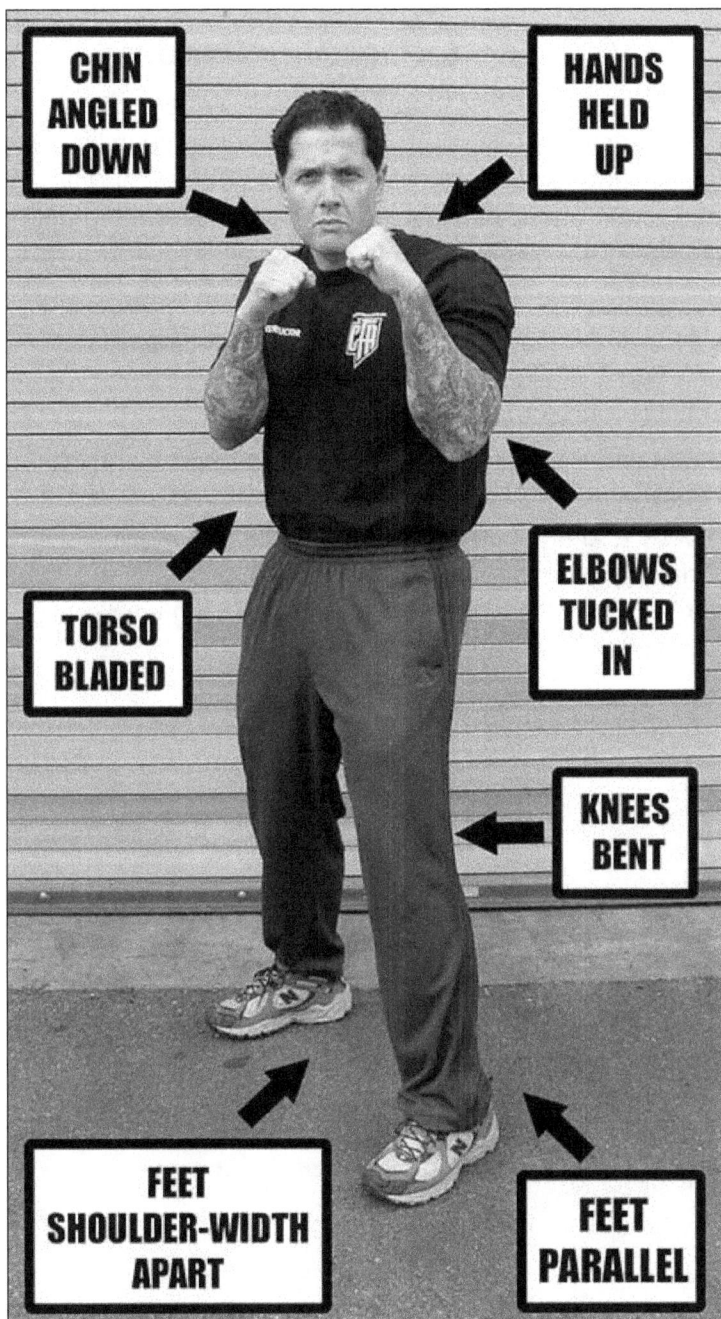

CHIN ANGLED DOWN

HANDS HELD UP

TORSO BLADED

ELBOWS TUCKED IN

KNEES BENT

FEET SHOULDER-WIDTH APART

FEET PARALLEL

DE-ESCALATION STANCE
(Kicking & Punching Ranges)

The *de-escalation stance* is used when attempting to defuse a hostile situation. To assume this stance in kicking and punching ranges, begin by angling your body at roughly 45 degrees from the adversary (refer to the photo on the opposite page).

Keep your feet shoulder-width apart, with knees slightly bent and your weight evenly distributed. Your hands should remain open, relaxed, and raised to protect the upper targets of your centerline.

Maintain an upright posture with your torso, pelvis, head, and back aligned. Stay calm, relaxed, and in control of both your body and emotions. Avoid any muscular tension, especially in your shoulders, neck, arms, or thighs, as this can hinder your breathing and movement, draining your energy and limiting your ability to respond quickly.

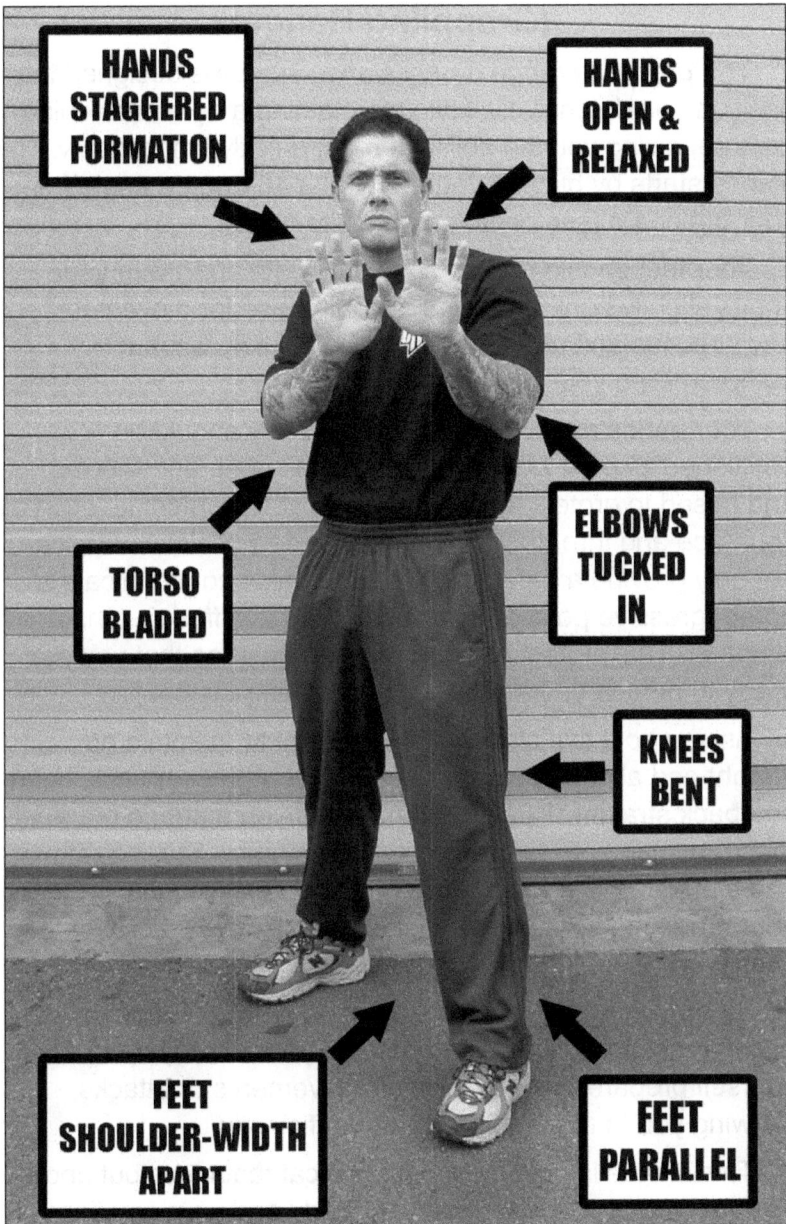

HANDS STAGGERED FORMATION

HANDS OPEN & RELAXED

TORSO BLADED

ELBOWS TUCKED IN

KNEES BENT

FEET SHOULDER-WIDTH APART

FEET PARALLEL

DE-ESCALATION STANCE
(Grappling Range)

The *grappling range de-escalation stance* is designed to position you defensively while maintaining a non-threatening posture, giving you the ability to react quickly if necessary. This stance starts by blading your body at a 45-degree angle from your opponent (see photo on opposite page).

Your feet should remain shoulder-width apart with your knees slightly bent, providing a stable base for movement in any direction and allowing you to react fluidly without compromising your balance.

Your hands are key in this stance. They should be positioned side-by-side, with your palms open and relaxed, and raised to protect the vital areas of your centerline, such as your face and throat. Open hands in a de-escalation stance not only provide a defensive shield but also communicate a non-aggressive posture, which can help to diffuse a tense situation. This protective hand position ensures that you are ready to defend yourself without escalating the conflict.

As you hold this stance, it's important to maintain an upright and aligned posture - keeping your torso, pelvis, head, and back straight. This alignment gives you a strong physical foundation and reinforces mental composure. Staying relaxed and alert is essential, as tension in your muscles can restrict your breathing and reduce your ability to move quickly or evasively.

By remaining loose and fluid, particularly in your shoulders, neck, arms, and thighs, you preserve your energy and keep yourself prepared for any sudden movements or attacks, allowing you to respond swiftly and efficiently.

This stance is not just about physical readiness but about maintaining control over both your body and your emotions, ensuring that you can act decisively if the situation escalates.

HANDS
SIDE BY SIDE

HANDS
OPEN &
RELAXED

TORSO
OPEN

ELBOWS
TUCKED
IN

KNEES
BENT

FEET
SHOULDER-WIDTH
APART

FEET
PARALLEL

THE FIRST STRIKE STANCE

The *First Strike stance* is identical in form to the de-escalation stances, with the key difference being your *intent:* rather than focusing solely on defense or diffusing a situation, you are now preparing to preemptively launch an attack.

The stance positions your body at a 45-degree angle to your opponent, feet shoulder-width apart, knees slightly bent, and hands raised to protect your centerline. This physical posture remains non-threatening to avoid escalating the situation prematurely, but it puts you in the ideal position to strike swiftly and decisively.

The primary purpose of the First Strike stance is to allow you to initiate an attack before your adversary has a chance to act, gaining the upper hand. Your mindset should shift from one of defense to controlled aggression, ready to deliver a preemptive blow if the situation warrants.

This stance is designed to minimize telegraphing your intentions, keeping your opponent unaware of your readiness to strike. By maintaining a calm and non-aggressive appearance, while mentally preparing for immediate action, you set yourself up to catch your opponent off-guard, delivering a quick and decisive strike before they can react.

FOOTWORK

A skilled self-defense practitioner must be able to move quickly and efficiently. Mobility is essential, as it allows you to maneuver your body with speed, balance and control. This is achieved through basic footwork, which involves taking swift, economical steps while staying balanced and relaxed, always moving on the balls of your feet.

The Basics of Footwork

Footwork serves both offensive and defensive purposes, and it revolves around four primary directions: advancing, retreating, sidestepping to the right, and sidestepping to the left.

Moving Forward (Advancing): From your stance, bring your front foot forward by approximately 24 inches, followed by your rear foot, moving the same distance.

Moving Backward (Retreating): From your stance, bring your rear foot back by approximately 24 inches, then move your front foot the same distance to maintain balance.

Moving Right (Sidestepping Right): From your stance, move your right foot 24 inches to the right, followed by your left foot, covering the same distance.

Moving Left (Sidestepping Left): From your stance, move your left foot 24 inches to the left, then bring your right foot an equal distance to follow.

To master these movements, practice them daily in front of a full-length mirror until your footwork becomes quick, balanced, and second nature. Refer to the following photos for demonstrations of proper footwork in action.

TO ADVANCE: From the starting position, first move your front foot forward (approximately 24 inches) and then move your rear foot an equal distance.

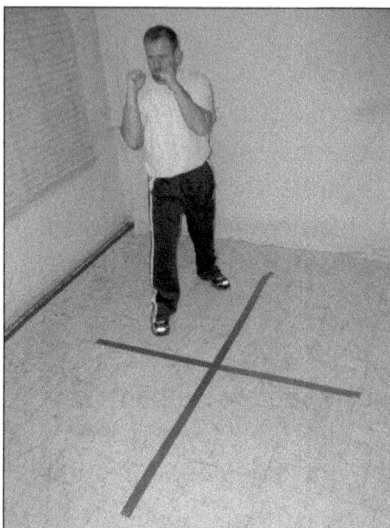

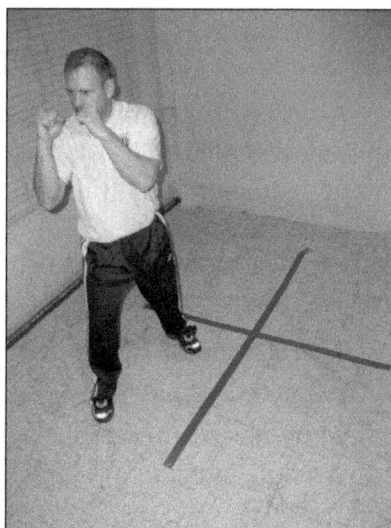

TO RETREAT: From your stance, first move your rear foot backward (approximately 24 inches) and then move your front foot an equal distance.

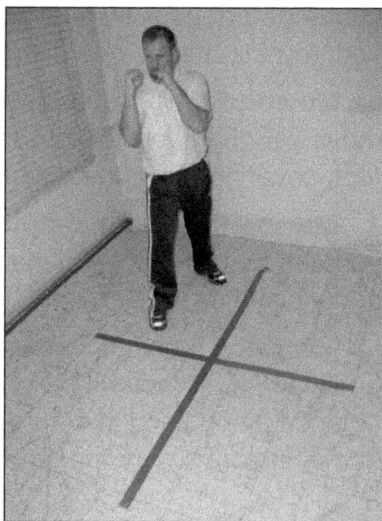

MOVING RIGHT (sidestepping right): From a stance, first move your right foot to the right (approximately 24 inches), and then move your left foot an equal distance.

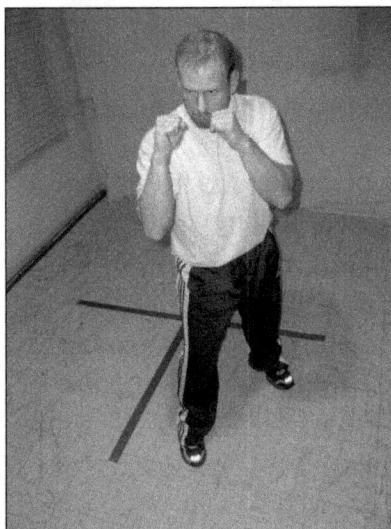

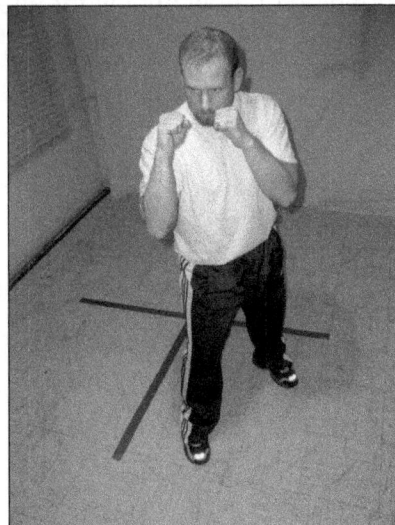

MOVING LEFT (sidestepping left): From a stance, first move your left foot to the left (approximately 24 inches) and then move your left foot an equal distance.

ADVANCED FOOTWORK

After mastering basic footwork, you can begin incorporating strategic circling into your skill set. Strategic circling is an advanced form of footwork that uses your lead leg as a pivot point, allowing you to maneuver with efficiency.

This footwork can be used both defensively, to evade an overwhelming attack, or offensively, to strike your opponent from advantageous angles. It can be performed from either a right or left stance, giving you flexibility in combat.

Circling Right (from a right stance): Starting in a right lead stance, step 8 to 12 inches to the right with your right foot. Use your right leg as a pivot and rotate your rear leg to the right until you've returned to a proper stance and position. Remember to keep your hands up at all times for protection.

Circling Left (from a left stance): Starting in a left lead stance, step 8 to 12 inches to the left with your left foot. Use your left leg as a pivot, swinging your rear leg to the left until you've achieved the correct stance and positioning.

Again, this advanced footwork allows you to move fluidly around your opponent, maintaining balance and control while opening up new angles for attack or defense.

COMBAT ATTRIBUTES

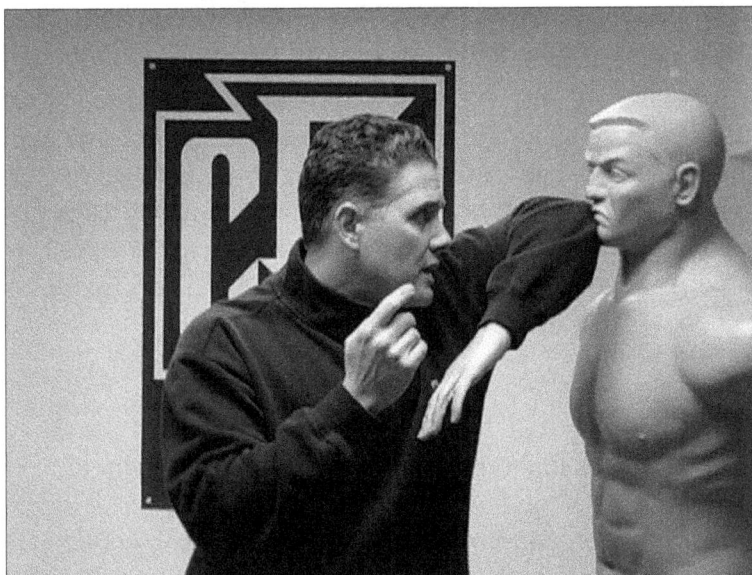

For any fighting technique to be truly effective, it must incorporate essential combat attributes. These qualities enhance the efficiency and effectiveness of your techniques, turning a basic strike into a powerful, precise tool.

Key attributes like speed, power, timing, non-telegraphic movement, rhythm, coordination, accuracy, balance, and range specificity all play a critical role in determining the success of a self-defense technique in high-risk combat situation.

While there are many more attributes to consider, I will focus on five fundamental ones: speed, power, timing, balance, and non-telegraphic movement.

Speed

To land an effective strike, you must possess speed. Speed refers to how quickly your body weapon reaches its target. A fast strike should be like a snake's bite - felt before it's seen.

While some people naturally have great speed, you can maximize your potential by training. One way to enhance speed is by relaxing your body before executing a strike.

For example, when delivering a palm heel strike to the chin, your arm should shoot out and back with no muscular tension. Though it sounds simple, many people struggle to stay relaxed under the stress of fighting. Another way to develop blinding speed is to practice throwing your strikes quickly in the air, focusing on fast execution and retraction. With consistent practice, you will see significant improvement.

Power

Power refers to the impact force you generate when striking a target. Power doesn't rely solely on size or strength - a smaller person can deliver devastating strikes by combining speed with proper technique. This is why a well-trained fighter, like a small hammer striking with precise force, can break through tougher materials just as easily as a heavier one swinging without focus. The key is to use speed and technique to maximize impact.

To generate maximum power, drive your entire body into the blow and aim beyond your target. Well-timed footwork, along with a strong rotation of your hips and shoulders, will further increase force. In self-defense, your strike should land with the impact of a 12-gauge shotgun, not a pellet gun.

Timing

Timing is your ability to execute a strike or other combat movement at the perfect moment. There are two types of timing: defensive and offensive. Defensive timing is the time between your assailant's attack and your defensive response. Offensive timing is the time between recognizing an opening and delivering your attack.

To develop timing, train with stick and knife fighting, sparring, double-end bags, and focus mitt drills. Mental visualization is also a powerful tool - imagining self-defense scenarios that require precise timing helps improve your fighting instincts.

Balance

To attack and defend effectively, you must maintain balance throughout your movements. Balance is your ability to stay in control whether stationary or moving. This requires mastering body mechanics, controlling your center of gravity, and maintaining proper skeletal alignment.

To develop balance, practice your techniques slowly to become familiar with how your weight shifts during each strike. For example, when executing an elbow strike, keep your head, torso, and legs properly aligned, following through the target without overextending.

Non-Telegraphic Movement

Surprise is one of the most valuable tools in self-defense, especially during a first strike scenario. A successful strike relies on avoiding telegraphing your intentions to the assailant. Common telegraphing cues like clenching your teeth, widening your eyes, cocking your fist, or tensing your shoulders can alert your opponent.

To eliminate telegraphic movements, maintain a poker face and avoid giving away any cues before executing a technique. Practicing in front of a mirror or reviewing video recordings of yourself can help identify and eliminate these signals. Patience and practice will help you master this crucial fighting attribute.

TARGETING

Knowing how and when to strike your enemy is crucial for street survival, but knowing *where* to hit is just as vital. It's like knowing how to swing a hammer but not aiming at the nail— you won't get the job done. Anyone serious about neutralizing a violent attacker in a self-defense crisis must understand the vulnerable body targets on the human anatomy.

Contrary to popular belief, the human body has numerous weak points that are highly susceptible to attack. It's not built to withstand the kind of punishment that a well-placed strike can deliver. Think of it like a chain: no matter how strong the chain is, it will always have a weak link. Similarly, no matter the size, strength, skill, or mental state of your attacker, they will always have vulnerable targets that can be exploited.

It's important to mention that every martial artist, self-defense practitioner, and combat instructor has a moral and legal responsibility to understand the medical implications of their offensive techniques. You must know which targets can stun, incapacitate, disfigure, cripple, or even kill an adversary. This knowledge will not only help you make informed decisions in a self-defense scenario but will also make you a more efficient and responsible self-defense technician.

Unfortunately, there are some misguided martial arts and self-defense instructors who teach ineffective striking targets. For example, hitting the biceps, collarbone, chest, kidneys, or coronal suture yields poor results in a real fight. These targets won't neutralize a violent criminal - they'll likely only anger him, provoking a more vicious and determined response.

This is why it's essential to strike anatomical targets that will immediately incapacitate the enemy. Anything less could leave you seriously injured or even dead. The key targets on your opponent are divided into three zones:

Zone 1 (Head Region): Targets related to the senses, such as the eyes, temples, nose, chin, and back of the neck.

Zone 2 (Neck, Torso, Groin): Targets that affect breathing and vital functions, including the throat, solar plexus, ribs, and groin.

Zone 3 (Legs and Feet): Targets that affect mobility, such as the thighs, knees, shins, insteps, and toes.

Now, let's take a closer look at these anatomical targets and explore the medical implications of striking each one.

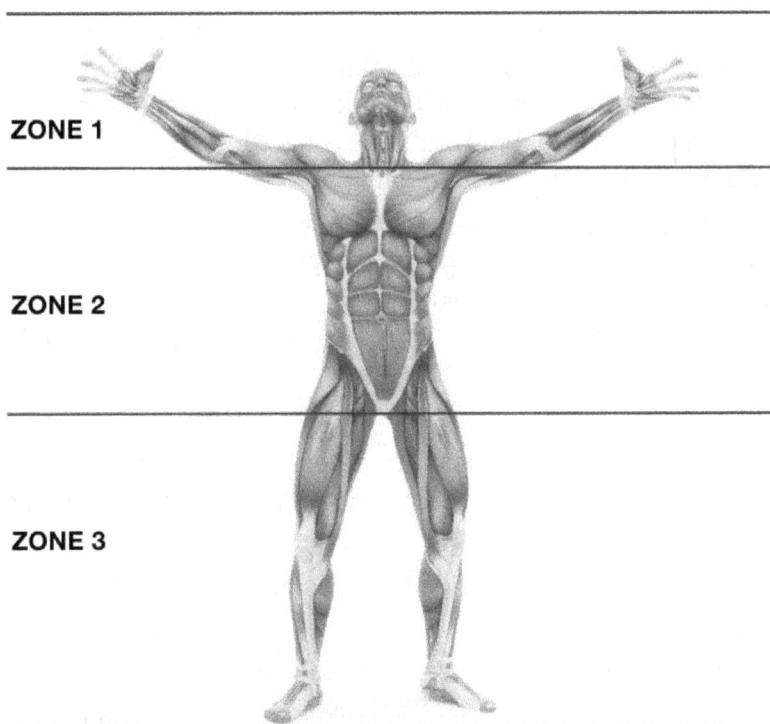

ZONE 1

ZONE 2

ZONE 3

EYES

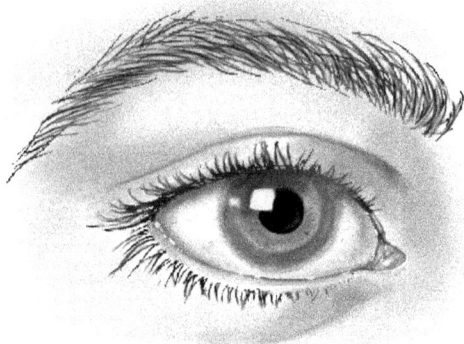

The eyes, nestled within the orbital sockets of the skull, are among the most vulnerable and vital targets in street combat. These delicate organs are essential for your assailant to fight effectively, and their sensitivity makes them an ideal focal point for self-defense. Not only are the eyes extremely difficult to protect, but they also require minimal force to damage.

Eye strikes can be delivered from various angles - whether poking, clawing, or gouging - each with devastating effects. Even a light strike can cause intense watering, blurred vision, or temporary blindness, while more forceful blows can result in hemorrhaging, permanent blindness, ruptured tissue, excruciating pain, and shock or unconsciousness.

The common reactions to a well-executed eye strike are predictable and provide a crucial opening for further attack or escape. Your assailant may:

• Bend forward, closing his eyes shut while screaming in pain.

• Instinctively cover his eyes with his hands.

• Freeze in shock, momentarily paralyzed by the pain.

In combat, targeting the eyes not only incapacitates your opponent but also shifts the entire dynamic in your favor.

EARS

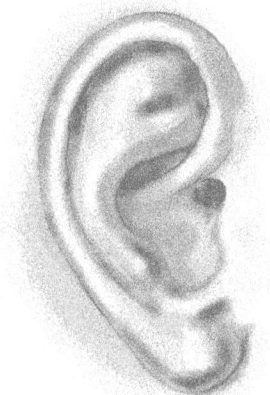

Like the eyes, the ears are extremely sensitive to attack. The opponent's ears can be punched, popped and torn. When struck with a moderate amount of force, the tympanic membrane (eardrum) will easily rupture.

Striking the ear can also result in percussive shock, extreme pain, unconsciousness, partial or complete loss of hearing, bleeding, disorientation, and loss of balance. You can use the following body weapons to attack the ears: cupped palm strike, punches, elbow strikes, and in some cases, the knee strike.

The assailant's probable reaction dynamic from a well targeted ear strike may include the following:

- He bends forward, covers his ears.

- He collapses to the ground.

- He freezes from shock, momentarily paralyzed by the pain.

45

TEMPLE

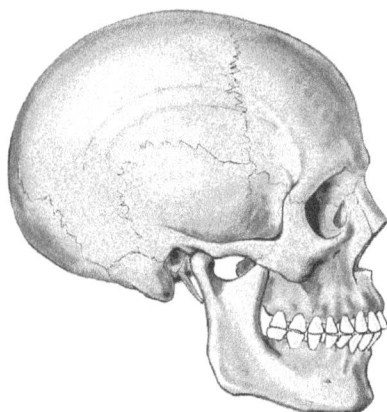

The temple or sphenoid bone is a thin, weak bone located on both sides of the skull approximately one inch from the assailant's eye. Because of its inherently weak structure and close proximity to the brain, a very powerful strike to this anatomical target can be deadly.

Other possible injuries include unconsciousness, hemorrhage, concussion, shock, and coma. You can use the following body weapons to strike the assailant's temple: elbow strikes, hook punches and in some cases the knee strike.

The opponent's probable reaction dynamic from a strike to the temple may include the following:

- His head and body fall sideways.
- His torso becomes exposed.
- His eyes shut from the impact.
- His arms and hands drop.
- He's knocked out cold.

NOSE

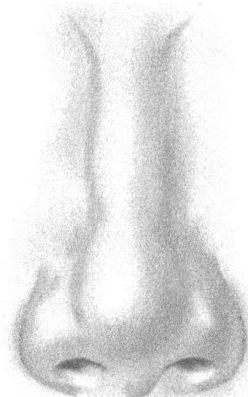

The nose is made up of a thin bone, cartilage, numerous blood vessels, and many nerves. It is a particularly good impact target because it stands out from the assailant's face and can be struck from three different directions (up, straight, down).

A moderate blow can cause stunning pain, watering of the eyes, temporary blindness, and hemorrhaging. A powerful strike can result in shock and unconsciousness. Lead straights, rear crosses, palm heels, upper cuts, hammer fists, elbow and knee strikes can be delivered effectively to the assailant's nose.

The opponent's probable reaction dynamic from a nose strike may include the following:

• He bends forward.

• He shuts his eyes.

• He covers his face with both his hands.

• He becomes temporarily immobilized.

• If temporary blindness occurs, he might grab hold of you.

CHIN

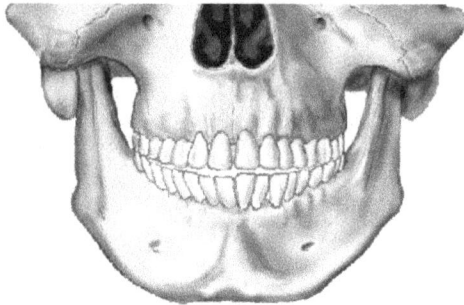

In boxing, the chin is often referred to as the "knockout button," a vulnerable target that has ended the careers of countless fighters. It's also an excellent target in unarmed combat. A well-placed strike to the chin at a forty-five-degree angle can send shockwaves to the brain's cerebellum and cerebral hemispheres, causing paralysis and immediate unconsciousness.

Depending on the force of the strike, additional injuries may include a broken jaw, a concussion, or whiplash to the neck. Some of the most effective body weapons for targeting the chin include uppercuts, elbow strikes, knee strikes, palm heels, and even head butts.

The opponent's probable reaction dynamic from a powerful chin strike may include the following:

- His head reels backward.
- His throat and torso become exposed.
- His centerline opens up.
- His arms and hands drop.
- He's knocked out cold.

BACK OF NECK

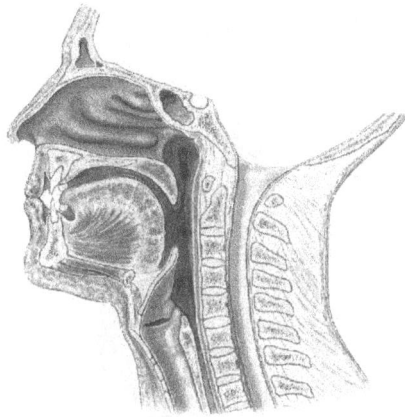

The back of the assailant's neck, composed of the first seven vertebrae - known as the cervical vertebrae - serves as a crucial conduit for nerve impulses between the brain and the body. This area is highly vulnerable in combat due to the limited protection surrounding the vertebrae, making it a potentially lethal target.

A well-executed and forceful strike to the cervical vertebrae can result in severe outcomes, including shock, unconsciousness, a broken neck, paralysis, coma, or even death. Among the most effective body weapons for targeting this region are hammer fists and elbow strikes, both capable of delivering significant impact to this sensitive area.

The assailant's probable reaction dynamic from a powerful strike to the back of the neck may include the following:

• His head drops forward.

• His arms and hands drop.

• He's knocked out cold.

THROAT

The throat is a highly vulnerable area, protected by only a thin layer of skin and containing vital structures such as the thyroid, hyaline, and cricoid cartilage, as well as the trachea and larynx. The trachea, or windpipe, is a cylindrical tube about 4 ½ inches long and roughly one inch in diameter.

A powerful, direct strike to the throat can lead to severe consequences, including unconsciousness, blood drowning, massive hemorrhaging, air deprivation, and potentially death. Crushing the thyroid cartilage can cause rapid swelling of the windpipe, leading to suffocation and death.

The probable reaction dynamics of an assailant following a throat strike may include:

• His head and body dropping forward.

• Instinctively grabbing or covering his throat with both hands.

• Struggling for air or going into shock.

SOLAR PLEXUS

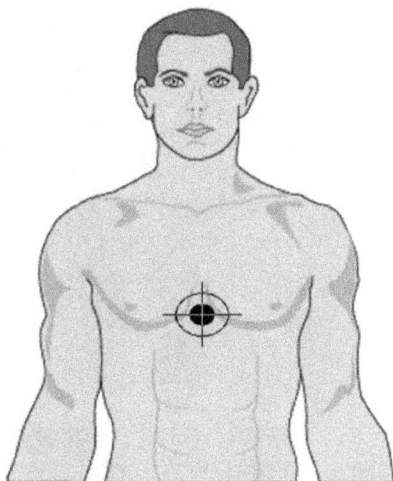

The solar plexus is a dense network of nerves located just below the sternum in the upper abdomen. A moderate strike to this area can cause intense pain, nausea, and shock, significantly impairing the opponent's ability to breathe. A more forceful blow to the solar plexus can lead to severe abdominal pain, muscle cramping, air deprivation, and shock, effectively incapacitating the adversary.

The opponent's probable reaction dynamic from a strike to the solar plexus may include the following:

• He grabs and covers his chest with his hands.

• He doubles over in pain.

• His body bends forward.

• He drops down on one knee.

• He struggles for air.

RIBS

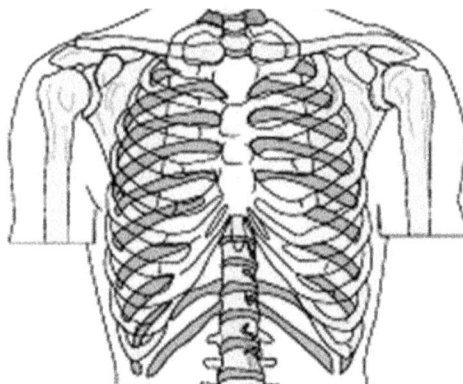

The human body contains twelve pairs of ribs. With the exception of the eleventh and twelfth ribs, the ribs are long, slender bones connected to the vertebral column at the back and the sternum and costal cartilage at the front. Since the eleventh and twelfth ribs, also known as floating ribs, are not connected in the front, strikes should be directed toward the ninth and tenth ribs for maximum impact.

A moderate strike to the front of the ribcage can cause severe pain and shortness of breath. However, a powerful blow at a forty-five-degree angle could break a rib, potentially driving it into the lung. This could lead to a collapsed lung, internal bleeding, air deprivation, excruciating pain, unconsciousness, and in extreme cases, death.

The opponent's probable reaction dynamic from a strike to the ribs may include the following:

- He covers the afflicted rib with his hands.
- He doubles over in pain.
- His body bends forward.
- He drops down on one knee.
- He struggles for air.

TESTICLES

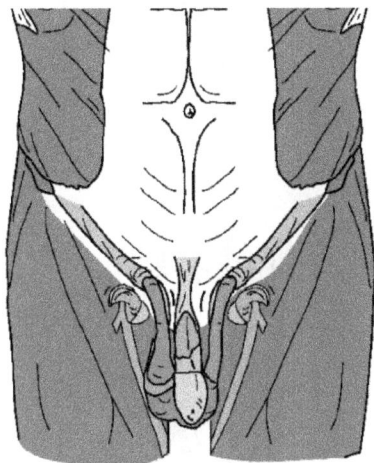

Every man understands that the testicles is an exceptionally sensitive target. The groin area, specifically the testes, can be kicked, stomped, punched, or crushed, making it a highly effective zone for disabling an assailant. A moderate strike to the groin can trigger severe pain, nausea, vomiting, shortness of breath, and even potential sterility. A more forceful blow, however, could crush the scrotum and testes against the pubic bones, potentially causing shock, intense pain, and even unconsciousness.

The assailant's probable reaction dynamic from a strike to the groin may include the following:

• His head and body violently drop forward.

• He grabs or covers his groin region.

• He struggles for breath.

• He momentarily freezes from shock.

THIGHS

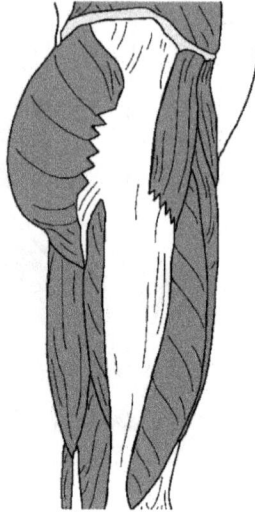

Many fighters overlook the thighs as an impact target. In fact, because the thighs are a large and difficult to protect, they make excellent striking targets in a fight.

While you can kick the thighs at a variety of different angles, the ideal location is the assailant's common peroneal nerve located on the side of the thigh, approximately four inches above the knee. Striking this area can result in extreme pain and immediate immobility. An extremely hard kick to the thigh may result in a fracture of the femur, internal bleeding, severe pain, intense cramping, and long-term immobility.

The opponent's probable reaction dynamic from a strike to the thigh may include the following:

• His afflicted leg buckles.

• His body weight shifts backwards.

• His body drops forward.

• His arms drop down to his sides.

KNEES

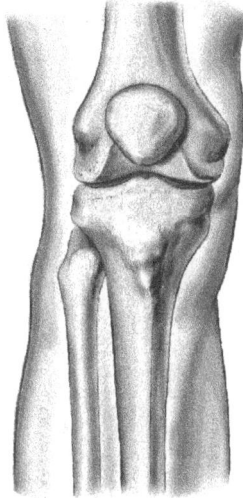

The knees are relatively weak joints that are held together by a number of supporting ligaments. When the assailant's leg is locked or fixed in position and a forceful strike is delivered to the front of the joint, the cruciate ligaments will tear, resulting in excruciating pain, swelling, and immobility.

Located on the front of the knee joint is the patella, which is made of a small, loose piece of bone. The patella is also vulnerable to possible dislocation by a direct, forceful kick. Severe pain, swelling, and immobility may also result.

The assailant's probable reaction dynamic from a strike to the knee may include the following:

• His afflicted leg locks in place.

• His body weight shifts backwards.

• His head and body drops forward.

• His arms drop down to his sides.

SHINS

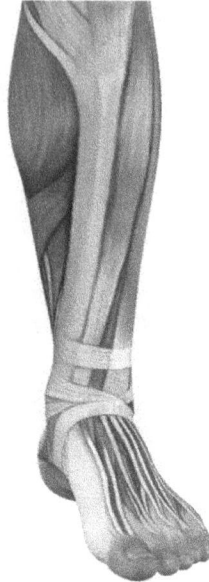

Everyone, at one time or another, has knocked his or her shin bone into the end of a table or bed accidentally and felt the intense pain associated with it. The shin is very sensitive because the bone is only protected by a thin layer of skin. However, a powerful kick delivered to this target can easily fracture it, resulting in nauseating pain, hemorrhaging, and immobility.

The opponent's probable reaction dynamic from a shin kick may include the following:

- His afflicted leg locks in place.
- His body weight shifts backwards.
- His body drops forward.
- His arms drop down to his sides.

TOES/INSTEP

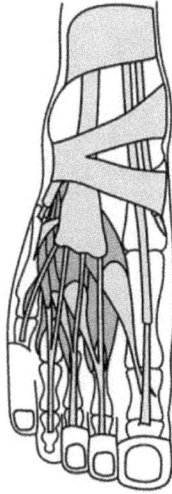

With a powerful stomp of your heel, you can break the small bones of an assailant's toes and/or instep, causing severe pain and immobility. Stomping on the toes is an excellent technique for releasing many holds. It should be mentioned, however, that you should avoid an attack to the toes/instep if the attacker is wearing hard leather boots, i.e., combat, hiking, or motorcycle boots.

The opponent's probable reaction dynamic from a shin kick may include the following:

- He'll raise his afflicted leg off the ground.
- His attention will shift to the ground.
- He'll be unable to walk or support his bodyweight.

HANDS/FINGERS

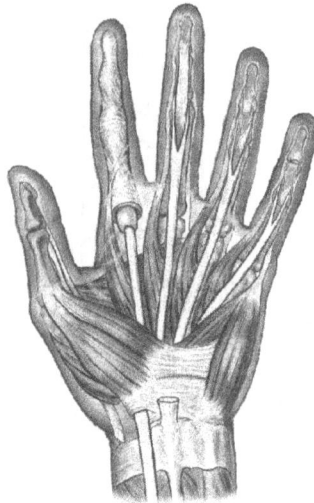

The hands and fingers are considered weak and vulnerable targets that can easily be jammed, sprained, broken, torn, and bitten. While a broken finger might not stop an attacker, it will certainly make him release his hold. A broken finger also makes it difficult for the assailant to clench his fist or hold a weapon. When attempting to break an assailant's finger, it's best to grab the digit and forcefully tear backward against the knuckle.

The probable reaction dynamic from a hand or finger injury may include:

- He instinctively retracts his hand into his body.
- He covers/protects his afflicted hand with his other hand.
- He's incapable of clenching his fist.
- He's unable to maintain a grip on his weapon.
- If he's holding or grabbing you, he'll release his grip.

DEFENSIVE TECHNIQUES

Defense is a fundamental concept in every martial art. In some systems, it serves as the foundational philosophy; in others, it's a strategic approach to combat. For instance, many self-defense instructors, both traditional and modern, emphasize defensive responses over offensive actions during violent street encounters. It's noteworthy that most katas in Karate begin and end with a block, symbolizing the defensive attitude deeply ingrained in many Karate systems. Defense, without a doubt, remains the cornerstone of most conventional martial arts styles.

However, relying solely on a defensive strategy in real-life combat can be dangerously misguided. A self-defense practitioner who adopts a purely defensive mindset risks severe injury - or worse. Allowing a criminal assailant to make the first offensive move is akin to giving a gunslinger the first draw - it's a reckless and potentially fatal decision. The harsh reality is that, in most violent encounters, the fighter who strikes first often gains the upper hand. It's a fundamental rule: the one who initiates usually wins. I'll explore this concept further in the next chapter.

59

That said, defense remains an essential component of any self-defense system and must be properly developed. A well-rounded fighter needs the ability to block, evade, and counterattack efficiently. Even in an offensive-based combat system, such as Contemporary Fighting Arts, strong defensive skills enhance your ability to protect yourself while positioning you for an effective counterattack. The key lies in balancing offense with defense, ensuring that you're prepared to survive any confrontation.

There are seven key components of defense that must be mastered to effectively protect yourself in combat. They are:

Stances – the strategic posture you assume prior to or during combat.

Distance – the spatial relationship between you and your adversary.

Mobility – the ability to move your body quickly and freely while balanced.

Blocking – defensive tools designed to intercept your assailant's oncoming blow.

Parrying – defensive tools that redirect your assailant's blows.

Evading – maneuvers designed to strategically move your targets away from your assailant's strike.

Attacking – offensive action intended to neutralize the threat, gain physical control, and incapacitate your assailant(s), if necessary.

Since we've already covered stances, distance, and mobility in earlier sections, we will now dive right into blocking techniques, essential for intercepting and neutralizing your opponent's attacks. As for attacking, this vital component will be thoroughly explained in the upcoming chapters, where we'll explore various offensive techniques tailored to different combat scenarios.

BLOCKING TECHNIQUES

Blocking techniques serve as essential defensive tools used to intercept an assailant's attack by positioning a non-vital limb - typically your arm - between the opponent's strike and its intended target.

There are four key blocks you must master: high blocks, mid blocks, low blocks, and elbow blocks. To ensure maximum effectiveness with hand blocks, always keep your hands open and relaxed. Let's start by exploring the high block.

High Blocks

The high block is designed to defend against overhead strikes. To perform the lead high block, raise your lead arm and extend your forearm above your head, ensuring that your head remains protected behind your arm. Avoid positioning your arm in a way that leaves your head exposed. Keep your hand open, not clenched, as this increases the surface area of the block and allows for a quicker counterattack. The same mechanics apply for the rear high block: raise your rear arm and extend your forearm above your head, maintaining proper coverage and readiness for a counterstrike.

Mid Blocks

The mid block is designed to defend against circular strikes aimed at the head or upper torso and can be executed with either the right or left arm. However, since most attackers are right-handed, you will most likely find yourself using the left mid block to intercept their dominant strikes.

To perform the block, raise your arm to approximately a 90-degree angle while rotating your forearm toward the incoming blow. Your goal is to meet the assailant's wrist or forearm with the belly of your forearm, maximizing structural integrity. Keeping your hand open increases the surface area of the block and allows for a faster transition to a counterattack.

Timing is critical - the rotation of your arm must be precisely coordinated with the attack. The mid block can be adjusted vertically and horizontally to account for the specific angle of the strike. Once the block is in place, be ready to counterattack immediately to maintain your advantage.

Low Blocks

The low block is designed to defend against powerful linear strikes aimed at your midsection. To perform the lead low block, lower your lead arm so that your forearm is parallel to the ground, with your fingers pointing upward to prevent jamming or fractures.

When executing a low block, make contact with the belly of your forearm, not the palm. The same mechanics apply to the rear low block: simply drop your rear arm down to intercept the assailant's strike.

Although low blocks are less frequently used, they remain a crucial part of your defensive toolkit. Be sure to include them in your training regimen.

Elbow Blocks

The elbow block is designed to defend against circular strikes aimed at your midsection, such as uppercuts, shovel hooks, and some kicks.

To perform the elbow block, drop your elbow downward while simultaneously twisting your body toward your centerline. Ensure your elbow remains perpendicular to the floor, and keep your hands relaxed and close to your chest. This technique can be executed on both the right and left sides for versatility in defense.

CAUTION: Elbow blocks should only be used when you're certain your opponent is not armed with a knife or edged weapon. If you cannot clearly see their hands, it's best to avoid using this block, as it leaves you vulnerable to hidden weapons.

PARRYING TECHNIQUES

A parry is a swift and forceful defensive maneuver used to intercept and redirect your opponent's linear attacks, such as jabs, lead straights, rear crosses, or even direct knife stabs. Unlike blocking, which absorbs the impact of a strike, a parry uses a quick, decisive slap to deflect the attack away from your body, creating an opening for counterattacks.

There are two types of parries for street self-defense: horizontal and vertical. Both can be executed with either the right or left hand, providing flexibility in any combat situation.

Horizontal Parry

To execute a proper horizontal parry, follow these steps: From your stance, move your lead hand across your body, sweeping horizontally along your centerline to deflect and redirect the assailant's punch. After the parry, immediately return your hand to its guard position to maintain defense readiness. Ensure that you make contact with the palm of your hand for maximum control and precision. With consistent training, you can seamlessly integrate the horizontal parry into your slipping maneuvers, enhancing your defense.

Vertical Parry

To properly execute a vertical parry, follow these steps: From your stance, move your lead hand in a downward motion along your centerline to deflect and redirect the assailant's punch. This motion is particularly effective against strikes aimed at your midsection or lower body, such as body jabs or straight punches.

As you deflect the strike, make sure to use the palm of your hand for contact, keeping your fingers tight and compact to avoid injury and maintain control over the parry. Once the punch has been redirected, immediately return your hand to its guard position to maintain defensive readiness and protect against follow-up attacks.

It's crucial to practice fluidity and timing when executing the vertical parry. Proper coordination between the parry and your overall defense allows for quicker counters and smoother transitions into offensive movements. With regular practice, the vertical parry can be incorporated into more complex defensive strategies, ensuring you stay protected while remaining poised to strike back at your opponent.

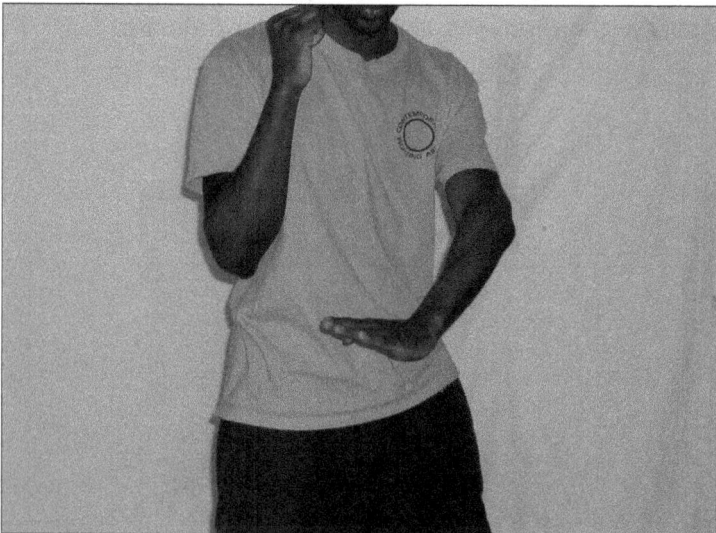

EVASION TECHNIQUES

Evading skills are fundamental defensive maneuvers that allow you to strategically move out of the path of your assailant's attack without making physical contact. Unlike blocking or parrying, evasion relies entirely on body movement to avoid incoming strikes, helping you maintain mobility and control during a confrontation. These skills are crucial for conserving energy while minimizing the risk of injury, as you avoid absorbing the full force of an opponent's strike.

Slipping

Slipping is a swift and highly effective defensive maneuver that allows you to evade an assailant's linear strikes - such as jabs, lead straights, rear crosses, and palm heels - while maintaining your position and staying within range. Unlike stepping back or sidestepping, which create distance, slipping keeps you in close proximity to your opponent, ready to counterattack immediately.

To execute a proper slip, timing is crucial. The movement is initiated by quickly snapping your head and upper torso to either the right or left, just enough to make the oncoming blow

67

miss its target. The key is to move your head off the centerline, where most punches are aimed, while keeping your feet grounded and your body balanced. This allows you to avoid the strike without wasting unnecessary energy or losing your position.

Effective slipping requires more than just head movement - your upper body should rotate slightly as well to ensure full evasion. For example, when slipping to the right, you can rotate your right shoulder slightly, keeping your chin tucked and eyes focused on your opponent. This subtle rotation helps you stay balanced and ready to retaliate.

Additionally, slipping requires practice to develop the necessary speed, timing, and muscle memory. Regular training will improve your ability to read your opponent's movements and react with the precision needed for effective slipping, ultimately making you a more elusive and dangerous fighter.

MENTAL TOUGHNESS IN SELF-DEFENSE

Mental toughness is a critical element of self-defense, often overlooked in favor of physical techniques. Yet, without the mental fortitude to withstand fear, stress, and the unpredictability of real-world violence, even the most physically adept fighter can falter. Mental toughness allows an individual to confront adversity, manage stress, and execute under pressure, which are crucial attributes when faced with life-threatening scenarios.

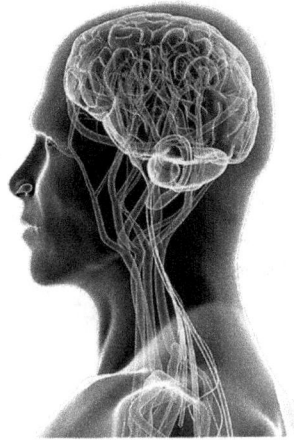

What is Mental Toughness?

Mental toughness refers to a collection of psychological skills and qualities that enable a person to cope, perform, and prevail through extreme adversity. It is not just about enduring pain or discomfort; it involves maintaining composure, making quick decisions, and continuing to function effectively under intense pressure. In the context of self-defense, mental toughness manifests in the ability to maintain control over one's emotions and actions when facing violent attacks.

As you train your body to perform under stress, you must also train your mind. The chaotic nature of street encounters often leads to panic, indecision, or hesitation, which can have fatal consequences. Developing mental resilience allows you to stay calm, assess the situation, and act with precision and purpose.

KEY ELEMENTS OF MENTAL TOUGHNESS

Coping with Adversity: The first step in developing mental toughness is learning to cope with the stress and fear that arise in dangerous situations. This involves recognizing fear and anxiety, controlling these emotions, and preventing them from clouding judgment. Techniques like visualization, controlled breathing, and positive self-talk are essential in managing this stress.

Performing Under Pressure: In self-defense, being able to perform in high-crisis situations is paramount. This requires efficiency, effectiveness, and safety in your actions. Mental toughness enables you to focus on the immediate task at hand - whether it's neutralizing an attacker or escaping a dangerous situation - without being overwhelmed by distractions.

Prevailing Against the Odds: True mental toughness goes beyond just survival. It is about prevailing in the face of adversity. In a self-defense scenario, this means not only enduring the physical and emotional stress of the encounter but also emerging victorious by executing the right techniques at the right moment.

BUILDING MENTAL TOUGHNESS THROUGH TRAINING

Just as you condition your body for combat, mental toughness can be developed and sharpened through consistent training.

Stress inoculation drills, scenario-based training, and full-contact sparring under realistic conditions are all excellent methods for building this mental resilience. These drills not only prepare you for physical confrontation but also train your mind to handle the psychological stressors that accompany real-world violence.

Mental toughness also prepares you for the long-term impact of violence. Surviving a violent encounter is not just about winning the fight- it is about maintaining your psychological health afterward. A well-trained mind is better equipped to cope with the trauma and stress that can follow a horrific altercation, enabling you to move forward without being crippled by fear or anxiety.

A LOOK AHEAD

As we conclude Chapter One, it's important to note that specific offensive techniques have not been covered here. These will be explored in detail in the following chapters, each focused on a different extreme combat methodology. This approach allows you to gain a deeper understanding of how to apply offensive techniques within the context of each unique system.

By learning offensive techniques in the framework of their respective methodologies, you'll not only understand the mechanics but also the appropriate situations to use them in real-world self-defense scenarios.

With this solid foundation in place, we're now ready to dive into the specifics of each CFA combat methodology in the chapters ahead.

SINISTER SELF-DEFENSE

CHAPTER TWO

First Strike

The Ultimate Preemptive Power Play

HIERARCHY OF COMBAT METHODOLOGIES

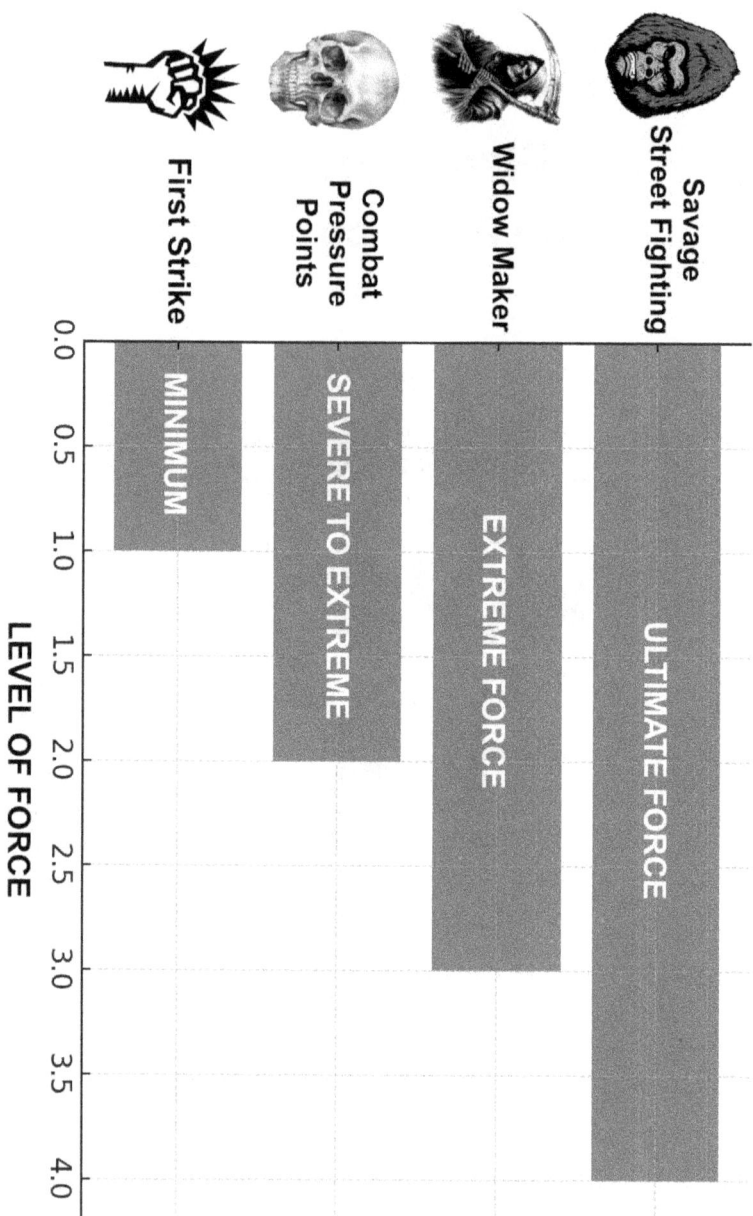

First Strike

Combat Pressure Points

Widow Maker

Savage Street Fighting

MINIMUM	
SEVERE TO EXTREME	
EXTREME FORCE	
ULTIMATE FORCE	

LEVEL OF FORCE

0.0 0.5 1.0 1.5 2.0 2.5 3.0 3.5 4.0

THE HIERARCHY OF COMBAT METHODOLOGIES

Before we dive into the specific techniques and strategies of the *First Strike* methodology, it's important to understand where it fits within the broader framework of self-defense.

Self-defense is not a one-size-fits-all approach; different situations demand different responses. In this book, I use a structured hierarchy to explain how force should be escalated based on the severity of the threat you face. This is known as the **Hierarchy of Combat Methodologies** (see chart).

At the foundation of this hierarchy is First Strike, which represents the least extreme, but still highly effective, use of force. As the threat escalates, so do the methodologies, moving from the more measured response of First Strike to the more severe and extreme responses such as Combat Pressure Points, Widow Maker, and ultimately Savage Street Fighting. This hierarchy ensures that your response to a violent situation is proportionate to the danger you're facing.

Hierarchy of Combat Methodologies

First Strike – Minimal Force

Combat Pressure Points – Severe Force

Widow Maker – Extreme Force

Savage Street Fighting – Ultimate Force

Each methodology builds upon the last, progressively increasing the intensity of force in response to more dangerous and life-threatening scenarios.

As we move through the book, you'll learn when to apply each level of force and how to adapt your techniques based on the escalating threat level.

THE STAGES OF SELF-DEFENSE

Now that we understand the overall structure of combat methodologies, it's essential to recognize the two primary stages of self-defense: the pre-contact stage and the contact stage. Each stage plays a critical role in shaping your response to a real-world self-defense situation.

Pre-Contact Stage

The *pre-contact stage* refers to the critical moments before physical engagement with an assailant. During this time, awareness of the looming threat gives you precious seconds to assess the situation and prepare mentally and physically for a potential confrontation.

In the awareness phase of the pre-contact stage, your goal is to assess the situation, determine the level of threat, and possibly engage in some dialogue with the assailant in an attempt to de-escalate the situation. Strategic stances, such as the natural, de-escalation, or the first strike stances, are particularly useful during this phase. These stances help you remain non-threatening while positioning yourself for swift defensive or offensive action if the situation escalates.

76

Contact Stage

The *contact stage* begins the moment physical contact occurs between you and your adversary—the fight is on. This often takes the form of an ambush attack or direct combat. At this point, there's no room for negotiation; you must act swiftly to protect yourself.

In this stage, the fighting stance becomes critical, among other techniques, to launch strikes, blocks, and evasive maneuvers. Your ability to seamlessly transition from pre-contact awareness to full physical engagement is key to surviving and controlling the confrontation.

THE ART OF STRIKING FIRST

The *First Strike methodology* is unique to my CFA system and it's designed for the pre-contact stage, when a threat is imminent but before your assailant has made his move. This approach allows you to act proactively, taking control of the situation before it escalates to full physical contact. By striking first, you maintain the element of surprise, disrupt your attacker's plans, and gain an early advantage. Though it's the least extreme of the combat methodologies in this book, it's no less effective in neutralizing threats quickly and decisively.

The philosophy behind the First Strike is simple: don't wait for violence to come to you. By striking first, you seize control and prevent the attacker from escalating the situation. Timing and precision are critical here, ensuring that you deliver your strike at the perfect moment to disable the threat without allowing them time to react.

Why Striking First Matters

In a self-defense confrontation where there's no safe escape, you must strike first, strike fast, strike with authority, and keep the pressure on. This offensive strategy is essential for neutralizing a dangerous adversary before they can mount a counterattack. A prolonged fight increases the chances of serious injury or death, so it's crucial to end the confrontation as swiftly as possible. Striking first allows you to incapacitate your opponent while minimizing their ability to retaliate, saving precious time and reducing unnecessary risk.

The First Strike methodology is about commitment. You're not throwing out jabs or feeler strikes; you're fully engaging with a series of decisive blows that take advantage of your attacker's vulnerabilities. In street combat, hesitation or half-measures can be fatal. A committed first strike, executed with confidence and precision, ensures that you dominate the encounter from the outset.

First Strike Justifications

The most challenging aspect of the First Strike Principle is knowing when to act. Every self-defense scenario is unique, and there's no universal answer. However, there are critical factors that must be present before launching a first strike.

First and foremost, force should only be used when it is legally justified. You must distinguish between lethal and nonlethal force - lethal force being the level of violence that can cause serious injury or death, while nonlethal force is designed to protect without inflicting permanent harm.

Understand that using force in self-defense carries legal risks. Even in situations where you are justified, there is always the possibility of civil lawsuits or criminal charges. Those trained in martial arts or self-defense may face even higher standards of conduct in the eyes of the law. It's crucial to recognize when force is necessary and justified, particularly when considering a first strike.

The First Strike Principle should only be applied when you are defending yourself against an immediate, unlawful threat. You need to be absolutely certain that launching a preemptive strike is necessary to protect yourself from imminent harm. Remember, the decision to strike first must always be a last resort, after all other means of avoiding violence have been exhausted.

Assessing the Situation

Before launching a first strike, you must quickly assess both the environment and your adversary. Assessment involves gathering information rapidly and analyzing it in terms of threat and danger. In terms of environment, you need to consider escape routes, barriers, makeshift weapons, and the terrain around you. These factors can either aid or hinder your ability to defend yourself and should be evaluated in the heat of the moment.

When assessing your adversary, pay attention to nonverbal cues such as clenched fists, heavy breathing, or an aggressive stance. These signs can indicate an imminent attack. You must also evaluate the range between you and your attacker— are they within striking distance, or do they have a weapon that could increase their reach? Understanding these factors will allow you to determine whether a first strike is necessary and how to time it effectively.

Why Hesitation Can Be Fatal

One of the biggest mistakes self-defense practitioners make is waiting for their adversary to make the first move. This reactive mindset can lead to disaster, as giving the attacker the initiative puts you on the defensive from the start. In a real-life confrontation, this hesitation can cost you your life.

Many practitioners hesitate to strike first because they are uncertain about the legal ramifications or lack confidence in their ability to execute a first strike successfully. Others may be hesitant due to moral or psychological concerns about being the one to "start" the physical confrontation. However, in self-defense, waiting can be fatal. You must have a solid understanding of when a preemptive strike is justified and be confident enough to act when the situation demands it.

Moral and Legal Considerations

When it comes to self-defense, understanding the legal and moral implications of your actions is paramount. While defending yourself is a natural right, it must be exercised responsibly and within the boundaries of the law. Using force, especially deadly force, comes with significant consequences, both legally and morally.

Each state or country has its own self-defense laws, and it's your responsibility to familiarize yourself with the laws where you live or travel. Failing to do so can lead to serious legal repercussions, even if your actions were intended to protect yourself or others.

For example, in many jurisdictions, using deadly force is only justified when facing an immediate and unlawful threat to your life or the life of someone else. Misjudging this level of threat could lead to charges ranging from excessive force to manslaughter or murder.

Consider a real-world scenario where an individual believed they were acting in self-defense but faced severe legal consequences. In a case in Florida, a man used deadly force during a road rage altercation, believing his life was in danger. However, upon review, the court determined that the threat was not imminent, and he was convicted of manslaughter. This case illustrates the importance of understanding what constitutes an immediate and unlawful threat, as well as the level of force permissible under the law.

Morally, you must also weigh the consequences of your actions. The decision to use force, especially deadly force, is not just a physical response - it is a moral one that can have lasting effects on you, your family, and your community. The aftermath of a violent encounter, even one justified by law, can lead to emotional trauma, legal battles, and public scrutiny.

Therefore, before employing any of the techniques described in this chapter or book, it's crucial to recognize that self-defense must always be a last resort. The primary goal should always be to de-escalate or avoid conflict when possible.

When force is necessary, it must be proportionate to the threat you face and executed within the legal framework of your jurisdiction. Understanding this balance between legal justification and moral responsibility is a critical component of effective self-defense.

FIRST STRIKE TECHNIQUES

Now that you're familiar with the prerequisites for the first strike, it's time to explore the tools themselves. First strike tools are specialized offensive techniques designed for initiating a preemptive strike against your adversary. Unlike the other techniques in your arsenal, these first strikes have been selected for their speed, destructiveness, and near invisibility. Let's begin with the vertical kick.

Vertical Kick

The vertical kick is executed from the lead leg, traveling in a direct vertical line to target the assailant's groin. To perform the kick, shift your weight onto your rear leg while simultaneously lifting your lead leg straight up towards the target. Once contact is made with the instep of your lead foot, immediately return your leg to the ground for stability. Ensure that your supporting leg remains bent to maintain balance throughout the movement. Be cautious not to snap your knee during the delivery of the kick - focus instead on a controlled, fluid motion that maximizes impact.

Here, Franco demonstrates the vertical kick.

Push Kick

The push kick is another effective first strike tool delivered from your lead leg. To execute the technique, shift your weight onto your rear leg while simultaneously raising your lead leg. Thrust the ball of your foot into your assailant's groin, quadriceps, knee, or shin with forceful precision. After making contact, immediately bring your leg back to the ground to maintain stability. As always, keep your supporting leg bent to ensure proper balance throughout the movement.

Finger Jab

The finger jab is a rapid, non-telegraphic strike executed with your lead arm, making contact with your fingertips. To perform the finger jab, relax your arm and quickly extend it outward before snapping it back. Avoid tensing your muscles before execution to maintain fluidity. The primary targets for this strike are the assailant's eyes, making it highly effective for causing temporary or permanent blindness, severe pain, and shock. The key to a successful finger jab lies in speed, precision, and, most importantly, non-telegraphic movement, ensuring the strike is both fast and difficult to predict.

83

Rear Palm Heel

The rear palm heel strike is a powerful open-hand, linear blow aimed at your assailant's nose or chin. To execute this technique, make contact with the heel of your palm while keeping your fingers pointed upward. As you deliver the strike, rotate your shoulder, hips, and foot in unison toward your target for maximum force. Ensure your arm extends straight out, making solid contact with the heel of your palm. Once the strike is completed, retract your arm along the same line of attack, maintaining fluidity and control throughout the movement.

Short-Arc Hammer Fist

The short-arc hammer fist is a swift and forceful strike designed for close-range encounters. The primary target is the bridge of your assailant's nose. To execute the vertical hammer fist, raise your fist while keeping your elbow flexed. Then, sharply whip your clenched fist downward along a vertical path, aiming for the nose. Ensure your elbow remains bent upon impact to maintain control and power. Throughout the execution of the strike, be sure to maintain your balance, positioning yourself for follow-up actions if necessary.

Double-Thumb Gouge

The double-thumb gouge is an aggressive grappling-range tactic that can deliver devastating consequences, whether executed while standing or on the ground. To perform the technique, firmly place both hands on your assailant's face, securing your grip by wrapping your lower fingers around the sides of their jaw for stabilization. Once positioned, forcefully drive both of your thumbs into the eye sockets, applying increasing pressure. This tactic can lead to temporary or permanent blindness, severe shock, or even unconsciousness. **WARNING:** The double-thumb gouge is an extreme measure that should only be employed in life-or-death situations. Ensure that its use is legally warranted and justified before taking such decisive action.

Rear Web-Hand Strike

The rear web-hand strike is a close-quarters grappling technique capable of causing serious harm. Depending on the force applied, a strike to the throat may result in gagging, intense pain, difficulty breathing, nausea, and in extreme cases, death. To execute the strike, spread your thumb and index finger

apart, and drive the web of your hand directly into your assailant's throat, keeping your hand rigid with your palm facing down. After making contact, retract your hand quickly to its original position.

WARNING: The rear web-hand strike is a highly dangerous technique that should only be employed in life-or-death situations. Ensure its use is both legally justified and warranted before applying such force.

Rear Horizontal Elbow

The rear horizontal elbow is a powerful and devastating tool used effectively at grappling range. Its explosive nature makes it difficult for the assailant to defend against. The strike travels horizontally, targeting the assailant's face with the sharp point of your elbow. To execute this technique, rotate your hips and shoulders swiftly into the strike, generating force through the rotation of your body. Keep your palm facing downward, with your hand near the side of your head. The point of impact should be the tip of your elbow, ensuring maximum damage on contact.

Rear Diagonal Elbow

The rear diagonal elbow strike is a versatile and powerful blow, designed to travel diagonally downward to the assailant's head. This technique can be executed from either the right or left side, depending on your positioning. To perform the strike, rotate your elbow back and up, then whip it down forcefully toward your target. Bend your knees as you descend with the strike, ensuring that your body weight adds to the impact. Your palm should face away from you on contact, with the point of your elbow being the striking surface. This technique is particularly effective due to its downward momentum and the compact power of the elbow point.

SECONDARY STRIKE TECHNIQUES

Secondary-strike tools are offensive techniques that follow your initial first strike, forming the foundation of your compound attack. These follow-up strikes are crucial for maintaining pressure on your adversary, preventing his recovery, and ensuring a decisive outcome. The following 12 techniques form the backbone of your compound attack arsenal, starting with the hook kick.

Hook Kick

The hook kick is a powerful circular strike delivered from your rear leg, targeting either the adversary's knee or the common peroneal nerve. To execute, step at a 45-degree angle while twisting and driving your rear leg and hip into the target. Pivot on your base foot to generate momentum and follow through. Contact is made with your instep or shinbone. Striking the common peroneal nerve, located about four inches above the knee, will collapse the adversary's leg, causing temporary immobilization. Striking the knee itself can cause serious and permanent damage to cartilage, ligaments, tendons, and bones.

Lead Straight

The lead straight is a linear punch delivered with the center knuckle of your lead arm. To execute this technique, quickly twist your lead leg, hip, and shoulder forward, generating force from the ground up. Drive the punch directly into your assailant's target and immediately retract it back to the starting position. Be mindful not to let the punch deflect to the side - a common mistake that reduces its effectiveness. The primary targets for the lead straight include the

nose, chin, and solar plexus, offering the potential to disrupt your adversary's balance or breathing.

Rear Cross

The rear cross is one of the most powerful linear strikes in your unarmed combat arsenal. Delivered in a straight line, this punch targets the assailant's nose, chin, or solar plexus. Proper waist twisting and weight transfer are critical to maximizing its effectiveness. As you throw the punch, shift your weight from your rear foot to your lead leg, simultaneously torquing your rear foot, hip, and shoulder into the blow. Ensure that your fist is positioned horizontally for maximum impact.

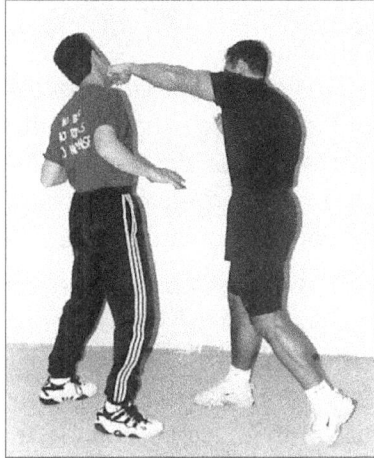

Lead & Rear Hooks

The lead and rear hook punches are among the most powerful and challenging strikes in your arsenal, requiring considerable time and practice to master. Both punches demand proper wrist, forearm, and shoulder alignment to avoid injury and ensure effective delivery. For each punch, your arm must be bent at least 90 degrees, with the wrist and forearm kept straight throughout the motion.

To perform either the lead or

rear hook punch, quickly and smoothly raise your elbow until your arm is parallel to the ground. Simultaneously, torque your shoulder, hip, and foot in the direction of the punch.

Lead & Rear Uppercuts

The lead and rear uppercuts are powerful, fight-ending punches that can be used effectively in both the punching and grappling ranges. Both strikes travel in a vertical direction, targeting the opponent's chin or body.

To execute either uppercut, twist and lift the corresponding side of your body (lead or rear) toward the target. Keep the punch tight with a short, compact arc, and avoid any winding-up or telegraphing movements to maximize speed and surprise.

Lead & Rear Shovel Hooks

The lead and rear shovel hooks are powerful diagonal punches that can be used to effectively target your opponent. To execute either punch, dip the corresponding shoulder (lead or rear) while simultaneously rotating the respective leg and hip toward the target. Drive your entire body into the punch while maintaining balance throughout.

Rear Vertical Hammer Fist

The long arc hammer fist is a powerful finishing technique delivered vertically to the opponent's neck or spine. To execute the rear vertical hammer fist, raise your clenched fist with your elbow bent. Drive it downward in a vertical line onto the back of your opponent's neck, bending at your hips and knees to generate power. Follow through the target, ensuring your elbow remains bent upon impact. Maintain your balance throughout the strike. **CAUTION:** Never throw a hammer fist with a straight arm, as it reduces speed and power and may result in severe elbow strain.

Rear Vertical Knee

The rear vertical knee strike generates immense force by utilizing the strength of your entire lower body, driving through the target with devastating effect. Timing and accuracy are essential to land this strike effectively, especially when targeting high-value areas like the face or ribs, where a well-placed blow can incapacitate an adversary instantly. Additionally, maintaining control of your opponent during the strike is crucial - grappling or holding them in place ensures that your knee lands precisely where intended, maximizing both power and effectiveness.

Rear Diagonal Knee

The rear diagonal knee strike is a highly effective close-quarters tool that moves along a diagonal path, much like the motion of a hook kick. This strike can be devastating when delivered with proper technique and precision. It is designed to target critical areas of your opponent's body, such as the common peroneal nerve, quadriceps, groin, ribs, and, in some cases, even the face.

To execute the rear diagonal knee strike effectively, begin by rotating your hips and pivoting your rear leg, generating power from your entire body. The knee should travel in a sharp, upward diagonal trajectory toward the intended target, utilizing the momentum from your hips and core. Proper body mechanics are crucial here - without them, the strike may lose its power and effectiveness.

Key to the success of this strike is the follow-through. Don't just aim to make contact; instead, aim to drive your knee through the target, as this will maximize the force and inflict more significant damage. Whether you are targeting the lower body, like the peroneal nerve or quadriceps, or higher targets like the ribs or face, the follow-through ensures that your opponent is incapacitated or destabilized, giving you a critical advantage in the encounter.

FIRST STRIKE SCENARIOS

The following section presents several first strike scenarios. Since every self-defense situation is different, these scenarios are intended as examples of potential combinations that can be used in combat. As you review the photographs, focus on how I take advantage of my opponent's reaction dynamics.

TACTICAL SEQUENCE 1

Vertical Kick/Rear Uppercut/ Lead Horizontal Elbow

Step: 1

Step: 2

Step: 3

TACTICAL SEQUENCE 2

Push Kick/Rear Uppercut/Lead Horizontal Elbow/
Rear Vertical Knee

Step: 1

Step: 2

Step: 3

Step: 4

TACTICAL SEQUENCE 3

Push Kick/Rear Hook/Lead Hook/Rear Vertical Knee

Step: 1

Step: 2

Step: 3

Step: 4

TACTICAL SEQUENCE 4

Finger Jab/Rear Cross/Lead Hook

Step: 1

Step: 2

Step: 3

Step: 4

TACTICAL SEQUENCE 5

Rear Palm Heel/Lead Hook/Rear Hook

Step: 1

Step: 2

Step: 3

Step: 4

97

TACTICAL SEQUENCE 6
Rear Palm Heel/Lead Straight/Rear Hook

Step: 1

Step: 2

Step: 3

Step: 4

TACTICAL SEQUENCE 7

Short Arc Hammer Fist/Lead Horizontal Elbow/
Rear Horizontal Elbow/Rear Vertical Knee

Step: 1

Step: 2

Step: 3

Step: 4

TACTICAL SEQUENCE 8

Rear Horizontal Elbow/Lead Horizontal Elbow/
Rear Diagonal Knee

Step: 1

Step: 2

Step: 3

Step: 4

FIRST STRIKE DECEPTIONS

In this section, I'll introduce you to two of the more than 30 ruses that are part of my first strike methodology. These tactics are designed to distract and confuse your opponent, lowering their guard and creating the opportunity to deliver a devastating first strike. These unorthodox tricks are highly effective, even against the most street-wise adversaries.

Every self-defense situation is different, so it's important to choose the ruse that best suits your circumstances. Use your best judgment when selecting the right approach for the moment.

THE GEMINI PRINCIPLE

Before you throw a first strike, there's often some level of dialogue between you and your opponent. This is where the *Gemini Principle* comes into play. The Gemini Principle involves strategically and deceptively using both verbal and nonverbal cues to set up a successful first strike. Much like the dual nature of the Gemini zodiac, this tactic requires you to summon the "dark twin" of your persona to engage in this type of deceptive behavior.

Once you assume your first strike stance, your goal is to manipulate or soften your opponent mentally. Speak in a calm, non-confrontational tone, telling them you have no intention of fighting. The trick is to prolong their thought process and distract them, lowering their guard. When they take the bait, deliver your first strike and continue applying pressure until they are fully incapacitated. Ideally, strike while speaking—

asking a question often creates the perfect distraction.

This form of deception requires a calm demeanor, precise timing, and a fair amount of acting. Be careful not to engage in heated or argumentative exchanges; remember, dialogue is simply another tool to weaken your opponent's defenses and create an opening for your attack.

WARNING: Like any tactic, the Gemini Principle can backfire if not executed with confidence and precision. Regular practice is essential to ensure it works when you need it most.

THE FIFTH-COLUMN TACTIC

The First Strike concept extends beyond protecting yourself - it can also be employed to safeguard a significant other, such as a close friend, spouse, acquaintance, co-worker, or partner. This approach is called the *Fifth-Column Tactic*, and it involves six crucial steps:

1. When a hostile adversary confronts your friend, side with the adversary in the argument, even if their position seems absurd. This manipulation helps soften the opponent.

2. Maintain a nonthreatening and passive posture, appearing calm and unaggressive to avoid raising suspicion.

3. Speak in a calm, non-confrontational tone, assuring the adversary that you and your friend have no desire to fight.

4. To further confuse and distract the adversary, pretend to get angry with your friend. Raise your voice and reprimand them for instigating the conflict - this will require some acting skill.

5. While showing sympathy toward the adversary, subtly reposition yourself into the best possible striking position.

6. Once you've secured the ideal position and your friend is safely out of harm's way, execute a first strike and continue applying pressure until the adversary is fully incapacitated.

THE WICKED JESTER
CHAOS AND CONTROL IN COMBAT

The *Wicked Jester* is a signature symbol in Contemporary Fighting Arts (CFA), reflecting the dual nature of chaos and control in combat. This iconic figure captures the CFA ethos, where unpredictability is embraced, yet every move is calculated. It's no surprise that the *Wicked Jester* has gained popularity in my clothing line designs, resonating with those who understand the balance between cunning deception and tactical precision. As both a trickster and a strategist, the *Wicked Jester* perfectly embodies the core principles of CFA, reminding us that true mastery comes not just from strength, but from the ability to dominate even in the most chaotic of circumstances.

In combat, chaos often emerges as aggression, confusion, and violence, manifesting through unpredictable attacks, sudden shifts in momentum, and the raw, unfiltered intensity of survival. Control, however, emerges in the fighter's ability to manipulate, deceive, and maintain focus amidst the turmoil. With its mischievous and cunning nature, the *Wicked Jester* thrives in chaotic environments, wielding unpredictability as a weapon to gain the upper hand—yet always with calculation and intent.

CONTEMPORARY FIGHTING ARTS

EST. 1989

STRIKE FIRST, SMOKE LATER

This duality mirrors how fighters must navigate real-world combat: creating or exploiting chaos in an adversary's mind while maintaining their own psychological control and tactical

103

advantage. The *Wicked Jester* symbolizes the art of masking intentions, luring opponents into a false sense of security, and striking decisively when least expected—blending the chaotic with the calculated to dominate in battle.

This is particularly relevant to CFA's First Strike methodology, which includes strategies like the *Gemini Principle* and *Fifth-Column Tactic*. Both tactics embody the essence of manipulation within chaos. The Gemini Principle uses deceptive dialogue and non-aggressive body language to mentally disarm opponents, creating confusion and concealing the fighter's true intentions. The *Wicked Jester*'s playful deception aligns perfectly with this method, as it encourages a fighter to manipulate their opponent's perception while preparing for a precise, preemptive strike.

Similarly, the Fifth-Column Tactic, where a fighter sides with the opponent to create a false sense of security before launching an unexpected counterattack, mirrors the Jester's trickery. The *Wicked Jester* thrives on creating this kind of strategic misdirection, where apparent disorder is simply a cover for calculated control. In combat, chaos can overwhelm an untrained mind, leading to impulsive reactions and missteps. The *Wicked Jester* reminds us that while chaos is inevitable, it can also be harnessed and directed. By channeling chaos in a controlled manner, a fighter can create openings, force their adversary into a reactive state, and disrupt their game plan. The jester's unpredictability isn't random; it's deliberate, calculated, and designed to undermine the adversary's confidence and decision-making skills.

On the other hand, control is the foundation that keeps a fighter grounded amidst the chaos. Just as the *Wicked Jester* can deceive with misdirection, the fighter must remain anchored in their techniques, knowing when to strike, how to exploit the chaos, and when to retreat or escalate. The *Wicked Jester* personifies the balance between those two extremes— between the unexpected chaos they introduce to their adversaries and the tactical control they maintain over their own actions.

This duality is especially relevant to the First Strike methodology. The unpredictability of the First Strike not only disorients the opponent but also establishes immediate control over the flow of the encounter. The ability to strike preemptively is rooted in this blend of chaos and control— creating confusion for the opponent while maintaining sharp focus and calculated decision-making.

By adding the *Wicked Jester*'s philosophy to the chapter, self-defense practitioners are encouraged to embrace both elements, mastering the art of deception while maintaining control in the most chaotic moments of combat. This mastery ensures they can dictate the terms of the engagement, just like the *Wicked Jester*, who thrives in chaos yet remains the ultimate manipulator—laughing all the while.

ESCALATING TO THE NEXT LEVEL
COMBAT PRESSURE POINTS

While the First Strike method can be followed by conventional strikes, there are moments when the adversary's escalation of violence requires a far more severe response. When the threat becomes life-threatening, or the assailant's intent is to cause grave harm, Combat Pressure Points offers techniques designed to neutralize the threat with decisive force. These deadly or maiming techniques go beyond the scope of conventional strikes and focus on incapacitating the attacker swiftly, ensuring your safety in extreme scenarios.

As we progress through each chapter, you'll notice an

escalation in the use-of-force with each combat methodology. We began with the preemptive and less extreme First Strike approach, and now transition to the more severe Combat Pressure Points. Later chapters will explore the Widow Maker Program and Savage Street Fighting, each pushing the level of force and intensity in response to the increasingly dangerous situations you may face.

It's important to clarify that this book focuses exclusively on unarmed combat methods. While the ultimate use-of-force may involve weapons such as firearms or knives, those are reserved for future works, where we'll cover armed combat and how to incorporate these tools into your self-defense strategy.

However, with each escalation in force, the responsibility lies with you to assess the situation accurately. Your actions must always be legally and morally justified in the eyes of the law. The decision to escalate to the Combat Pressure Points level should only be made when the circumstances demand it - when protecting your life or the life of a loved one leaves you no other option.

CHAPTER THREE
Combat Pressure Points
The Art of Precision Destruction

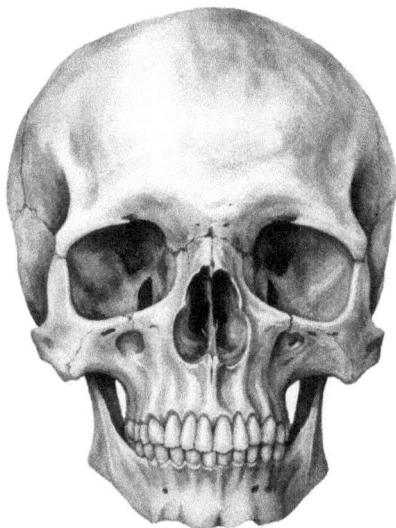

Factors That Justify Escalation to Combat Pressure Points

Before diving into the Combat Pressure Points methodology, it's crucial to understand the conditions that justify escalating from First Strike to this next level of force.

Street combat is rarely a straightforward encounter. Multiple variables can dramatically shift the dynamics of a fight within seconds, necessitating more severe force to neutralize criminal threats effectively.

Let's explore the key factors that could justify the escalation to Combat Pressure Points:

1. Multiple Attackers

Facing multiple attackers is one of the most dangerous scenarios in street combat. Attempting to overwhelm each adversary with broad, powerful strikes - like those used in First Strike - can leave you vulnerable to the others. Combat Pressure Points offers a way to deal with multiple attackers quickly and efficiently by targeting specific points that disable them immediately and decisively.

109

For example, while one attacker may be neutralized with a quick strike to the throat, and a second attacker could be stopped with a precise strike to the temple. These precision strikes cause immediate incapacitation, allowing you to stay in control of the fight and prevent multiple attackers from overwhelming you. Technique selection, timing and accuracy are critical in these high-risk situations.

2. Armed Attackers

When faced with an armed attacker, the stakes are drastically higher. A knife, club, or firearm can turn a simple confrontation into a life-threatening situation. In these moments, escalating to Combat Pressure Points is not just justified but necessary. Armed opponents present unique challenges that demand calculated strikes.

By targeting vital targets and breaking fingers off, you can disarm your opponent quickly and efficiently without engaging in prolonged combat. The goal is to neutralize the attacker before his weapon can be used against you, often by attacking his central nervous system. Combat Pressure Points enables you to disable and disarm an armed adversary by exploiting their body's weaknesses, reducing the risk of them using their weapon against you.

3. Opponents Under the Influence

Street combat often involves opponents under the influence of drugs or alcohol, rendering them impervious to pain and traditional striking techniques. First Strike might not be enough to incapacitate someone in this state. However, Combat Pressure Points allows you to bypass their altered pain thresholds by targeting the body's functional vulnerabilities.

For instance, an opponent high on PCP might not feel a strike to the nose, but a precise hit to the throat can still disrupt their body's ability to function. This can cause them to lose control of their limbs, collapse, or experience temporary paralysis - regardless of their diminished pain response. Precision becomes the great equalizer in such encounters, allowing you to incapacitate even the most resilient opponents.

4. Combat with Larger, Stronger Opponents

Facing a larger, stronger opponent presents a significant challenge in street fights. Overpowering them with broad strikes can be difficult, as their size and strength allow them to absorb more punishment than a smaller adversary. Combat Pressure Points provides an advantage by neutralizing their strength through precision targeting.

Instead of attempting to overwhelm them with a flurry of

blows, you focus on points that disable specific body parts, rendering their strength useless. For example, a strike to the kneecap can cause their leg to collapse, eliminating their ability to stand or move effectively. This neutralizes their size advantage and gives you control over the encounter. The beauty of Combat Pressure Points lies in its ability to bring down even the strongest opponent with targeted strikes that disable rather than overwhelm.

5. Prolonged Fights

When a confrontation lasts longer than expected, fatigue sets in. The longer you fight, the more your ability to deliver powerful, broad strikes diminishes. Combat Pressure Points offers a way to escalate the fight with calculated, efficient strikes that conserve energy while targeting critical areas.

This is particularly useful when dealing with an opponent who has managed to withstand your initial First Strike assault. As exhaustion starts to weigh on you, Combat Pressure Points allows you to finish the fight without relying solely on overwhelming force. Instead, you rely on accuracy and targeting nerve clusters that incapacitate the opponent quickly, even as your energy wanes.

6. High-Risk Scenarios

Certain situations demand an immediate escalation to Combat Pressure Points due to the heightened level of danger involved. These include scenarios where your opponent uses the environment to gain an advantage - such as attempting to run you over with a car, submerging your head underwater, trapping you in a confined space, or engaging with lethal intent. In these moments, your survival depends on targeting your opponent's most vulnerable points with precise, devastating force.

High-risk scenarios require quick escalation of force to prevent serious harm to yourself or others. Combat Pressure Points provides you with the means to neutralize a threat swiftly and efficiently, before they can cause irreversible damage. Whether in a crowded bar, a narrow alley, or a confined area with limited mobility, precision becomes your greatest asset. A well-placed strike to a critical pressure point can stop the attacker cold, giving you the vital opportunity to escape or regain control of the situation.

7. When You're on the Verge of Passing Out

Street combat can push you to your physical and mental limits. There may be moments when exhaustion, injury, or even a well-placed strike from your opponent leaves you on the verge of losing consciousness. In these situations, Combat Pressure Points can be your last line of defense before succumbing to unconsciousness. You must act quickly, targeting pressure points that will incapacitate your opponent with minimal effort.

Imagine a scenario where you're pinned down, vision blurred, and seconds away from passing out. You muster the last of your strength and deliver a precise strike to your opponent's throat, causing them to choke and struggle for breath, giving you just enough time to regain control of the fight. In moments like these, Combat Pressure Points can mean the difference between survival and defeat.

8. When You're Severely Injured During the Fight

In the chaos of street combat, there's always the risk of sustaining severe injuries, whether it's from an opponent's weapon, a surprise attack, or just the brutal nature of the fight. When you're severely injured, your ability to generate power and deliver broad strikes, like those used in First Strike, diminishes significantly. In such situations, Combat Pressure Points becomes a crucial tool for survival.

With limited strength and mobility, devastating precision is your best ally. You no longer have the capacity to overpower your opponent, so you must rely on carefully targeted strikes to incapacitate them quickly. These calculated strikes allow

113

you to conserve energy and protect yourself while minimizing the physical demands of the confrontation. Combat Pressure Points becomes essential when your own injuries prevent you from using more forceful techniques.

FLEXIBILITY AND REASONABLE FORCE

While Combat Pressure Points is a methodology for severe to extreme force, it's essential to remember that the rules of escalation are not set in stone. Every situation is different, and your response must reflect the principle of reasonable force. This means that the amount of force you use should be proportional to the threat you are facing.

For example, while targeting critical pressure points might be necessary in situations involving multiple attackers, weapons, or life-threatening circumstances, in other situations, less severe measures may suffice. The key is to assess the threat in real-time and adjust your actions accordingly.

Understanding when and how to escalate your response is critical to ensuring that your actions are not only effective but also legally and morally justified.

BRIDGING THE GAP BETWEEN METHODS

By understanding the variables and factors that justify escalating to Combat Pressure Points, you create a bridge between different combat methodologies. When facing multiple attackers, armed opponents, or individuals who are impervious to pain, Combat Pressure Points offers a tactical, calculated escalation of force. This method leverages precision over power, making it the perfect response when the stakes are higher and your survival depends on exploiting your opponent's vulnerabilities.

Once you've identified the need to escalate from First Strike to Combat Pressure Points, the next step is to master the precision and control required to make every strike count. In the next section, we'll delve into the specific techniques, anatomy, and mindset necessary to wield Combat Pressure Points with lethal efficiency.

THE SLEDGEHAMMER VS. THE SCALPEL

Imagine two tools - a sledgehammer and a scalpel. Both have their purpose, but they are designed for vastly different tasks. The sledgehammer is used for demolition, delivering brute force to break down walls and barriers. The scalpel, by contrast, is designed for delicate, precise incisions. One miscalculated swing of a sledgehammer, and you risk smashing everything in sight. But with the scalpel, even the smallest cut, delivered in the right place, can sever a critical connection and cause catastrophic damage.

In combat, First Strike is your sledgehammer. It is meant to hit hard, fast, and powerfully, with the goal of overwhelming the opponent before they have time to react. You target broad, vulnerable areas like the chin, thighs, and groin because these spots are universally susceptible to impact. When it works, First Strike is devastating - many confrontations will never move beyond this point because the opponent is taken out of the fight with a single blow.

However, there are times when conventional strikes alone won't suffice. Some opponents are too resilient, too hardened, or simply too tough to be brought down by power alone. That's when you switch to the scalpel: Combat Pressure Points. Here, the key is precision. You're no longer aiming for broad targets but for highly specific vulnerable points on the body— nerve clusters, and other vulnerable areas that can incapacitate an opponent through internal damage rather than external force.

In Chapter One, I discussed a variety of critical targeting systems for effective self-defense. However, in this chapter, we will narrow our focus exclusively to the head, utilizing impact pressure point targets for the Combat Pressure Points methodology. This approach, which I refer to as "*head hunting*," centers on the most vulnerable points of the head, allowing for swift and decisive strikes in real-world self-defense situations.

Unlike in my previous book *Combat Pressure Points*, the ears, nose, and chin have been excluded from this list of targets. While strikes to these areas can cause severe pain and temporary disorientation, this current system focuses on extreme force applications, where more severe pressure points are needed to incapacitate an opponent. The targets in this chapter are designed for life-threatening situations, where maximum damage is necessary and justified.

The combat pressure point targets we'll focus on in this chapter include:

Eyes – A sensitive area where a strike can cause temporary or permanent blindness, intense pain, or incapacitation.

Temple – A vulnerable target that can lead to unconsciousness, disorientation, or even more severe consequences when struck forcefully.

Throat – Striking the throat can cause choking, extreme injury, and potentially death, making it one of the most lethal targets, reserved for life-threatening situations.

Back of Neck – This is another sensitive area that can lead to unconsciousness or even paralysis with a properly delivered strike.

By concentrating on these key head targets, you ensure that each strike counts, incapacitating the opponent quickly while reducing the duration and risk of combat. This *head hunting* strategy allows you to exploit the assailant's most vulnerable areas for maximum damage.

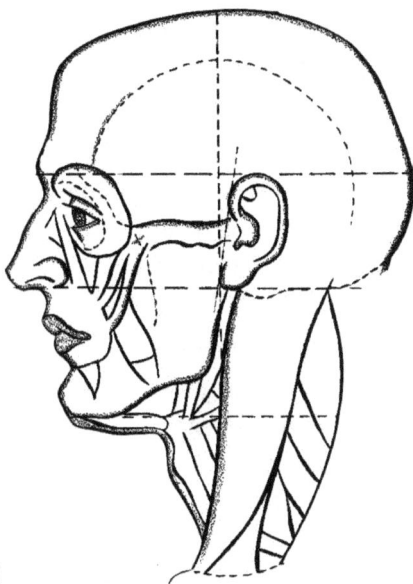

THE FLUID SHOCK PRINCIPLE

In Combat Pressure Points, maximizing the impact of your blow is paramount. To do this effectively, you must focus on transferring the full energy of your strike into the target.

This concept is known as the *Fluid Shock Principle.* When delivering an impact pressure points strike, allow your blow to sink into the target for a fraction of a second before retracting. This split-second pause ensures that the energy is fully absorbed by the target, causing maximum damage and incapacitation. By allowing the strike to settle into the opponent's target, you amplify its effect, making it far more devastating than a quick hit.

WARNING: Avoid jabbing or flicking punches, as these movements fail to transfer enough energy and leave you vulnerable to potential counterattacks. Such strikes may appear fast, but they are futile in delivering the kind of impact required to disable an adversary quickly and decisively.

By mastering the Fluid Shock Principle, you ensure that your strikes, whether to the eyes, throat, or other critical pressure points, deliver the maximum impact necessary to end the threat efficiently.

ATTACKING THE EYES

Let's take another look at the eyes (no pun intended) from the perspective of Combat Pressure Points. The eyes are perhaps the most vulnerable target on the human body, and a precise strike here can result in devastating consequences for your opponent. Whether you're aiming to temporarily blind or permanently incapacitate, attacking the eyes is an incredibly effective method for neutralizing a threat quickly.

When targeting the eyes, accuracy and intent are paramount. A direct finger jab, thumb gouge, or even a well-aimed thumb rake can cause severe pain, disorientation, and immediate loss of vision. The key is to ensure that your strike follows through, applying the Fluid Shock Principle - allowing the energy of your strike to sink into the eye socket for that crucial fraction of a second. This ensures maximum impact, transferring the full force of your blow into the opponent's most sensitive area.

The eyes represent a target that few attackers can defend against or recover from swiftly. A single strike can be enough to stop the fight entirely, making it one of the most critical pressure points in real-world self-defense.

Thumb Rake

The thumb rake is a powerful close-quarter technique aimed at quickly incapacitating an opponent. Using the thumb as the primary weapon, the practitioner applies firm pressure and rakes it horizontally across the opponent's eye, targeting severe irritation, pain, or even temporary blindness. Success in this technique depends on the use of the opposite hand to anchor the opponent's neck, providing stability and control. By securing the neck, the practitioner reduces the opponent's ability to evade or block the attack, ensuring precise and effective contact with the eye.

Thumb Gouge

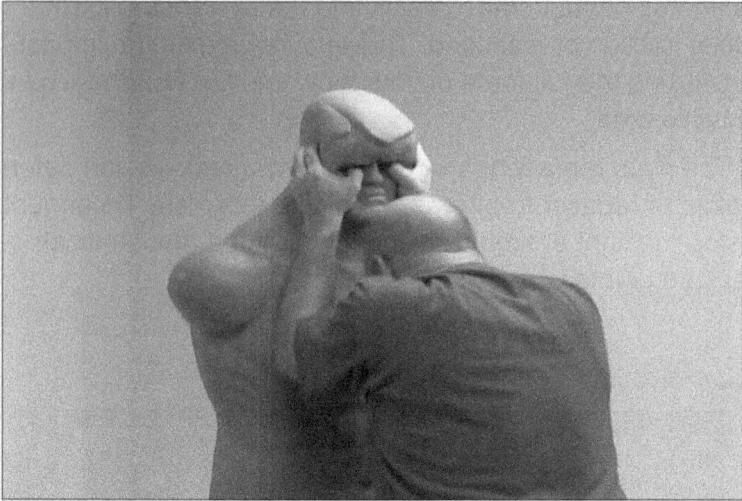

The double-thumb gouge is an extremely destructive close-quarter technique that can deliver devastating results, whether you're standing or on the ground.

To execute this technique, place both hands on the assailant's face and secure your grip by wrapping your lower fingers around their jawline. Then, drive both of your thumbs into the assailant's eye sockets with force, applying increasing pressure. This technique has the potential to cause temporary or permanent blindness, induce shock, and even lead to unconsciousness.

Eye Rake

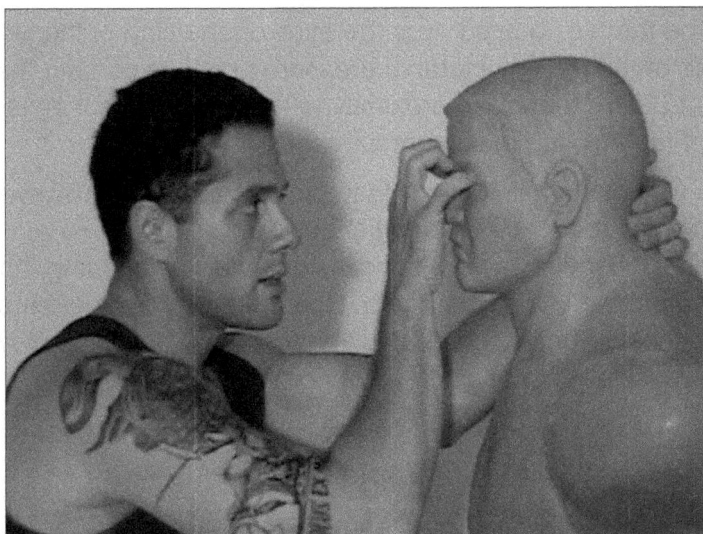

The eye rake is a brutal close-quarters technique aimed at temporarily or permanently blinding an assailant, giving you an immediate tactical advantage in a life-threatening situation.

To perform the eye rake, secure the opponent's neck with one hand while positioning your other hand on their face. With your thumb near the jawline, use your other fingers to rake vertically down their eyes in a swift, sharp motion. Apply steady pressure to drive force into the eye sockets. The movement should be fast, non-telegraphic, and unexpected to catch the opponent off guard.

ATTACKING THE TEMPLE

The temple, located near the eyes on the side of the skull, is one of the most vulnerable pressure points in combat. Its thin structure and close proximity to the brain make it an ideal target for inflicting maximum damage.

A well-placed strike to the temple can have serious, even deadly consequences. Potential outcomes include unconsciousness, severe concussion, internal bleeding, and in extreme cases, shock or coma. Due to its fragility, the temple is a critical target for combat scenarios, where a single blow can decisively incapacitate an opponent.

Temple Hook

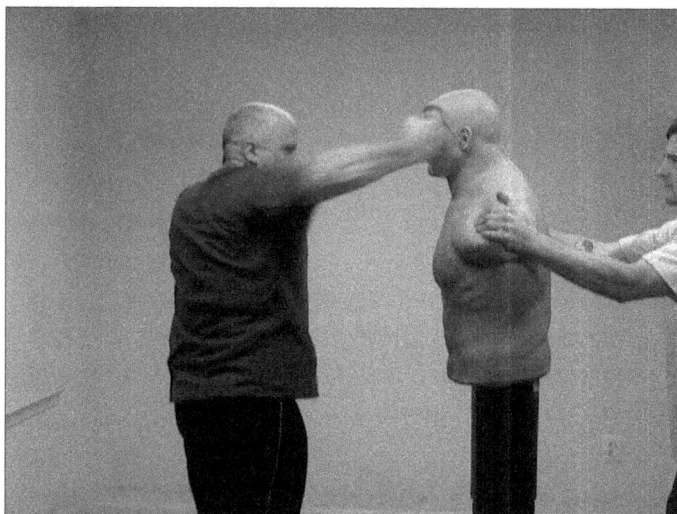

Throwing a hook punch to the temple is a highly effective technique due to the vulnerability of this pressure point. When executed with precision and power, the hook punch targets the thin bone structure of the temple, delivering significant force that can disrupt the opponent's equilibrium and cause disorientation, unconsciousness, or even more severe injuries. The curved trajectory of the hook punch allows it to bypass an opponent's guard, making it an ideal strike to exploit the temple's fragility. However, because of the potential for serious damage, this technique should be used with caution and only in situations where such force is justified.

Elbow to Temple

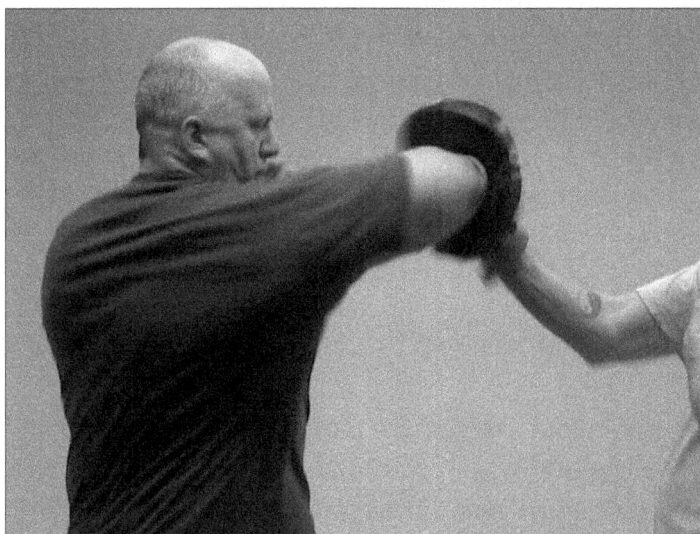

An elbow strike to the temple is an incredibly powerful technique, leveraging the hard bone of the elbow against one of the most fragile areas of the skull. The short, sharp motion of an elbow strike allows it to generate significant force at close range, making it ideal for targeting the temple. A well-placed elbow strike can lead to immediate disorientation, unconsciousness, or even more severe consequences such as a concussion or internal bleeding.

ATTACKING THE THROAT

As I discussed earlier, the throat is one of the most lethal pressure point targets in combat due to its minimal protection. It is shielded only by a thin layer of skin, leaving vital structures like the trachea, thyroid cartilage, and larynx highly vulnerable to damage. The trachea, or windpipe, is a cartilaginous tube about 4 1/2 inches long and 1 inch in diameter, making it especially susceptible to a forceful strike.

A powerful blow to the throat can result in a range of devastating consequences, including unconsciousness, massive hemorrhaging, air starvation, and even death. If the thyroid cartilage is crushed, the windpipe may swell shut, causing suffocation. Additionally, a severe strike can lead to blood drowning as internal bleeding blocks the airway. Due to the critical nature of these injuries, targeting the throat is reserved for life-threatening situations where extreme force is justified.

In the Combat Pressure Points methodology, attacking the throat delivers maximum damage with minimal effort, making it a vital target for incapacitating an opponent swiftly and decisively.

Web Hand Strike

To execute the strike, separate your thumb from your index finger, creating a "V" shape, and drive the web of your hand forcefully into the opponent's throat. Keep your hand stiff with the palm facing downward for maximum impact. After making contact, quickly retract your hand to the starting position to reset for further actions.

WARNING: The Web Hand strike is extremely dangerous and should only be used in life-threatening situations. Ensure that its use is legally warranted and fully justified before applying it.

Knife Hand Strike

The Horizontal Knife Hand is a powerful strike ideal for dealing with multiple attackers, particularly when flanked. To execute the strike, rotate your hips forcefully toward the approaching adversary, generating momentum. Make contact with the edge of your hand, targeting the opponent's throat, while ensuring your fingers remain out of the impact zone for maximum effectiveness and safety.

On the following page, a student demonstrates how to effectively incorporate a knife-hand strike in a close-quarters self-defense scenario. This technique focuses on generating momentum by forcefully rotating the hips toward the adversary, ensuring the strike is powerful and precise.

As shown in the steps, the edge of the hand targets the opponent's throat, maximizing both impact and safety by keeping the fingers out of the impact zone.

Step: 1

Step: 2

127

Throat Crush

To effectively execute the throat crush technique, begin by gaining control over the opponent. Use one hand to grip the side or back of their neck, stabilizing their movement and limiting their ability to escape or counter your actions. With your other hand, place your fingers and thumb on either side of the opponent's throat, specifically targeting the windpipe. Position your hand so that the web of your hand lines up directly with the Adam's apple, ensuring a firm grip.

As you apply pressure, squeeze your hand inward, compressing the trachea to restrict airflow and induce intense pain or panic. The goal is to incapacitate the opponent quickly by cutting off their air supply, leaving them unable to resist effectively.

Once the desired pressure has been applied and you've achieved the intended effect, evaluate the situation to determine whether to release the hold or escalate further, depending on the severity of the threat. This technique is extremely dangerous and should only be used in life-threatening situations where extreme force is justified.

Side Headlock Escape

You can utilize the throat crush technique to effectively counter a side headlock attack. Follow these step-by-step instructions to break free and gain control over your adversary.

Step 1: The assailant attacks with a side head lock.

Step 2: Turn your head into the attacker's centerline. Trap the attacker's striking hand with your right hand.

Step 3: Reach over the attacker's head, placing your middle finger firmly under the assailant's nose (septum region).

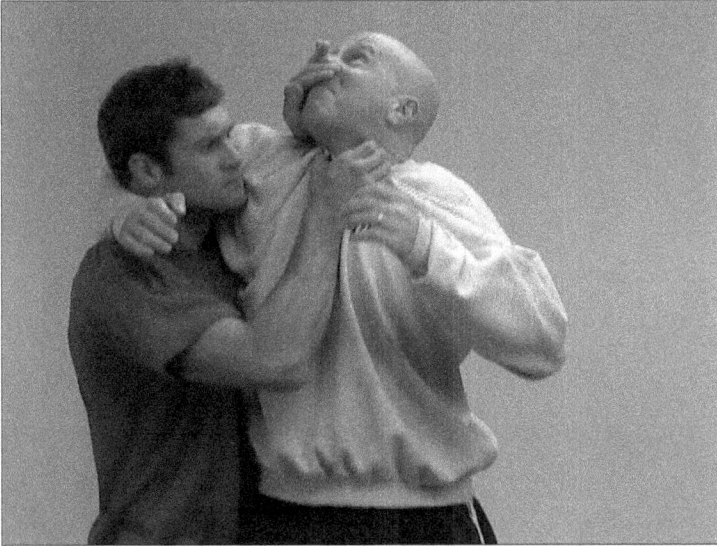

Step 4: *Force the attacker's head back, and immediately counter with a throat crush technique.*

Forearm Choke

Attacking the throat isn't limited to stand-up combat; you can also utilize the forearm choke effectively during ground fighting. When in close quarters on the ground, this technique allows you to apply pressure directly to your opponent's throat, using your forearm to restrict their airway and control their movements, making it a devastating option during a ground fight.

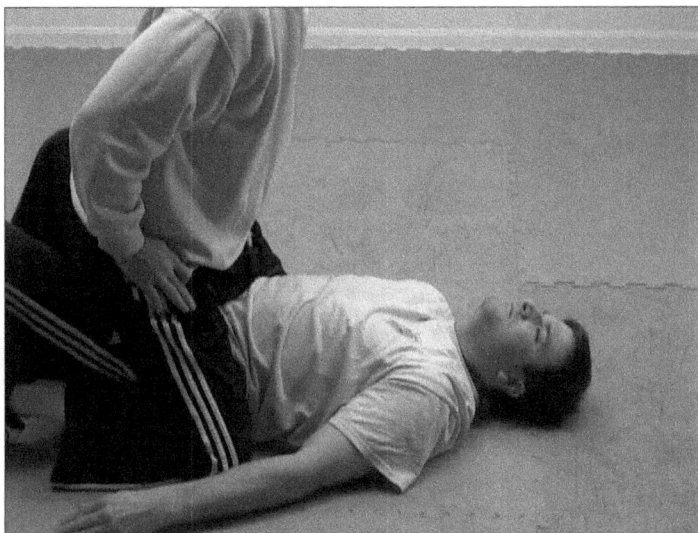

Step: 1

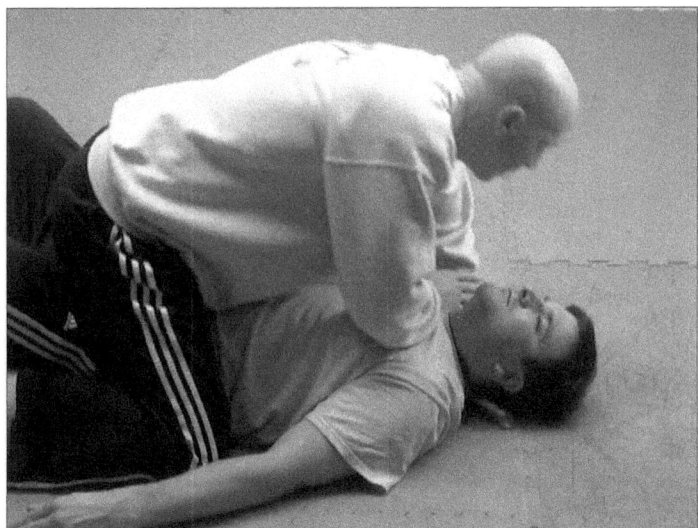

Step: 2

Step: 3

Step: 4

ATTACKING THE BACK OF NECK

The back of the neck is a critical target in combat pressure point methodology, housing the first seven vertebrae of the spinal column. These vertebrae function as a vital pathway for nerve impulses between the brain and the rest of the body, making this area especially vulnerable.

As a pressure point target, the back of the neck is particularly dangerous because the vertebrae are not well-protected. A powerful strike to this area can result in severe consequences, including shock, unconsciousness, a broken neck, complete paralysis, coma, or even death.

Long Arc Hammer fist

The Long Arc Hammer Fist strike to the back of the neck is a powerful finishing technique, designed to incapacitate an opponent quickly and decisively. Due to its potential to cause severe injury or even death, it should be reserved exclusively for situations where the use of deadly force is legally justified. This strike targets the vulnerable vertebrae at the back of the neck, making it effective in ending a life-threatening encounter when no other options remain.

In the following photos, observe how the focus mitts are positioned at the appropriate height for the striker. Additionally, note how the striker bends their knees and lowers their weight while delivering the blow, maximizing power and control.

Step: 1

Step: 2

ESCALATING TO THE NEXT LEVEL
THE WIDOW MAKER PROGRAM

As we transition from Combat Pressure Points to the next level of force, it's crucial to recognize that certain situations demand a more extreme response.

While Combat Pressure Points focus on precise, fine motor skill strikes to incapacitate an opponent, the Widow Maker Program shifts to a gross motor skill approach, utilizing the relentless and brutal *razing* method. This methodology is designed for life-or-death scenarios where the adversary's aggression requires an overwhelming, all-out attack.

Gross motor skills are generally simple, powerful movements that do not require fine precision, making them easier to perform under high stress or in adrenaline-fueled situations, where complex motor skills may deteriorate due to the body's natural stress response. In combat, gross motor skills are often preferred because they remain reliable and effective even when adrenaline is spiking.

The Widow Maker Program goes beyond precision strikes, focusing instead on delivering a continuous, strategically calculated assault through the razing method. Razing unleashes a rapid series of quarter-beat strikes, designed to overwhelm the opponent both physically and mentally, resulting in a total cognitive shutdown. The gross motor nature of these attacks - fast, aggressive, and unrelenting - ensures that the adversary is unable to process or defend against the onslaught.

As with all techniques in this book, it is imperative that the Widow Maker is used only in situations where lethal force is legally and morally justified. When the stakes are at their highest and survival demands an extreme response, the Widow Maker Program and its razing method become your ultimate line of defense.

So if you're ready to unleash the reaper, these techniques will ensure you're equipped to end any confrontation with unwavering resolve.

CHAPTER FOUR
The Widow Maker
Unleash The Reaper!

THE ART OF WEBBING

The Widow Maker Program features two distinct and powerful fighting methods: *Webbing* and *Razing*. Each method can function as a highly effective stand-alone approach to neutralize an attacker. However, when these methods are combined into a single, fluid assault, they become an unstoppable force. Let's begin by taking a closer look at Webbing.

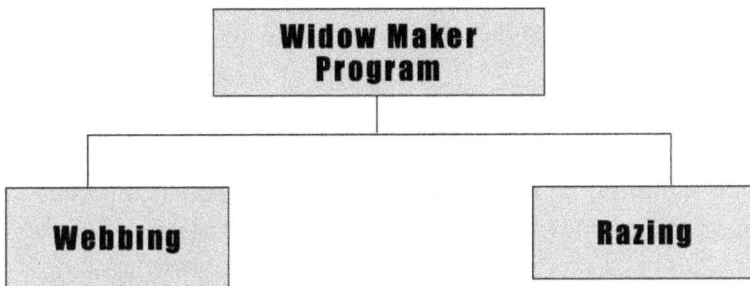

THE WEBBING STRIKE

The webbing technique is a signature element of my Contemporary Fighting Arts (CFA) self-defense system. While it may appear similar to a reinforced palm heel strike, it's far more powerful and complex. The body mechanics and footwork required for an effective webbing strike are fundamentally different from those of a standard palm heel. In fact, comparing a typical palm heel strike to the webbing technique is like comparing a firecracker to a grenade.

The name "webbing" comes from how the hands spread out like a large web, enveloping the opponent's face. This technique is incredibly versatile, serving multiple purposes in unarmed combat, including the following:

Entry Tool – To effectively use the razing method, you first need to close the distance gap between you and your adversary. Many confrontations will start outside of close-quarters combat (CQC) range, making it essential to bridge the distance safely. Thankfully, the webbing technique serves as a reliable and secure entry tool, allowing you to transition into the CQC range where razing techniques become most effective.

First Strike Weapon – As mentioned earlier, webbing is a powerful stand-alone striking technique. Its execution is nearly undetectable, making it an ideal choice as a first strike weapon. When applied correctly, the webbing strike is a safe, efficient, and highly effective technique. In fact, a properly delivered webbing strike can immediately incapacitate your adversary.

Sets Up Razing – If the webbing strike doesn't immediately incapacitate your adversary, it will undoubtedly weaken them both physically and psychologically, effectively preparing them for the subsequent phase of attack - *Razing*. This initial strike disrupts their balance and concentration, creating an opening for a relentless follow-up.

Pictured here, the Webbing technique.

THE WEBBING STANCE

Theoretically, the webbing strike can be executed from any standing position; however, two specific stances - First Strike and Natural Stance - significantly increase the likelihood of delivering a powerful and effective strike. These stances were covered in detail in Chapter One.

As discussed in some of my previous books, a skilled fighter avoids standing squarely in front of an adversary. When possible, it's always advantageous to adopt a strategic stance. A stance plays a critical role in your ability to either defend against or attack an opponent, and it can significantly influence the outcome of a fight.

That said, a stance is often a luxury in real combat. Situations may arise where you cannot assume a stance, so it is essential to be prepared to execute the webbing strike without any formal foundation or structure.

THE WEBBING TARGET

The webbing strike is specifically aimed at the adversary's chin, targeting it at a forty-five-degree angle to generate shock waves that travel to the cerebellum and cerebral hemispheres of the brain, leading to paralysis and immediate unconsciousness. This angle of impact not only increases the risk of severe injuries such as a broken jaw, concussion, whiplash, and neck fractures, but also destabilizes the adversary's entire physical structure. This disruption incapacitates and triggers intense disorientation, making any form of retaliation virtually impossible.

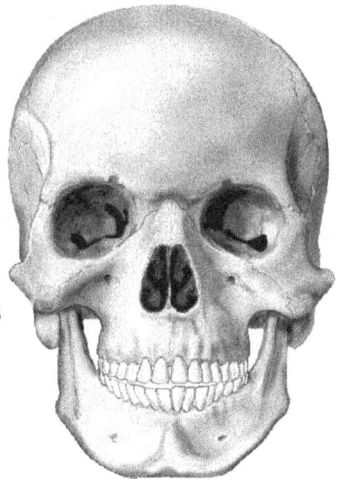

Striking the opponent's chin at a 45-degree angle will maximize damage to his brain and cervical vertebra.

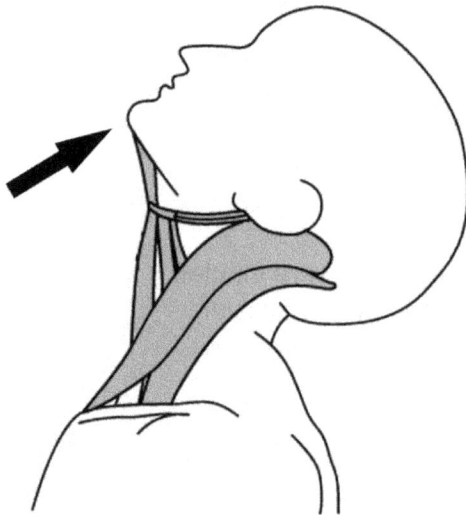

Optimal Angle for Webbing Strike: Aimed at a 45-degree angle to the chin, this trajectory directs force toward critical brain regions, maximizing the impact for immediate incapacitation.

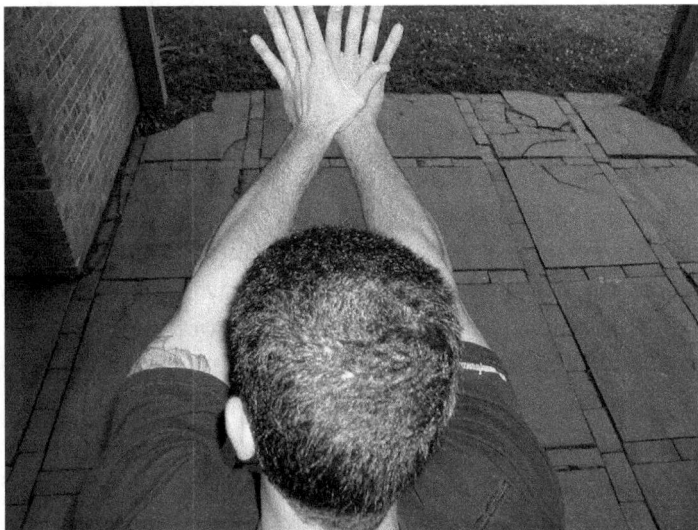

WEBBING BODY MECHANICS

The webbing strike involves precise hand and arm configuration, correct body mechanics, and timing. However, once you master these elements, webbing becomes second nature - an instinctive weapon you can deploy even under the pressure of a life-threatening attack.

The following section provides a detailed breakdown of the body mechanics necessary for effective webbing. Remember, proper execution of these mechanics should take less than one second.

Step 1: Begin from a right lead stance (with your right leg forward). Simultaneously position your left hand over your right hand, aligning your right thumb beneath the 5th metacarpal of your left hand (see illustration). In this setup, your right palm serves as the primary striking surface, while your left hand provides reinforcement to enhance the structural integrity of the strike. The

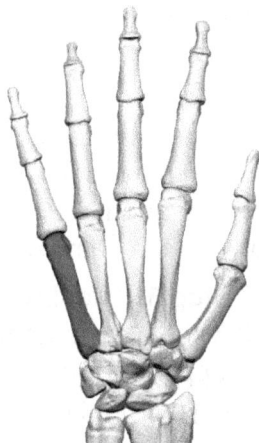

145

left hand plays a crucial role in this technique, as it not only reduces the risk of wrist or hand injuries but also amplifies the power of the blow.

Step 2: With your hands properly aligned, forcefully drive both arms toward the opponent's chin, ensuring your elbows remain slightly bent upon impact - do not fully lock them. Unlike conventional punches, the webbing strike does not involve any twisting or torquing of the body. Instead, its power is generated through the coordinated use of major muscle groups (including the back, chest, shoulders, and triceps) combined with forward momentum.

Step 3: Direct the webbing strike at approximately a 45-degree angle to the opponent's chin. The goal is to transmit shock waves to the cerebellum and cerebral hemispheres of the adversary's brain. Ensure that both of your palms remain perpendicular to the floor during the strike. This alignment helps minimize the risk of finger sprains and ensures a solid, flush connection with the target.

Step 4: Although the webbing strike can be executed from a stationary position, incorporating forward momentum significantly enhances its power. There are two ways to generate this momentum: the Half Step and the Full Step.

The Half Step: This movement generates substantial striking power. To perform the half step, move your lead foot forward approximately 24 inches while keeping your rear foot stationary.

The Full Step: This movement delivers the maximum striking power. To execute the full step, move your front foot forward about 24 inches, followed by moving your rear foot forward the same distance.

Step 5: After both hands make solid contact with the target, allow them to separate. Your left hand should grip the nape of the opponent's neck - this technique is known as "anchoring" - while your right hand transitions to initiate the razing phase.

WEBBING DEMONSTRATION

Step 1: *Begin from a first strike stance.*

Step 2: *Place your left hand over your right hand, aligning your right thumb beneath the 5th metacarpal of your left hand.*

Step 3: Once your hands are correctly positioned, drive both arms forward with force.

Step 4: Lower your head slightly as you step forward. Ensure that your elbows remain slightly bent upon making contact with the target.

BRIDGING THE GAP

After delivering the webbing technique, it's crucial to anchor your opponent. *Anchoring* means maintaining control over the adversary and preventing them from escaping the close-quarter engagement range. This step is vital for the Widow Maker program to function effectively, as it allows you to keep the pressure on the opponent.

Anchoring also serves as a critical link between the webbing and razing methodologies. There are two types of anchoring you need to master: *Offensive Anchoring* and *Defensive Anchoring*. Let's break down each one.

OFFENSIVE ANCHORING

Offensive anchoring is executed immediately after delivering the webbing strike. It involves grabbing hold of your opponent's neck with one hand while using the other hand to perform the razing technique. Anchoring is crucial for effective razing skills for the following five reasons:

1. It maintains the range necessary for continuous and effective razing, ensuring that each subsequent strike lands with precision.

2. It prevents the opponent from disengaging CQC range.

3. It stabilizes the opponent's head, allowing maximum pressure on facial targets when applying zero beat techniques, amplifying the overall damage.

4. It offers a tactile reference point if your vision becomes impaired during the course of the fight, allowing you to maintain control without relying on sight.

5. It establishes and conveys Alpha/Predator body language to the opponent, intensifying psychological dominance and weakening their resolve.

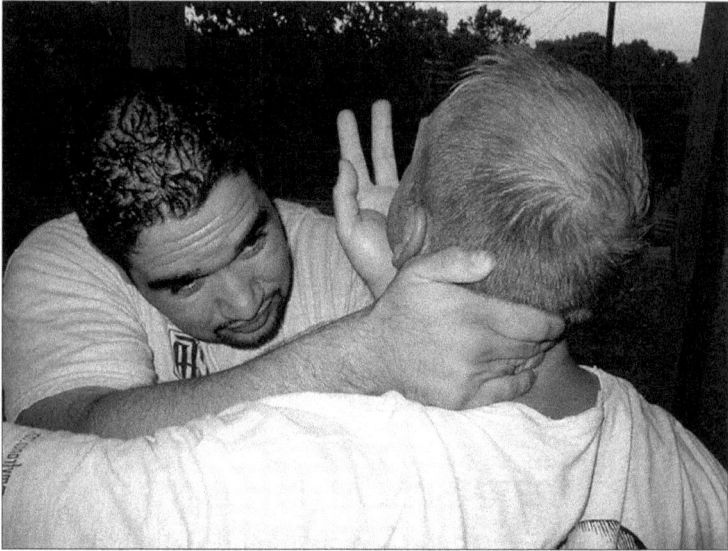

Pictured here, a student demonstrates offensive anchoring.

OFFENSIVE ANCHORING DEMONSTRATION

Step 1: *The author assumes a first strike stance.*

Step 2: He executes a webbing strike to the target.

Step 3: Once contact is made with the target, Franco's left hand anchors the back of the neck.

DEFENSIVE ANCHORING

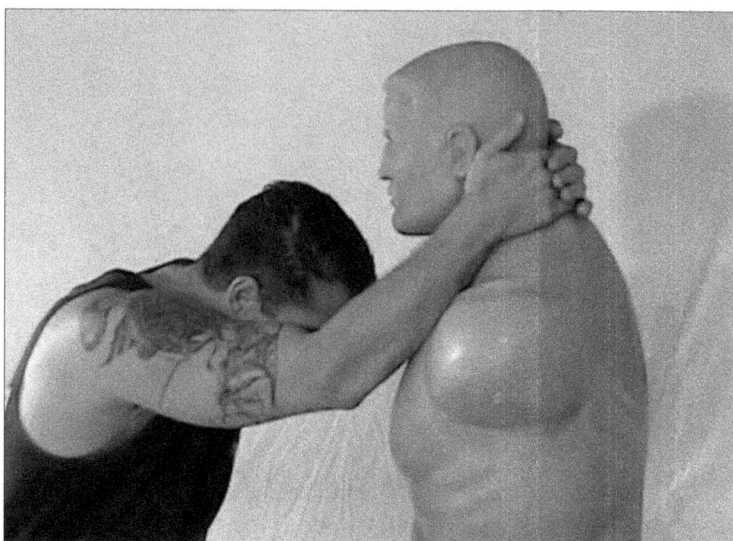

Next is defensive anchoring, which is employed in rare situations where your razing assault is interrupted, and the opponent panics and counters with a flurry of strikes.

This technique involves gripping the opponent's neck with both hands while tucking your head down between your biceps. Defensive anchoring serves as a temporary protective posture that shields your head, effectively minimizing the impact of the opponent's strikes.

Additionally, this technique allows you to maintain control over the opponent, preventing them from disengaging from close-quarters range or gaining momentum. The primary goal is to safeguard your head from incoming attacks until you can secure control over one of the opponent's arms, re-establishing your offensive advantage.

ANCHOR POINTS

Anchor points serve as crucial control mechanisms in close-quarters combat. By physically securing a part of the opponent's body, such as their neck or upper arm, you significantly reduce their ability to maneuver or escape.

The neck is an optimal anchor point because it allows you to control their center of gravity and balance while applying various techniques that compromise their posture and expose vital areas for attack. This level of control also gives you the ability to manipulate their head and upper body, preventing counterattacks while enhancing your own striking or submission capabilities.

In some cases, anchoring to the opponent's upper arm can be effective, particularly if the neck is not immediately accessible. Securing the upper arm allows you to neutralize their offensive arm, limiting their ability to strike or defend themselves. However, it's critical to avoid anchoring onto clothing, as fabric is prone to tearing, leaving you with little control over their actual movements.

By understanding and applying proper anchoring techniques, you position yourself to execute devastating attacks with precision while maintaining full control over the opponent's movements.

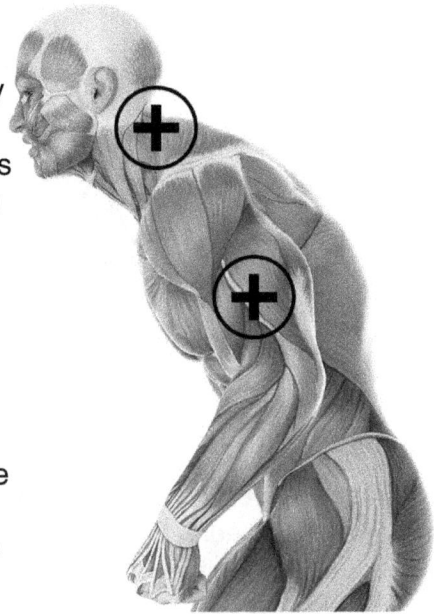

THE ART AND SCIENCE OF RAZING

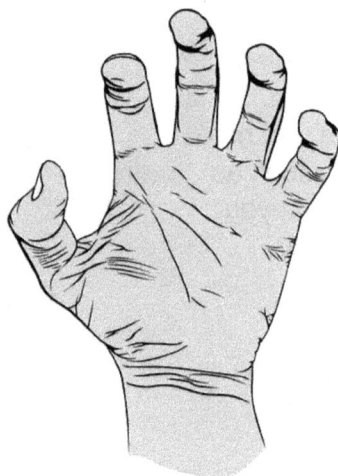

Once the webbing strike has been delivered and the opponent has been successfully anchored, it is imperative to transition immediately into the *Razing* method of attack.

Maintaining continuous offensive pressure without interruption is crucial. The primary goal is to seamlessly integrate webbing and razing into a single, relentless, and strategically calculated offensive sequence. This approach is designed to overwhelm and disrupt the opponent's cognitive processes, rendering him unable to respond effectively.

WELCOME TO THE DEEP END - NO TURNING BACK!

I have been teaching reality-based self-defense (RBSD) for over thirty-five years, and I can state with absolute confidence that razing is one of the most devastating forms of unarmed combat known. Its brutal and invasive nature inflicts severe physical and psychological trauma on its target. The sheer intensity of razing triggers immediate panic in the opponent, delivering a level of destruction that surpasses even that of a lethal and malicious criminal aggressor. When executed correctly, razing achieves the following objectives:

1. Cognitive Brain Shutdown - The intense and overwhelming nature of razing disrupts the opponent's cognitive processes, preventing any coherent thought or strategic response. The rapid and relentless nature of the razing technique overwhelms the opponent's ability to comprehend the unfolding situation.

2. Immediate Damage - Razing is exceptionally difficult to defend against due to the speed and close range at which quarter-beat strikes are delivered. The swift and relentless nature of these strikes makes it nearly impossible for the opponent to mount a defensive response. It can be compared to an aggressive swarm of wasps - leaving the opponent with little choice but to attempt to flee from the onslaught.

ADDITIONAL BENEFITS OF RAZING

Integrating the razing methodology into your self-defense repertoire offers numerous advantages. Here's a brief overview:

1. Unconventional Approach - Razing is a highly unorthodox and unusual fighting style. Even the most experienced martial artists or street fighters are unlikely to have encountered this form of combat. As a result, they're often unprepared to respond to it, both physically and mentally.

2. Low Maintenance - Razing techniques are exceptionally efficient and straightforward to execute, even under the stress of real-world combat situations. Unlike conventional strikes such as kicks and punches, mastering razing does not require extensive practice to perfect fine motor skills.

3. Reduced Risk of Injury - Unlike closed-fist strikes, razing techniques minimize the risk of injuries, such as sprained or broken wrists and hands, making them a safer option during the stress of physical confrontations.

What Exactly is Razing?

In Contemporary Fighting Arts, razing is defined as a sequence of aggressive close-quarter techniques intended to physically and psychologically dismantle a criminal assailant. These techniques are executed at various rhythms, including half-beat, quarter-beat, and zero-beat intervals, and encompass the following:

- **Eye raking**
- **Thumb gouging**
- **Hammer fists**
- **Palm Jolts**
- **Tearing**
- **Crushing**
- **Biting**
- **Hair pulling**
- **Elbow strikes**
- **Shaving forearms**
- **Head butts**
- **Bicep pops**
- **Neck cranks**
- **Finishing chokes**

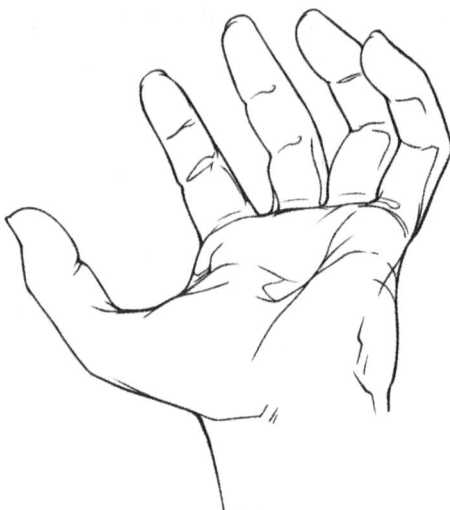

To the untrained observer, razing may appear erratic, disorganized, and chaotic, leading some to mistakenly label it as a 'haphazard' style of combat. However, beneath its seemingly wild nature lies a calculated and strategic approach designed to overwhelm the opponent both physically and mentally, rendering them incapable of effective defense.

In reality, razing is a close-quarters combat method that demands technical precision, timing, and coordination. It integrates advanced techniques that require dedicated training

156

and a deep understanding of human anatomy to achieve devastating effects in combat situations.

That said, it is possible to improvise with razing techniques, delivering a barrage of gross motor strikes against an opponent. In certain situations, this unrefined approach can be effective. However, to fully harness the devastating potential of razing, it must be delivered in a deliberate and calculated manner.

Moreover, razing is straightforward and can be seamlessly integrated into any fighting style. Regardless of the martial art or self-defense system you practice, razing can be incorporated into your existing approach with ease, adding a powerful layer of close-quarters combat effectiveness.

When Is It Appropriate to Use Razing?

It's important to address some crucial considerations regarding the use of razing. Due to its highly destructive nature, razing should only be employed in self-defense scenarios where the use of deadly force is justified.

Understanding Deadly Force

So, what constitutes deadly force? It is essential to emphasize that force should never be used against another person unless it is absolutely necessary. Force is categorized into two levels: deadly and non-deadly.

Deadly force refers to any violent action that is likely to result in a substantial risk of death or serious bodily injury. An individual is legally permitted to use deadly force in self-defense only when responding to another's use of deadly force. On the other hand, non-deadly force refers to actions that do not result in serious bodily harm or death.

It is crucial to understand that both webbing and razing have the potential to inflict serious bodily harm or even death. As such, they are considered techniques of deadly force and should only be used to protect yourself or a loved one from the imminent threat of unlawful deadly aggression.

Remember, the decision to use deadly force must always be a last resort, undertaken only after all other means of avoiding violence have been fully exhausted. Razing is not intended as an intermediate use-of-force option. It is not a technique that can be toned down for compliance or control. With razing, it's all or nothing - its effectiveness relies on being executed with overwhelming force and rapid speed. Anything less than full commitment to this approach may leave you vulnerable to serious injury from your adversary.

UNDERSTANDING THE WIDOW MAKER'S BEAT SYSTEM

To fully grasp the effectiveness of the razing fighting method, it's essential to understand the beat system I have developed. This system categorizes strikes into four distinct classifications:

- **Full Beat:** A strike that includes both an initiation and a retraction phase. Standard punches and blows, such as a lead straight or rear cross, fall into this category.

- **Half Beat:** A strike that is delivered during the retraction phase of the preceding strike, allowing for a faster follow-up.

- **Quarter Beat:** A rapid series of strikes that maintain continuous contact with the target. These strikes are primarily responsible for inducing psychological panic and trauma in the opponent.

- **Zero Beat:** Techniques that apply sustained pressure to a specific target until the adversary is fully incapacitated. Zero beat is generally used at the conclusion of a razing assault to ensure maximum effectiveness and complete the incapacitation of the adversary.

Although there are four distinct beat classifications, the razing methodology utilizes only three: half beat, quarter beat, and full beat.

Full Beat Demonstration

Step 1: Franco squares off in a fighting stance.

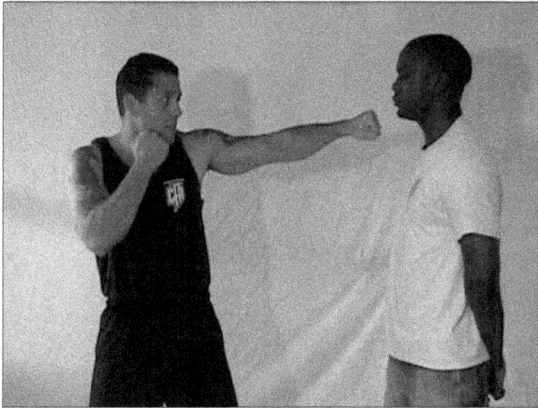

Step 2: He delivers a lead straight punch by extending his arm at his opponent.

Step 3: Franco retracts his arm back to the starting position.

Half Beat Demonstration

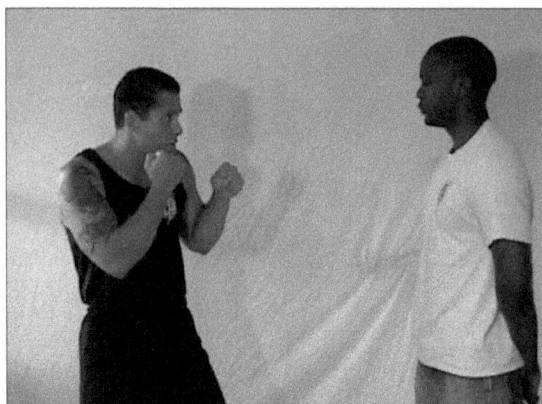

Step 1: Franco assumes a fighting stance.

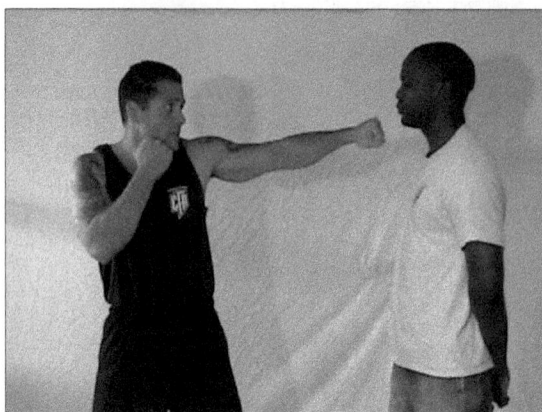

Step 2: He delivers a lead straight punch by extending his arm at his opponent.

Step 3: As Franco retracts his arm back, he converts it to a lead horizontal elbow strike.

Quarter Beat Demonstration

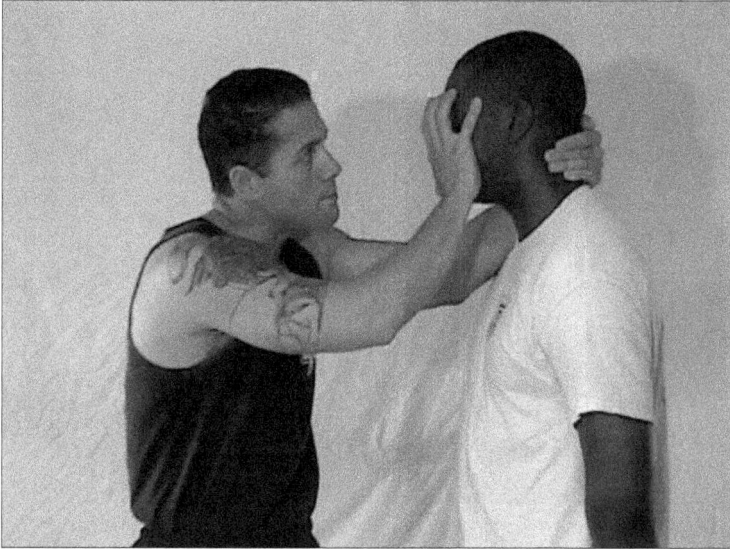

Step 1: *Franco begins his quarter beat assault by anchoring his opponent.*

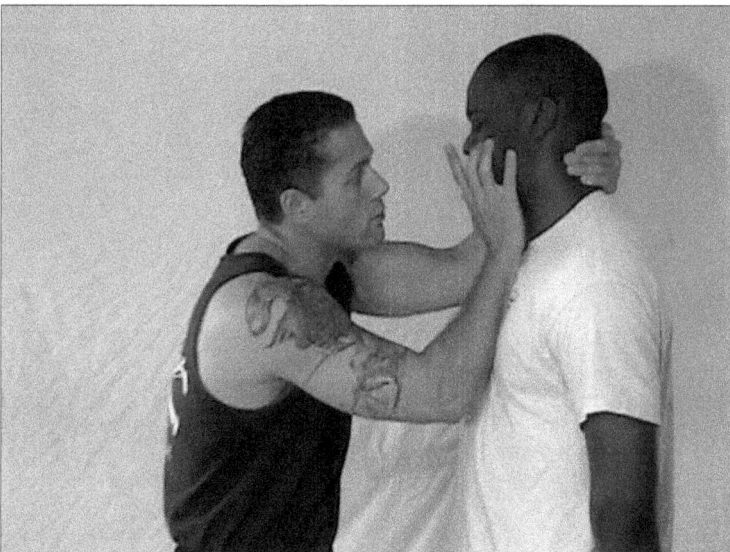

Step 2: *He rakes the opponent's eyes with a quick downward motion.*

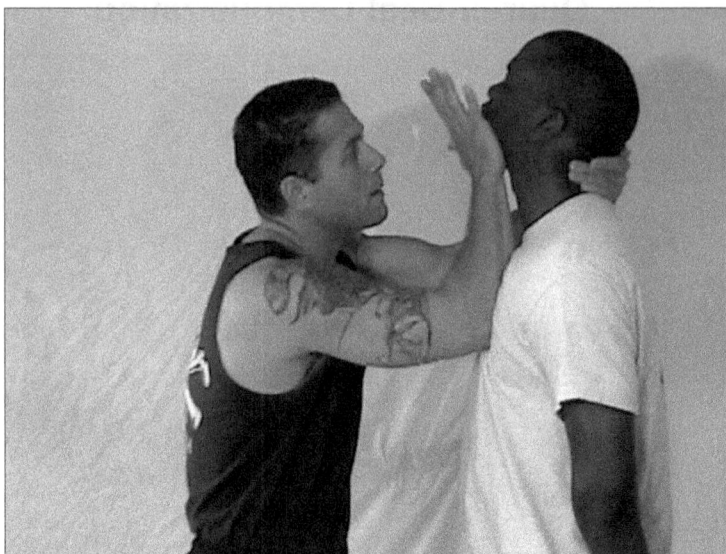

Step 3: *Without breaking contact with his opponent's face, Franco attacks with a palm jolt to the chin.*

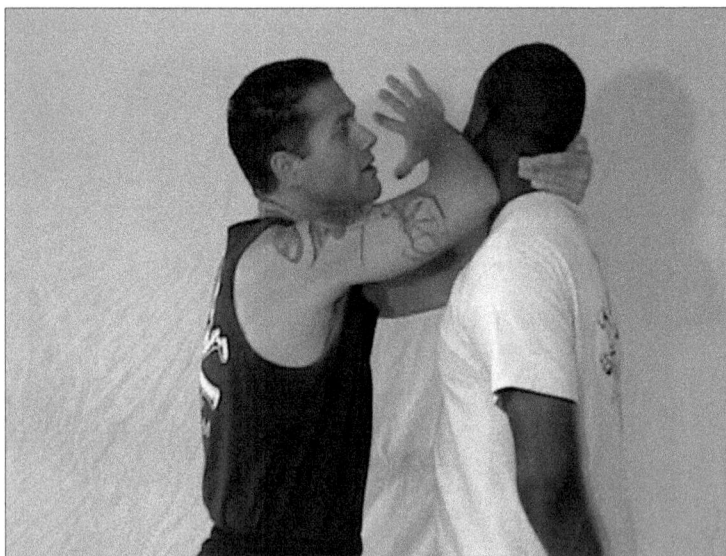

Step 4: *He immediately follows up with a shaving forearm across his opponent's face.*

Zero Beat Demonstration

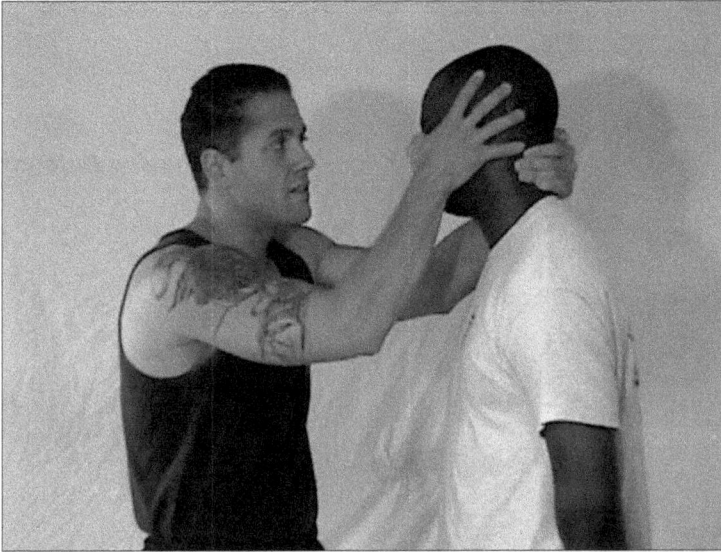

Pictured here, the author demonstrates a single thumb gouge technique.

The rear naked choke is another effective zero beat technique used at the completion phase of razing.

Razing Techniques

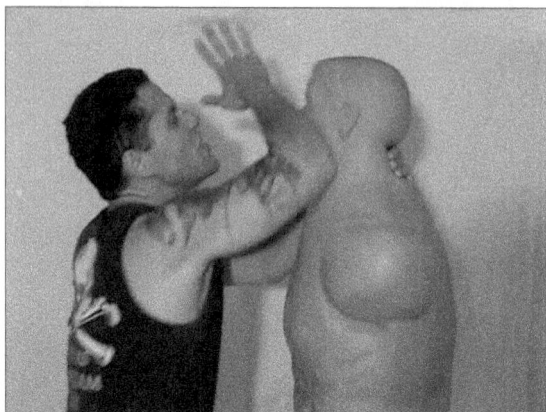

Shaving Forearm

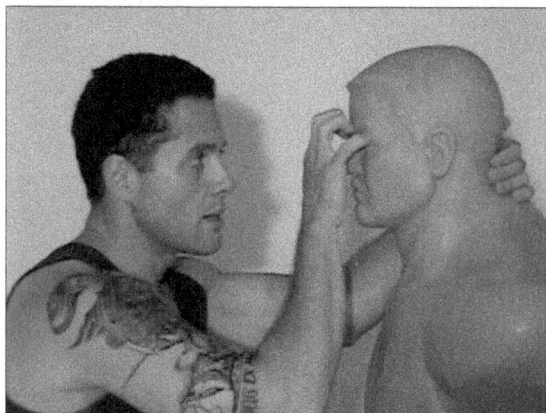

Eye Rake

*Short Arc
Hammer Fist*

Palm Jolt

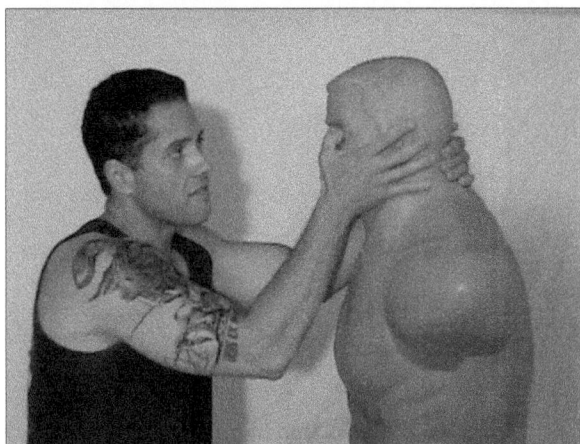

Thumb Gouge

Vertical Elbow

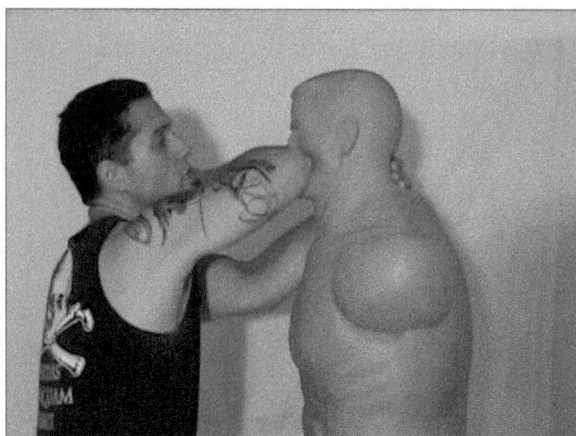

Horizontal Elbow

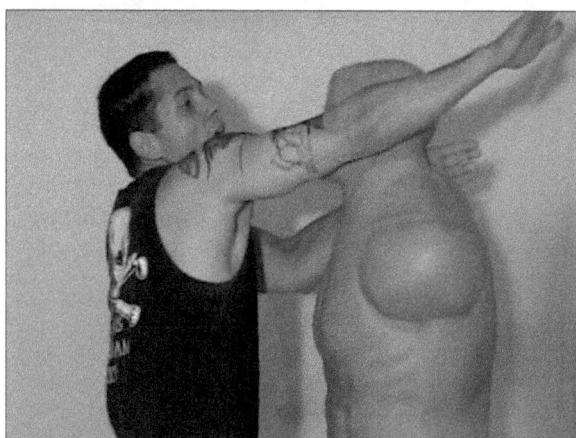

Biceps Pop

Biting

166

Head Butt

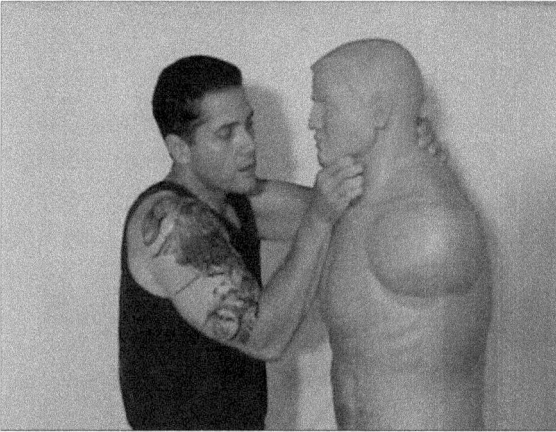

Throat Crush

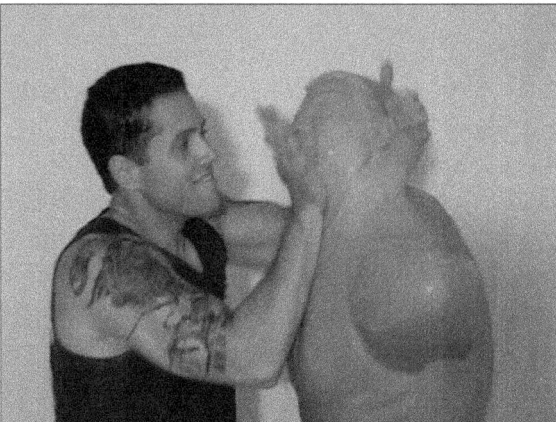

Neck Crank

Avoid Kicking Techniques

Kicking techniques should not be utilized during the execution of the razing method. Attempting to integrate kicks into a razing sequence disrupts the continuous offensive flow, potentially exposing you to significant risk.

As previously discussed, the effectiveness of razing lies in its ability to overwhelm the opponent, inducing a temporary cognitive shutdown. Achieving this effect requires maintaining constant pressure on the adversary. Kicking techniques, however, inherently remove you from close-quarter combat range, providing the opponent with an opportunity to regain his composure and counterattack.

Avoid Knee Strikes

While discussing techniques to avoid, it's important to refrain from using knee strikes during razing, as they present significant risks. Razing often forces the opponent to retreat quickly from the attack, and attempting a knee strike while they are pulling away can destabilize your stance and lead to a loss of balance. Additionally, incorporating a knee strike disrupts the continuous offensive flow that is critical to razing's effectiveness. In summary, knee strikes should be avoided during razing to maintain both stability and momentum.

Beyond the practical risks, knee strikes also shift focus and energy away from the upper-body dominance central to effective razing. Razing is designed to keep pressure applied directly to high-value targets, maintaining a close-quarters control that knee strikes inherently disrupt. By using only upper-body techniques, you retain complete control over range and positioning, allowing you to maintain relentless pressure on the opponent without exposing yourself to counterstrikes or losing the crucial upper-body advantage that razing requires.

The Chest-to-Back Position

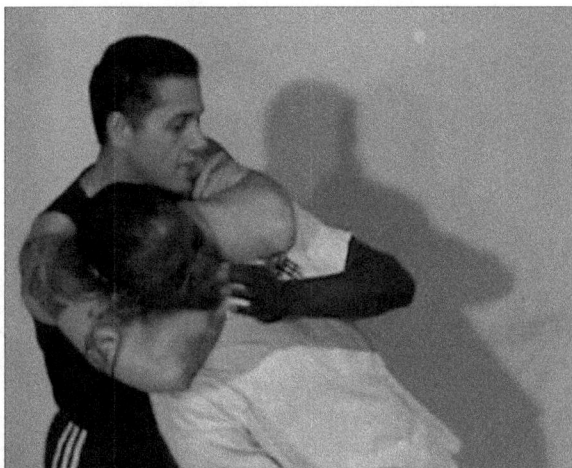

The chest-to-back position is the most advantageous position to assume after completing a razing assault. This position provides maximum control over the opponent while significantly limiting their ability to counterattack effectively. Additionally, the chest-to-back position allows for the application of a highly effective rear naked choke technique.

However, it's important to note that achieving the chest-to-back position is not a requirement for concluding a fight; rather, it is a strategically advantageous position. There are two primary methods for acquiring the chest-to-back position: the reflexive turn and the neck crank technique.

Reflexive Turn: During a razing assault, the overwhelming nature of the attack often causes the opponent's cognitive functions to shut down, prompting a reflexive turn away from the assault. Focused solely on escaping the pain of quarter-beat strikes, the opponent frequently makes a critical error by exposing their back to you.

Neck Crank Technique: Alternatively, the chest-to-back position can be achieved by applying a neck crank technique at the conclusion of the razing sequence. As the saying goes in my CFA system, *"When the neck turns, the body follows."*

Neck Crank Demonstration

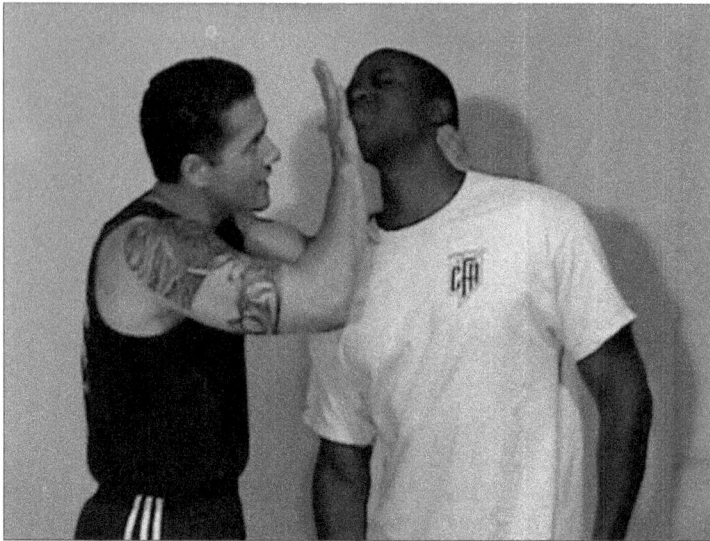

Step 1: Begin with your palm pressed against the opponent's chin.

Step 2: Next, push your opponent's chin in a counter clockwise direction.As your opponent's head and body turns, release contact from the chin.

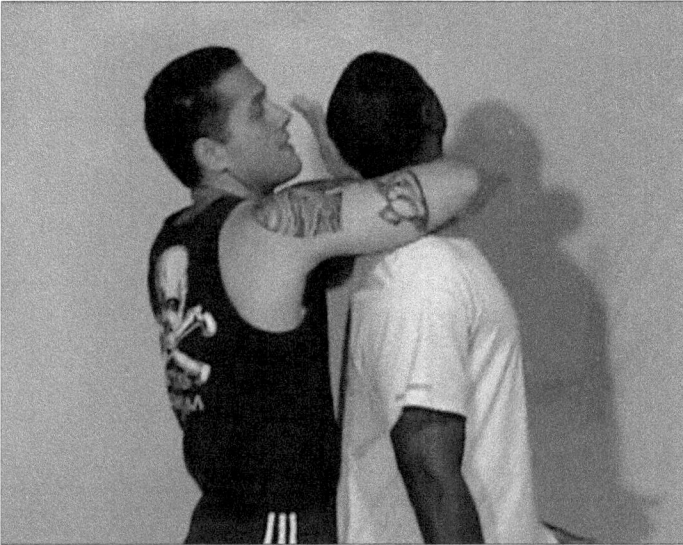

Step 3: *Once the opponent exposes his back, insert your arm against this throat and solidify the rear naked choke hold.*

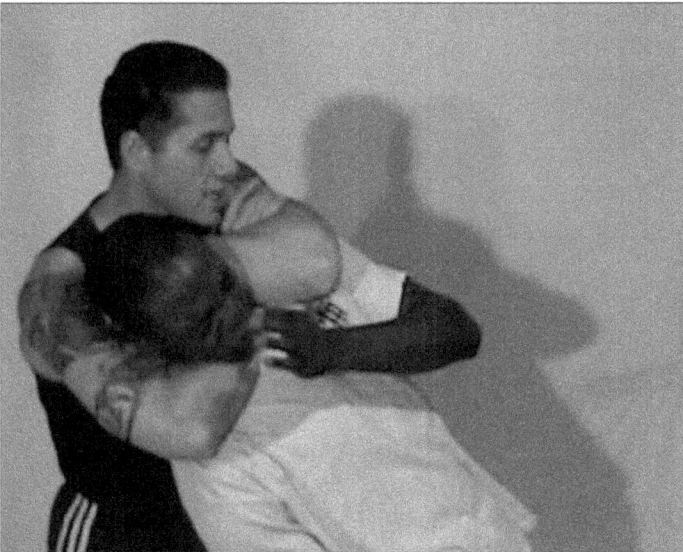

Step 4: *Apply pressure with both of your arms while forcing the opponent to the ground.*

Razing Targets

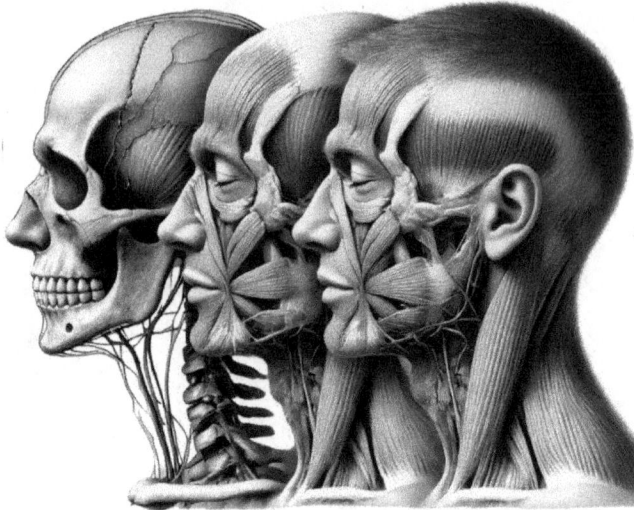

Razing techniques concentrate on a precise set of anatomical targets, all situated on the opponent's head and face. These targets were covered in detail in Chapter 1, so refer back to that chapter if you need a refresher. The key targets include:

- **Eyes**
- **Temple**
- **Nose**
- **Chin**
- **Throat**
- **Neck**

Important Note: The Mouth as a Target

The mouth is not a suitable target for razing. Avoid attempting any fish-hooking techniques during a razing assault. Keep your fingers away from the opponent's mouth, as there is a significant risk of losing a finger.

The Razing Stance

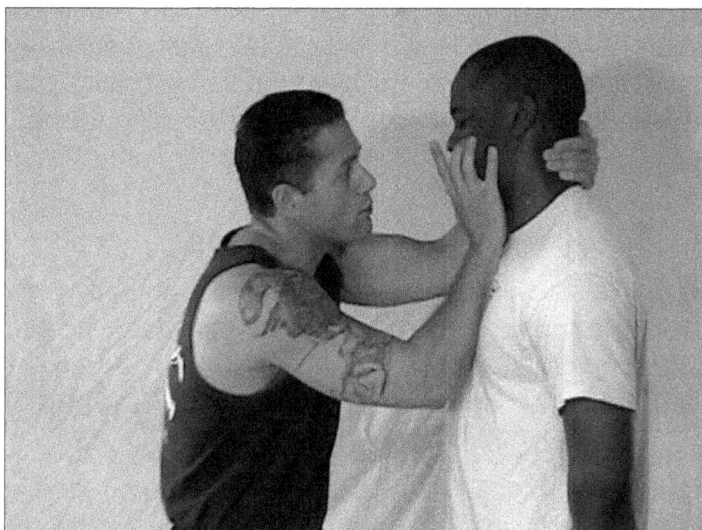

While it is possible to execute razing techniques from any standing position, utilizing a proper stance significantly enhances the effectiveness of your assault. A razing stance acts as a reference point from which you can deliver strikes while exploiting your opponent's reactions.

A solid stance not only optimizes the delivery of your razing techniques but also helps protect your vital areas from potential counterattacks. To assume an effective razing stance, position your body and feet at a 45-degree angle relative to your opponent. This alignment moves your vital targets back, reducing exposure to direct attacks, while keeping you in an advantageous position to launch your razing assault.

When adopting a razing stance, place your weaker side forward. For instance, if you are right-handed, position your left side toward the opponent. This orientation strengthens the stability of your anchor and maximizes the speed and power of your dominant razing arm. However, it's important to develop the ability to raze from both sides, so ensure you dedicate equal practice time to both left and right stances.

To achieve a balanced stance, place your feet slightly wider than shoulder-width apart, with your knees bent and flexible. Distribute your body weight evenly, keeping fifty percent on each leg, and maintain control of your balance throughout the engagement. Stability is essential when executing razing techniques, allowing for both power and precision.

Razing Limitations

Razing is a powerful and highly effective method in many self-defense situations, but it is important to recognize that has some limitations. Below are several situations in which the use of razing is not appropriate:

Non-Deadly Force Situations: As previously discussed, razing has the potential to inflict severe bodily harm or even result in death. It is classified as a form of deadly force and should only be employed when legally justified to use such force. Deploying razing in non-deadly force scenarios can lead to serious legal consequences.

Pain Compliance Situations: Razing is not suitable as an intermediate use-of-force technique. It is not designed to function as a compliance tool for subduing or controlling an opponent. Its purpose is far more aggressive, and using it outside of life-threatening situations is inappropriate.

Multiple Attacker Situations: Effective defense against multiple attackers relies heavily on mobility, enabling you to shift strategically between opponents, exploit openings, and avoid becoming encircled. Mobility allows you to reposition, keep attackers in a single line or limited arc, and deliver quick, targeted strikes without becoming vulnerable to a surrounding threat.

In contrast, razing requires a full commitment to one adversary, locking you into close quarters through anchoring techniques that immobilize your opponent but also restrict your own freedom of movement. This anchoring is ideal for overwhelming a single opponent; however, it limits your ability to react quickly to attacks from other directions, leaving you exposed to flanking attacks from additional adversaries.

Knife and Edged Weapon Situations: When faced with an opponent wielding an edged weapon, the foremost priority is to *control the weapon* before attempting to neutralize the attacker. Attempting to perform razing techniques while simultaneously trying to manage the weapon with one hand is a highly dangerous approach that could result in severe injury or death. Such situations demand a more specialized response. Remember, understanding these limitations is critical for integrating razing effectively into your self-defense strategy.

Razing Examples

To provide a clearer understanding of my razing method, I have included several different razing demonstrations. It's important to note that each of these sequences is executed in mere seconds. However, these examples are not meant to be memorized as a step-by-step sequence to replicate in a fight. Every move will depend on the reaction dynamics of the adversary during the confrontation and your ability to adapt in real-time.

About the Photographs

The following photographs were captured during a live razing demonstration, offering snapshots of rapid and dynamic movements in real time. These images are not staged or posed. However, still photographs alone cannot fully convey the intensity, brutality, and speed of razing. To truly appreciate its ferocity and effectiveness, I highly recommend watching the razing demonstrations available on my **SammyFrancoTV YouTube channel.** Viewing these techniques in action will give you a far deeper understanding of their true power and the relentless force that makes razing so effective in real-world scenarios.

Razing Demonstration #1

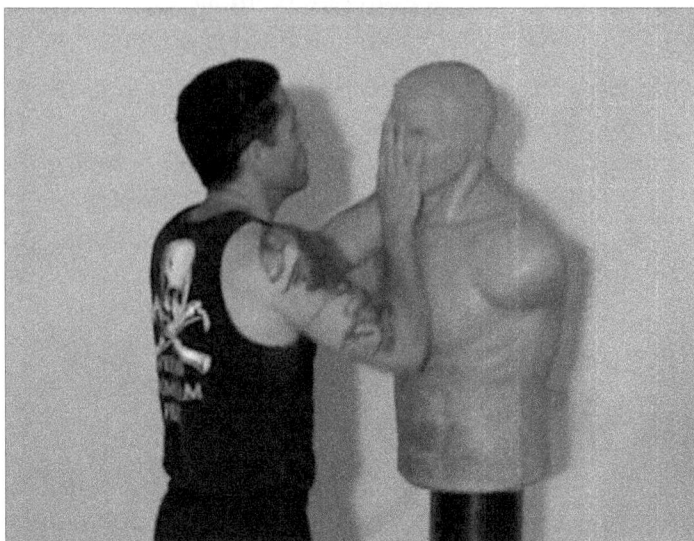

Step 1: *Franco begins with his left hand anchored behind the neck.*

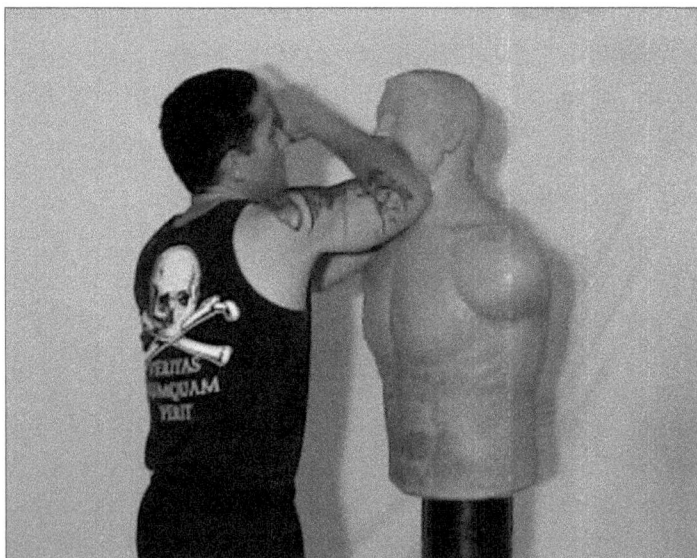

Step 2: *The razing begins with a shaving forearm across the face.*

176

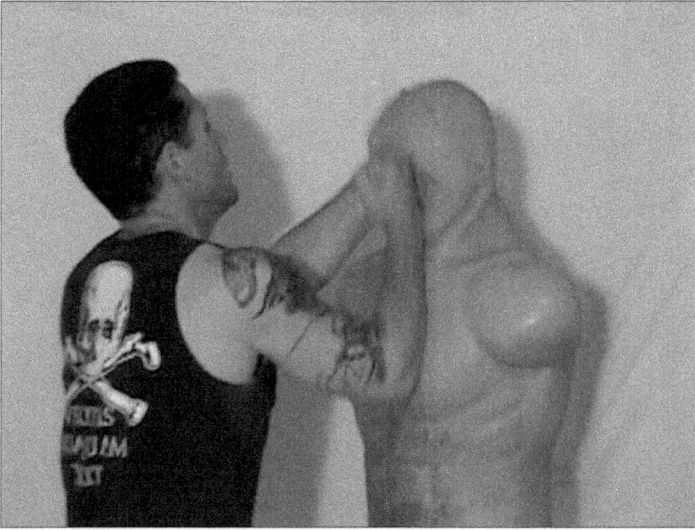

Step 3: *He follows up with a short arc hammer fist strike to the nose.*

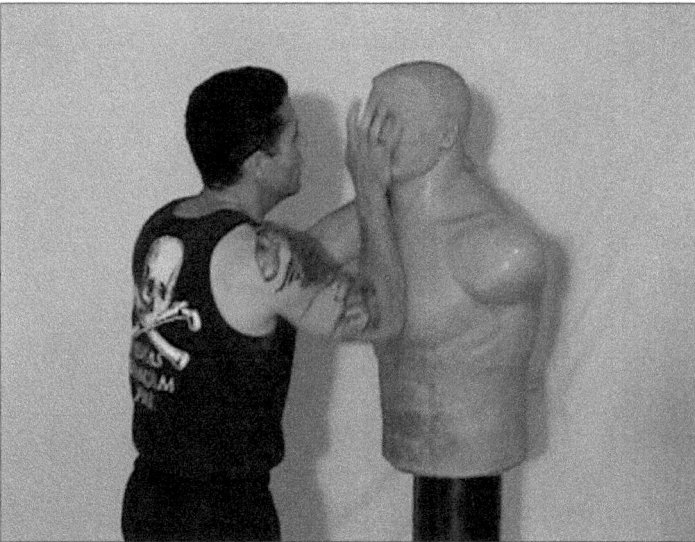

Step 4: *Next, a palm jolt to the chin.*

177

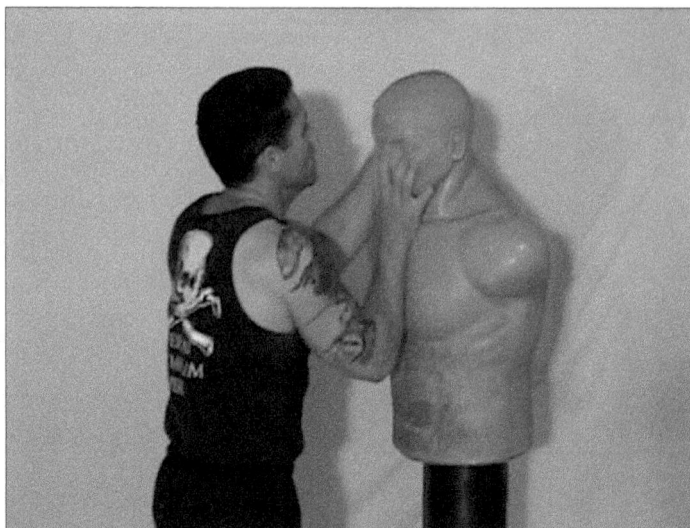

Step 5: He rakes the eyes.

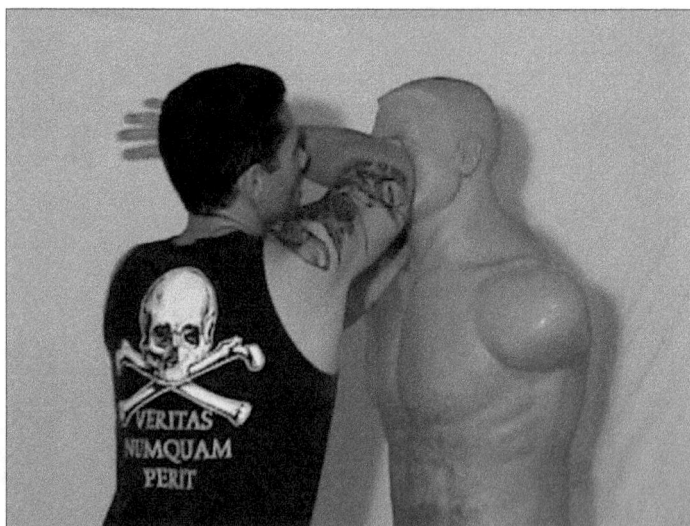

Step 6: Without breaking contact with the face, he delivers a diagonal elbow strike.

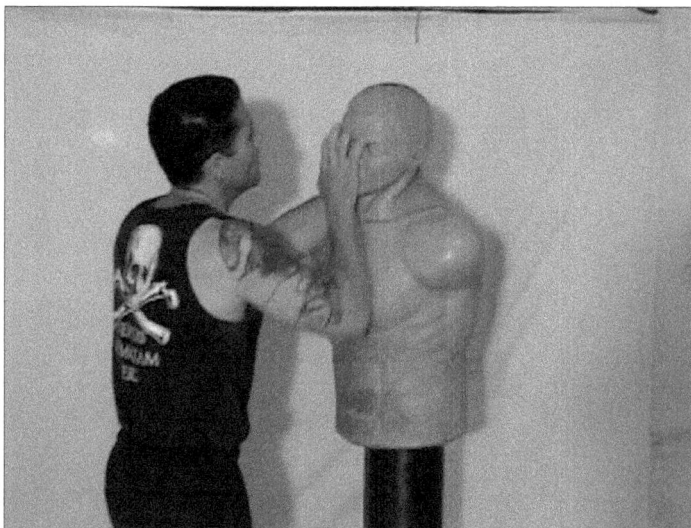

Step 7: *The diagonal elbows flows into another eye rake attack.*

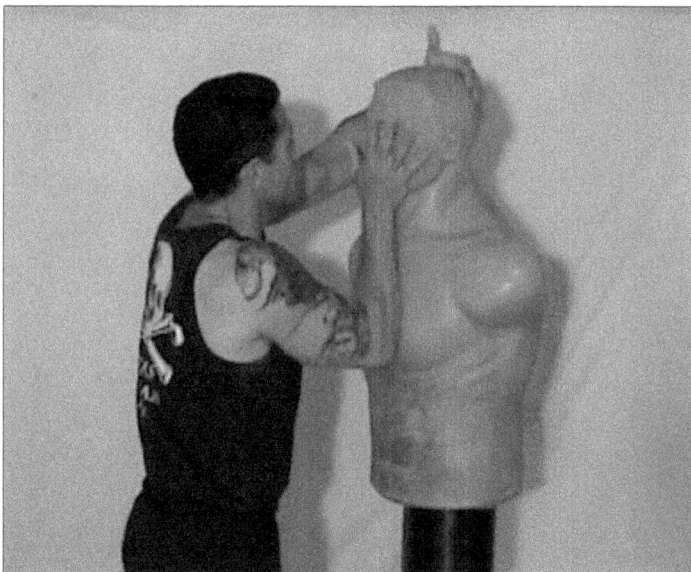

Step 8: *Without breaking contact, Franco sets up the neck crank.*

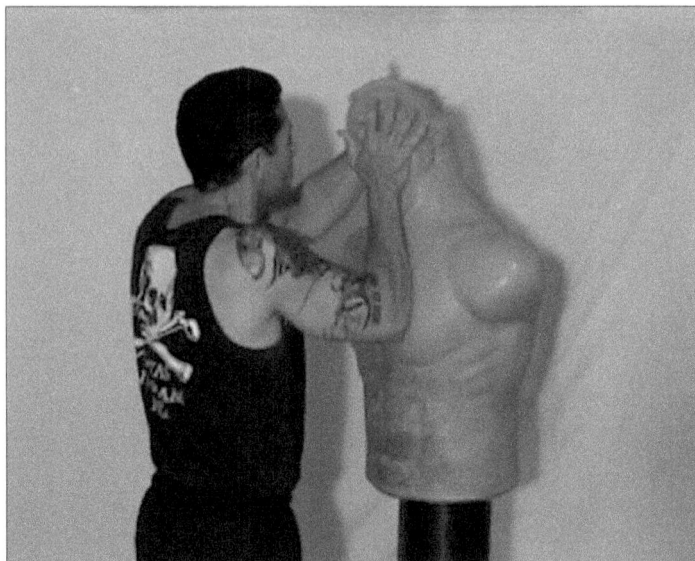

Step 9: *Franco cranks the neck counter clockwise with both of his hands.*

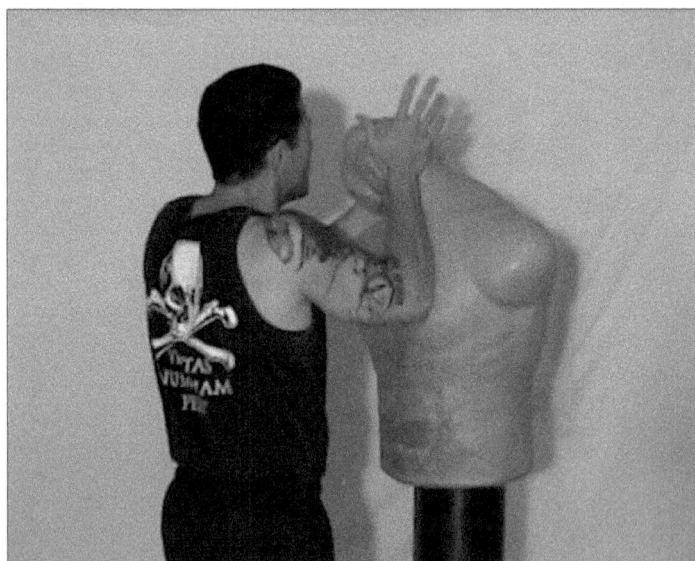

Step 10: *The razing sequence is complete.*

Razing Demonstration #2

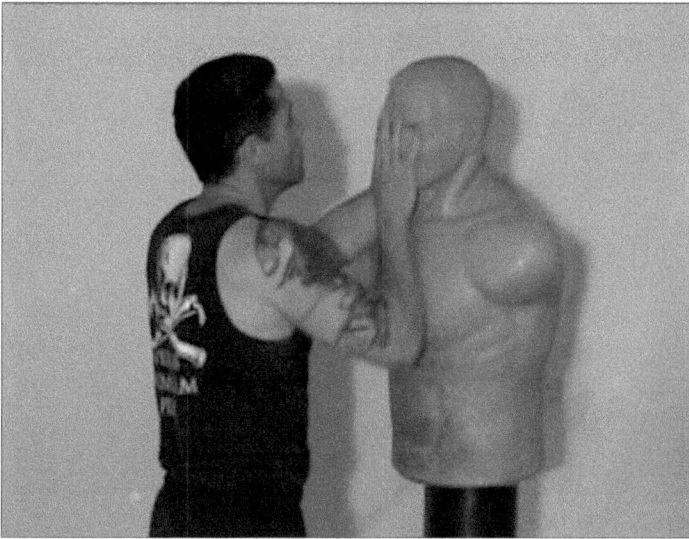

Step 1: *Franco begins with his left hand anchored behind the neck.*

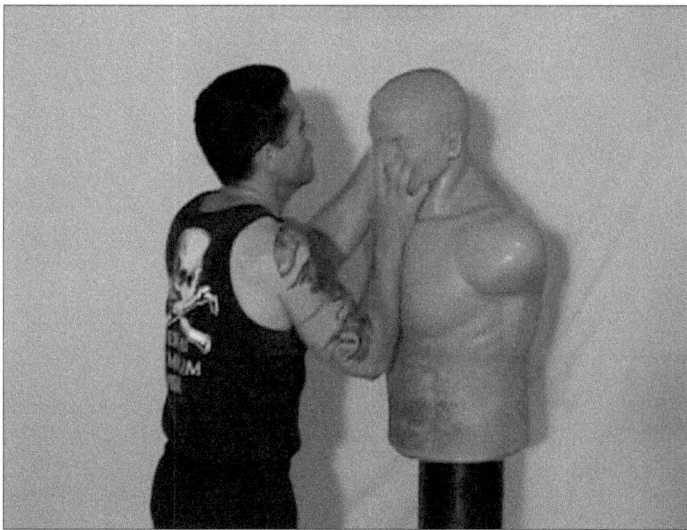

Step 2: *He begins with an eye rake.*

Step 3: Followed by a palm jolt to the chin.

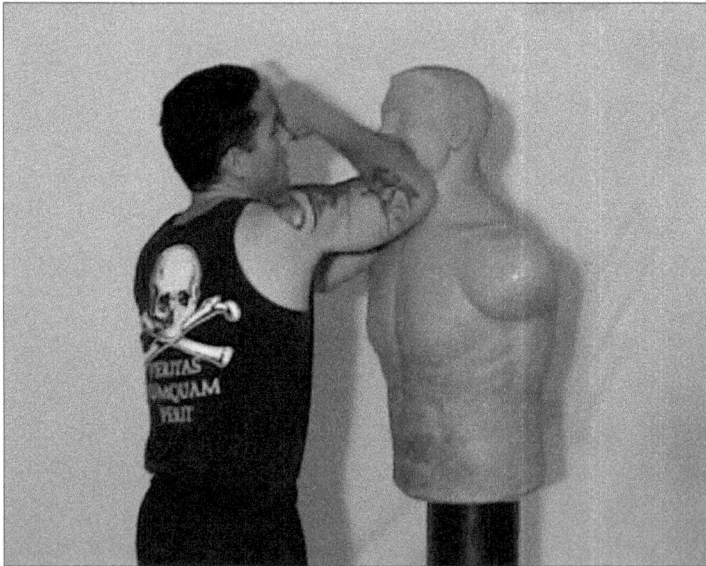

Step 4: Next, a shaving forearm across the face.

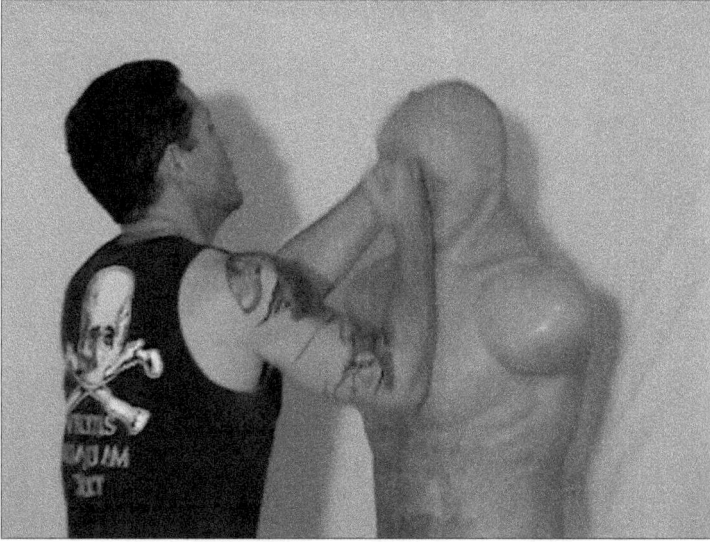

Step 5: *He follows up with a short arc hammer fist to the nose.*

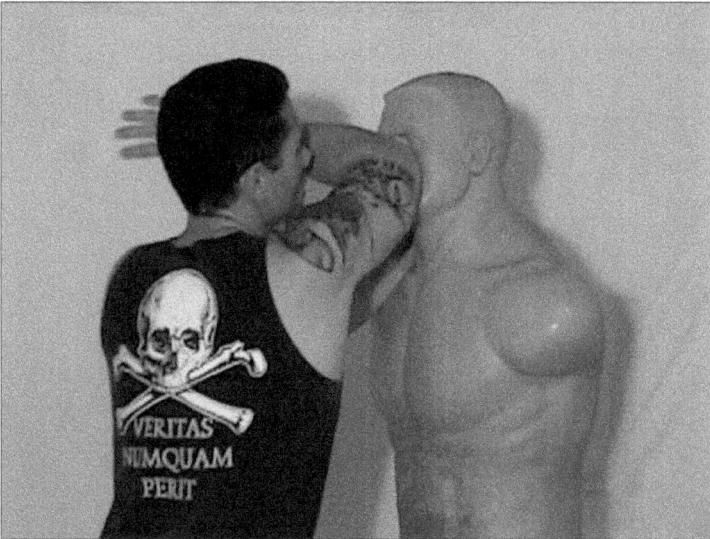

Step 6: *He attacks with a diagonal elbow strike.*

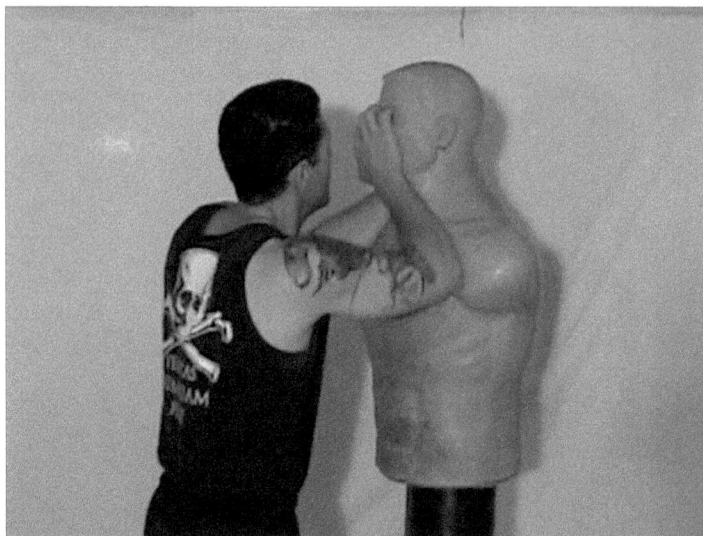

Step 7: He attacks with a diagonal eye rake.

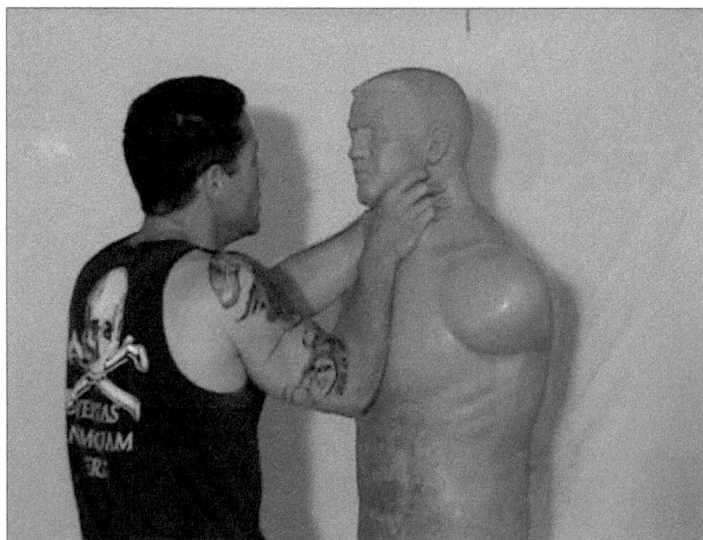

Step 8: The razing sequence is completed with a throat crush.

184

Razing Demonstration #3

Step 1: *Franco begins with his left hand anchored behind the neck.*

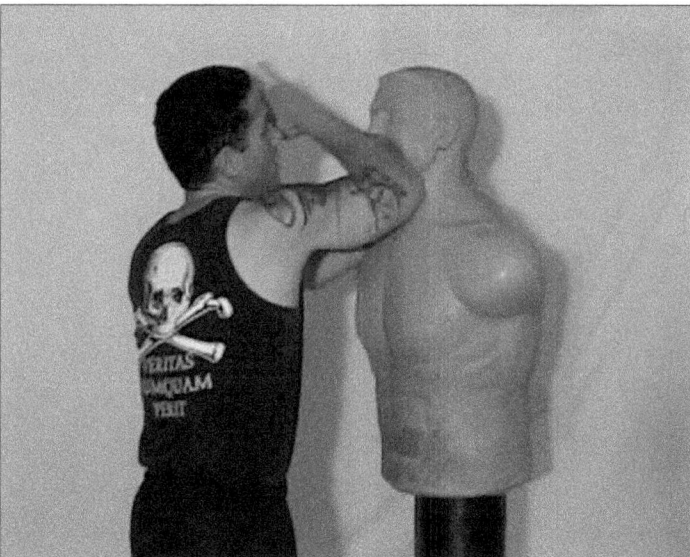

Step 2: *The razing starts with a shaving forearm across the face.*

185

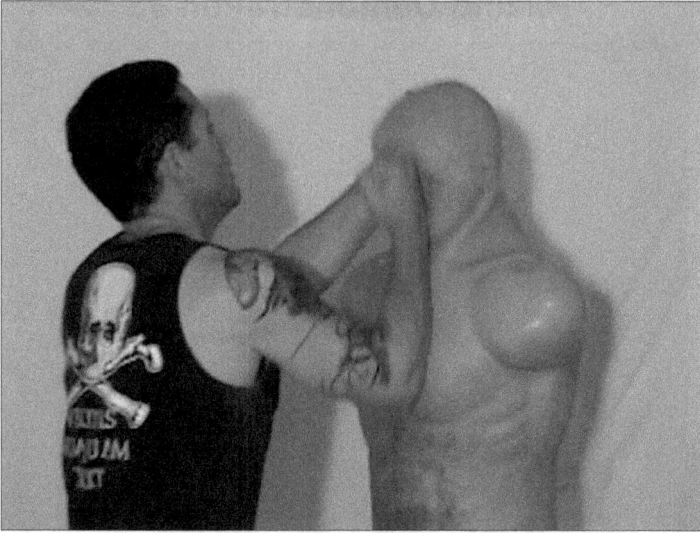

Step 3: *Next, he drives a short arc hammer fist to the nose.*

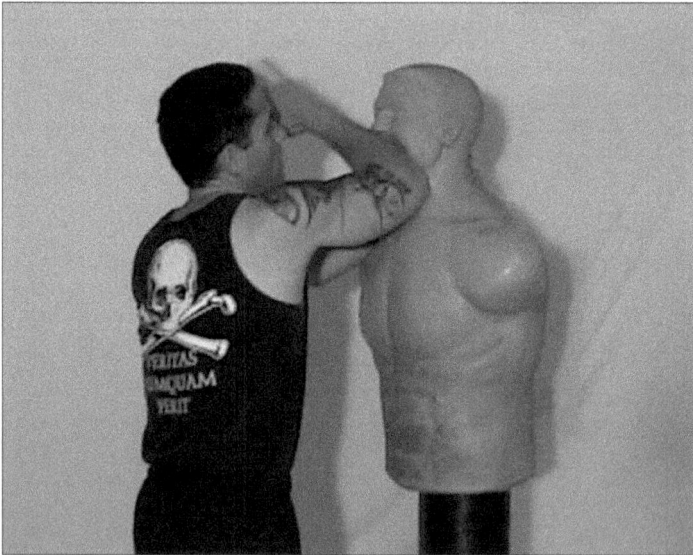

Step 4: *Followed by another shaving forearm.*

186

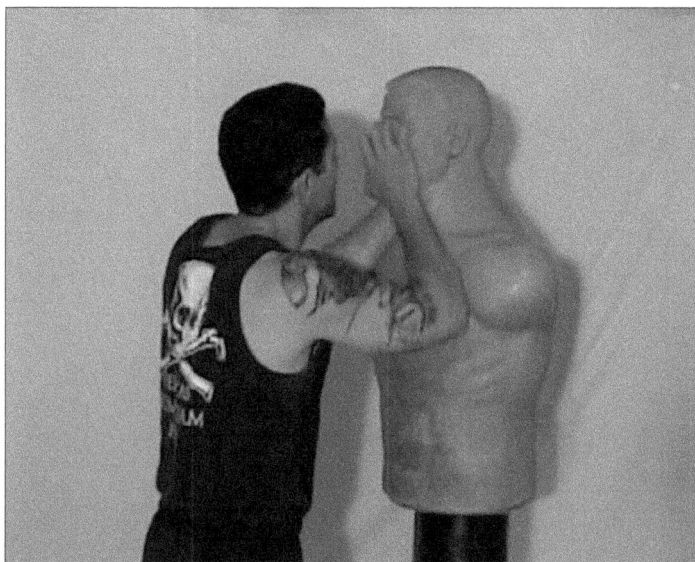

Step 5: *Without breaking contact, he rakes the eyes.*

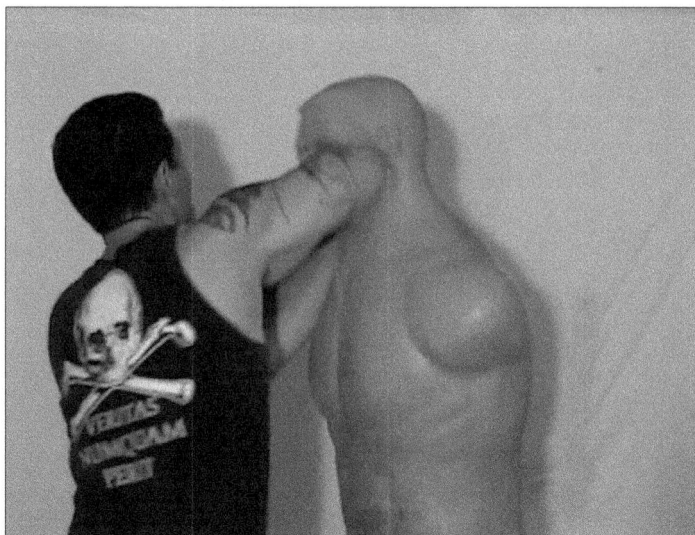

Step 6: *Franco follows up with an elbow strike.*

187

Step 7: *He releases the anchor from behind the neck and prepares to deliver a double thumb gouge.*

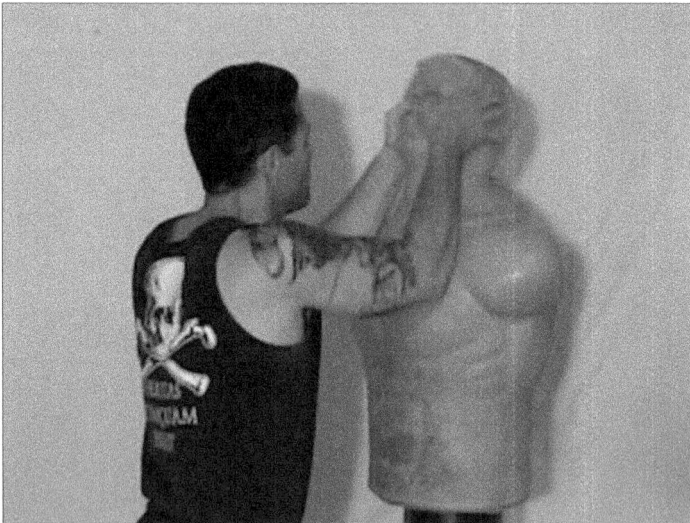

Step 8: *The razing sequence ends with a double thumb gouge into the eyes.*

188

Razing Demonstration #4

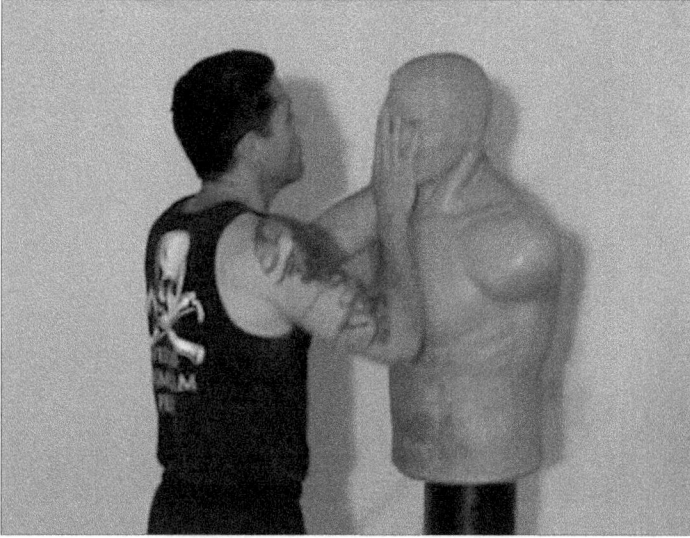

Step 1: *Franco starts with his left hand anchored behind the neck.*

Step 2: *He attacks with a diagonal elbow strike.*

189

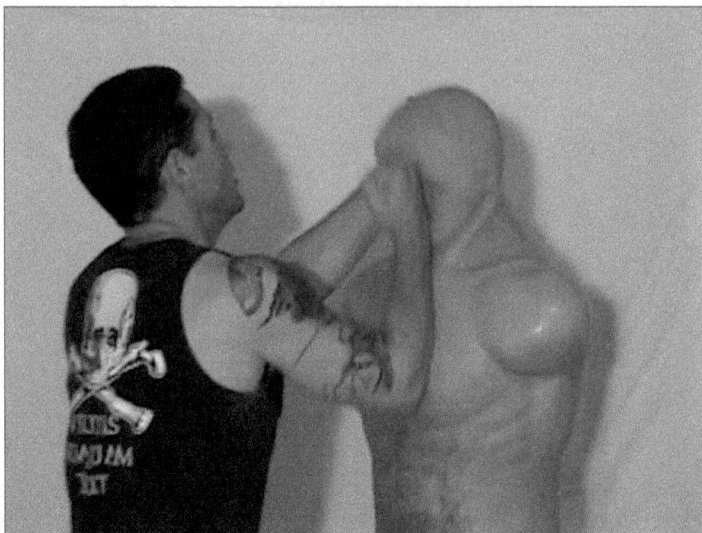

Step 3: *Followed by a short arc hammer fist to the nose.*

Step 4: *Next, a palm jolt to the chin.*

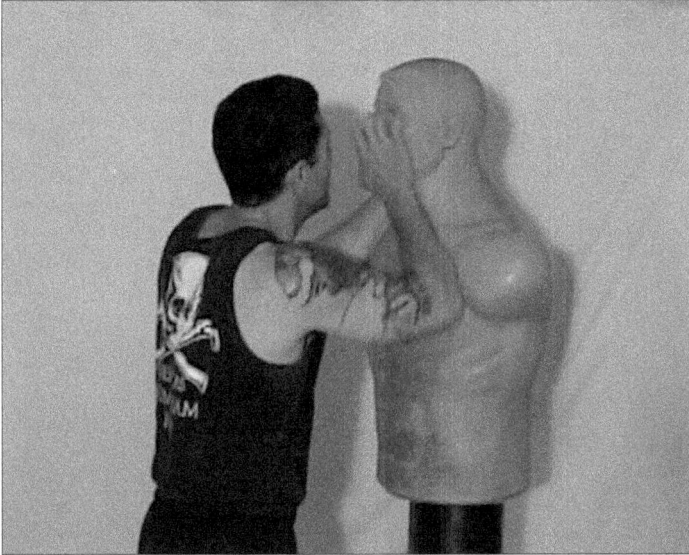

Step 5: *Without breaking contact, he rakes the eyes.*

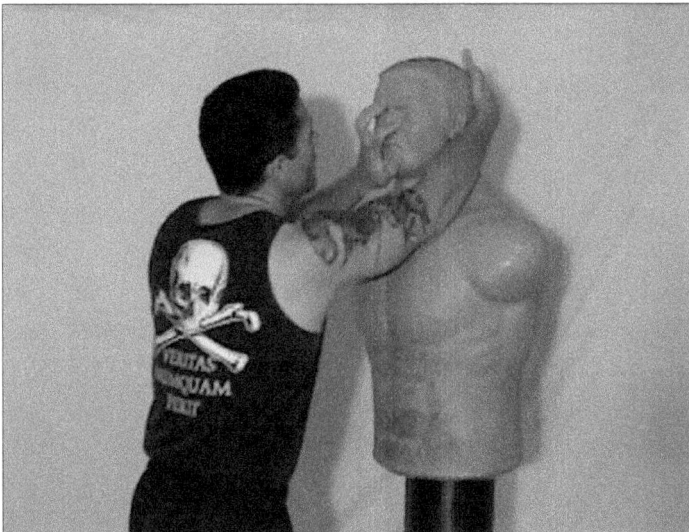

Step 6: *Franco switches anchoring hands and delivers another palm jolt.*

Step 7: *He immediately attacks with a head butt to the nose.*

Step 8: *Franco retracts his head and prepares to deliver another strike.*

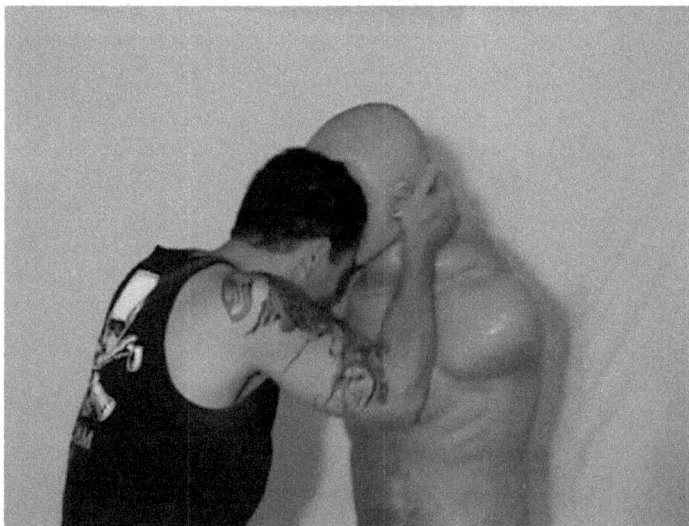

Step 9: *He drives another head butt strike.*

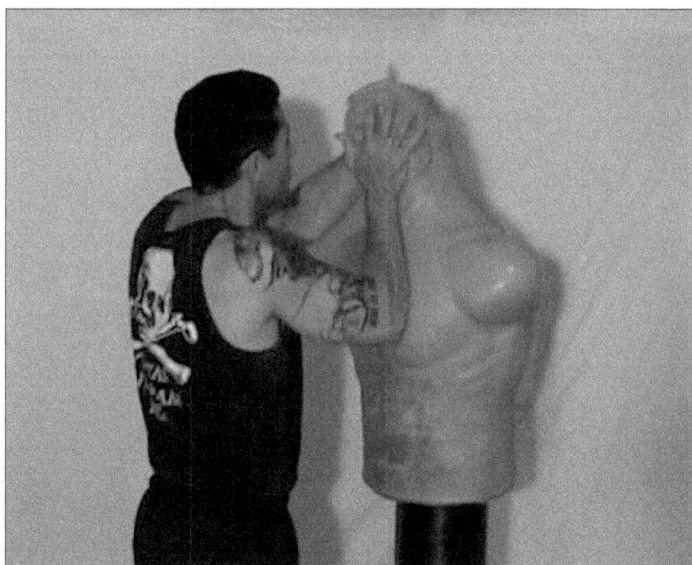

Step 10: *Franco cranks the neck counter clockwise with both of his hands.*

Razing Demonstration #5

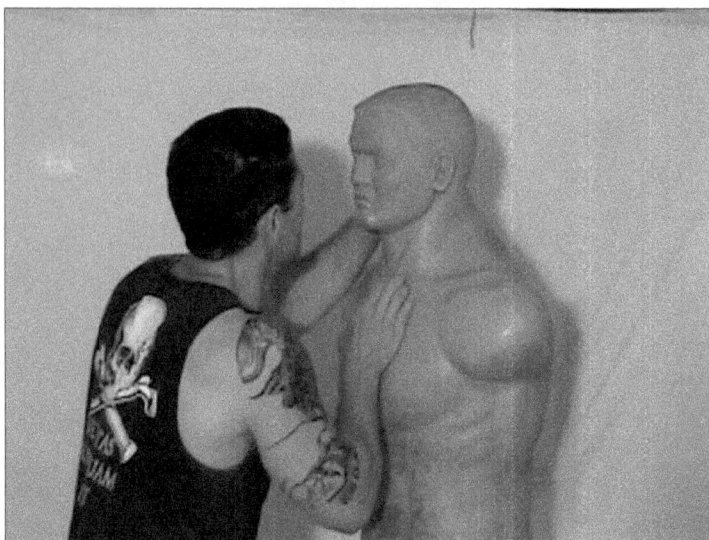

Step 1: Franco prepares to raze the body opponent bag.

Step 2: He delivers a palm jolt to the chin.

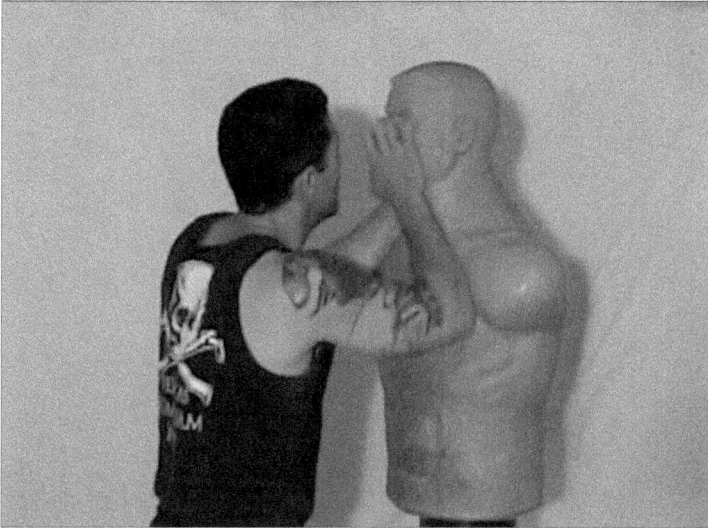

Step 3: *Without breaking contact, he rakes the eyes.*

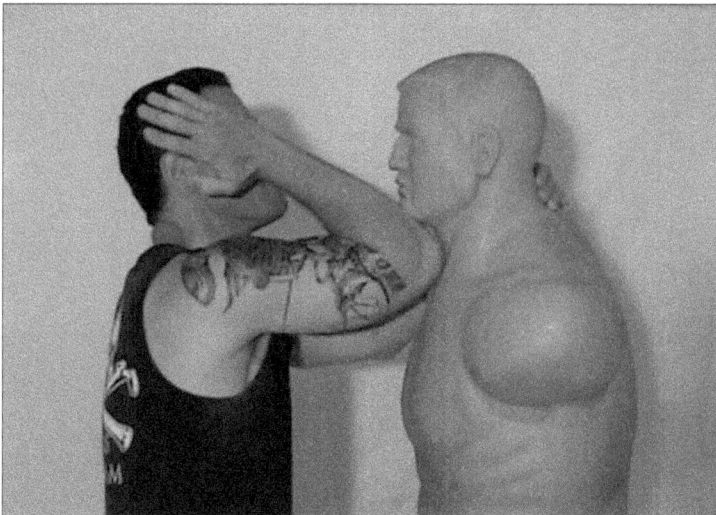

Step 4: *Followed by a vertical elbow to the chin.*

Step 5: *Next, a short arc hammer fist to the nose.*

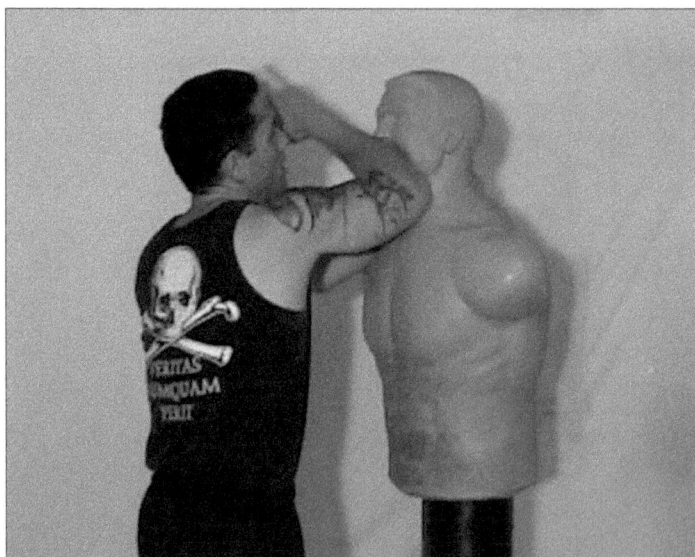

Step 6: *The razing continues with a shaving forearm.*

196

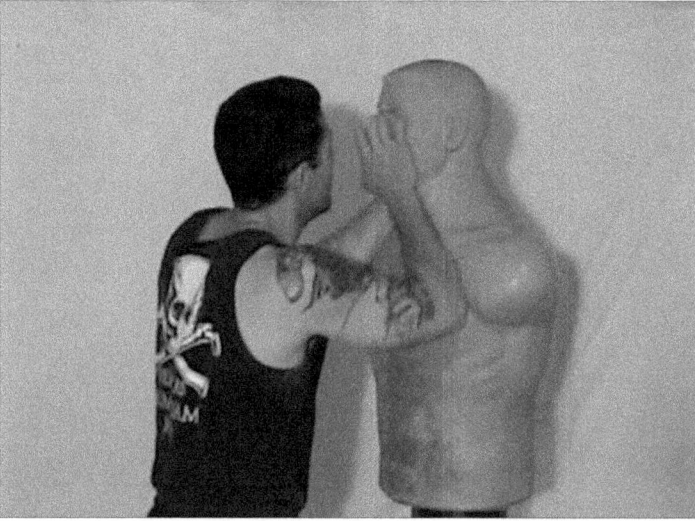

Step 7: *Without breaking contact, he rakes the eyes.*

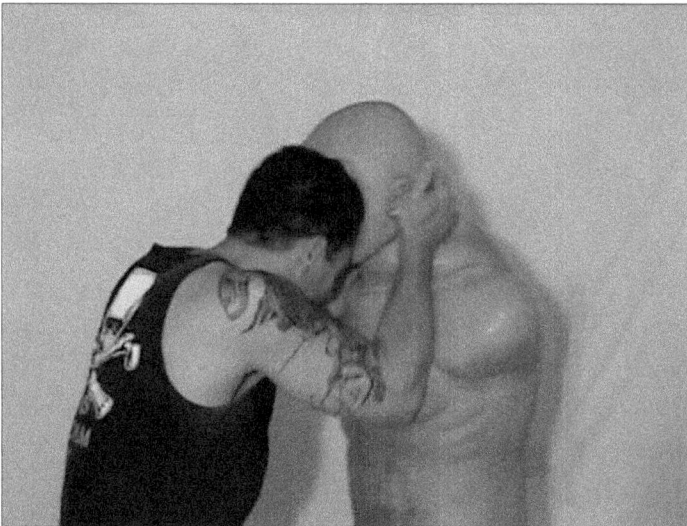

Step 8: *He attacks with a head butt to the nose.*

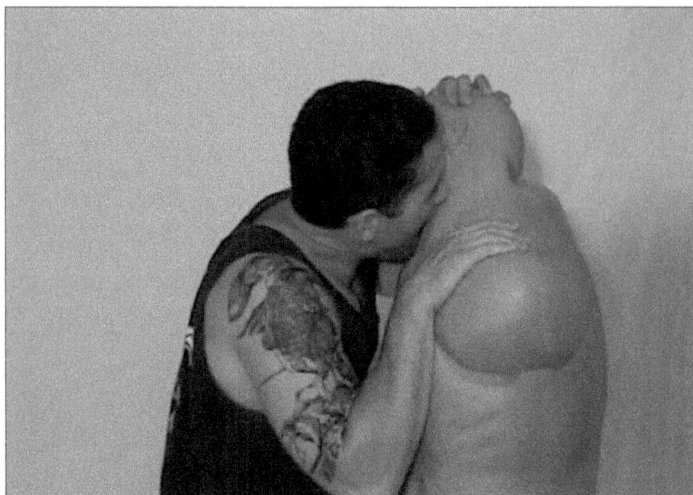

Step 9: Followed by a bite into the throat.

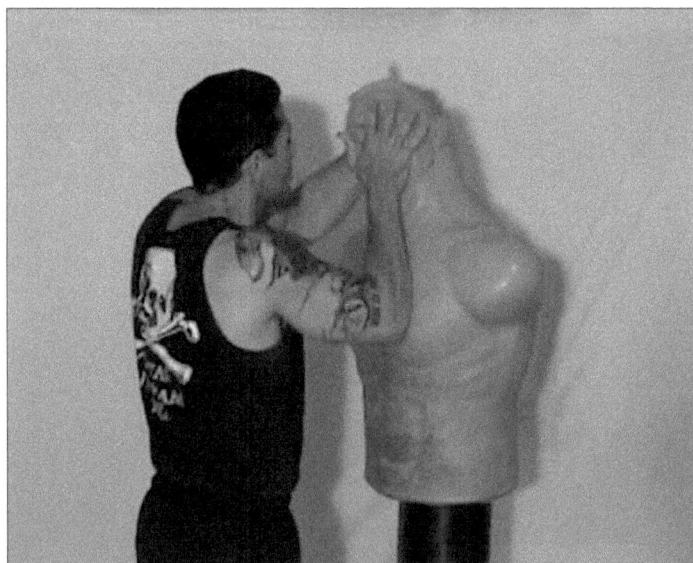

Step 10: The sequence ends with a neck crank.

Razing Demonstration #6

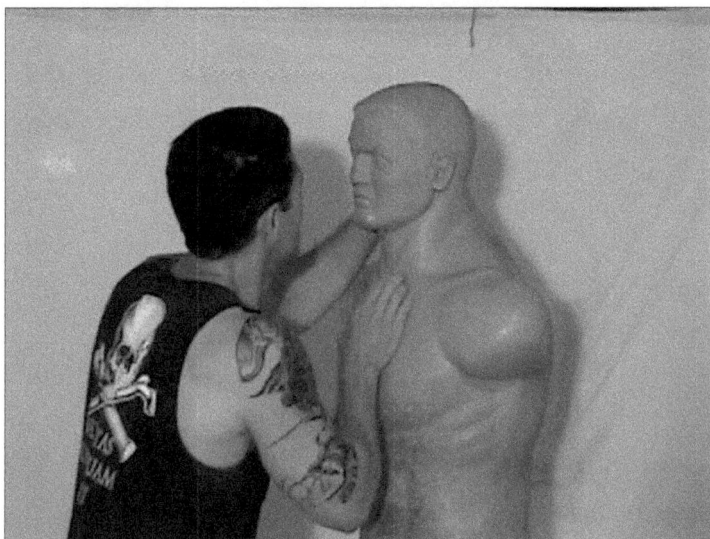

Step 1: *Franco prepares to raze the body opponent bag.*

Step 2: *He attacks with a vertical elbow to the chin.*

Step 3: *Followed by a short arc hammer fist to the nose.*

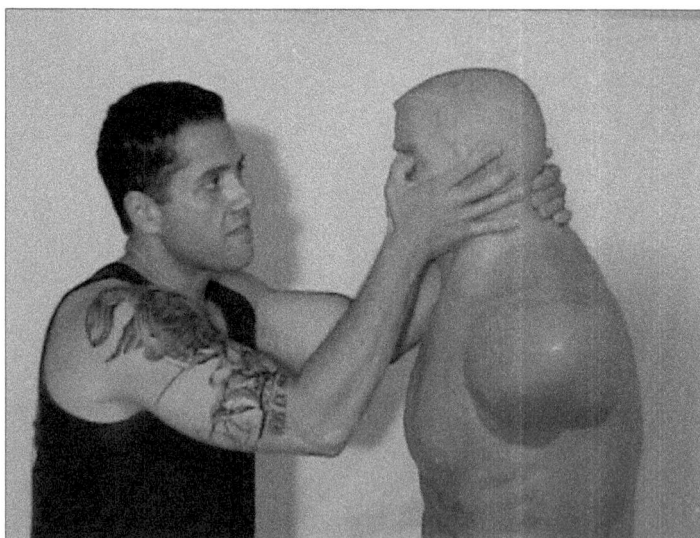

Step 4: *Next, a thumb rake.*

Step 5: *A head butt to the nose.*

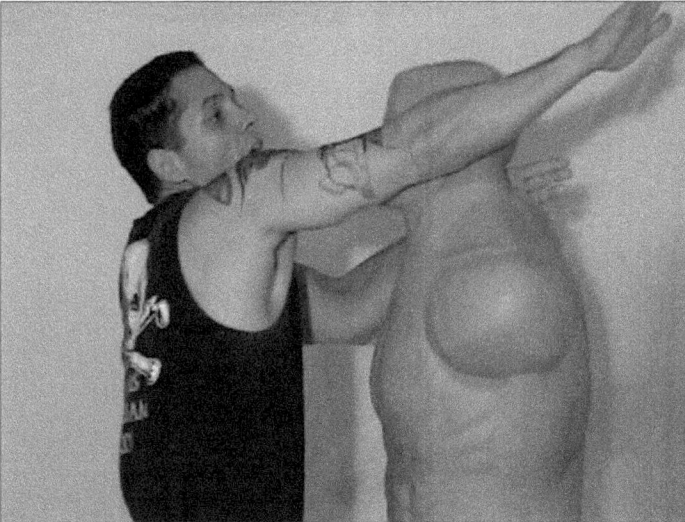

Step 6: *Followed by a biceps pop.*

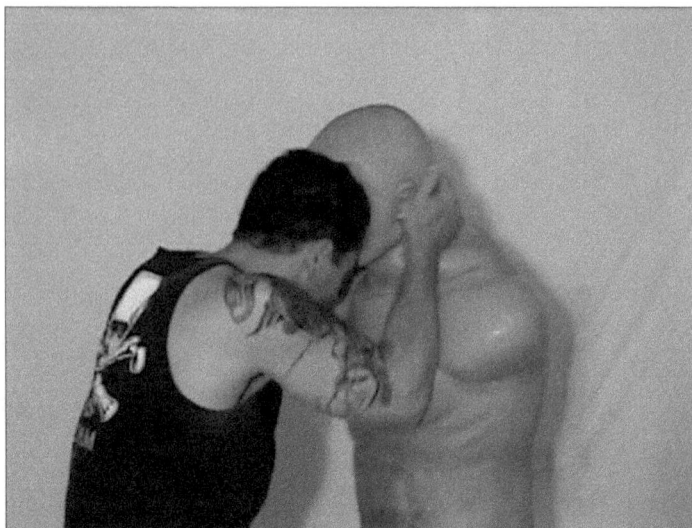

Step 7: *Another head butt to the nose.*

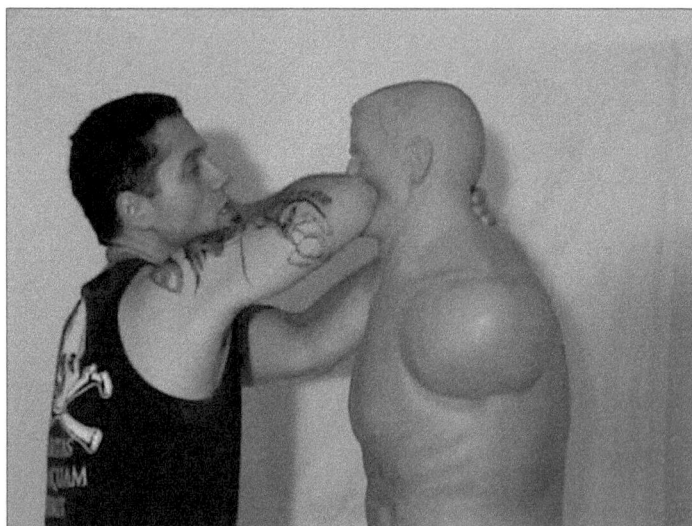

Step 8: *Next, a horizontal elbow.*

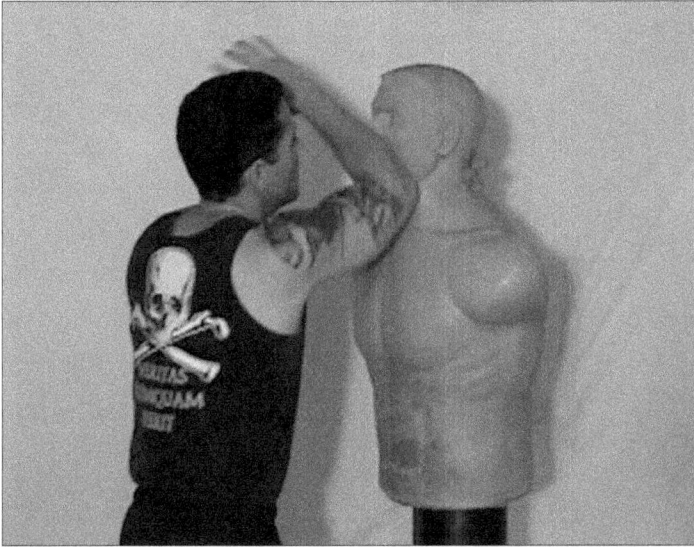

Step 9: *He follows up with a reverse shaving forearm.*

Step 10: *A short arc hammer fist to the nose.*

203

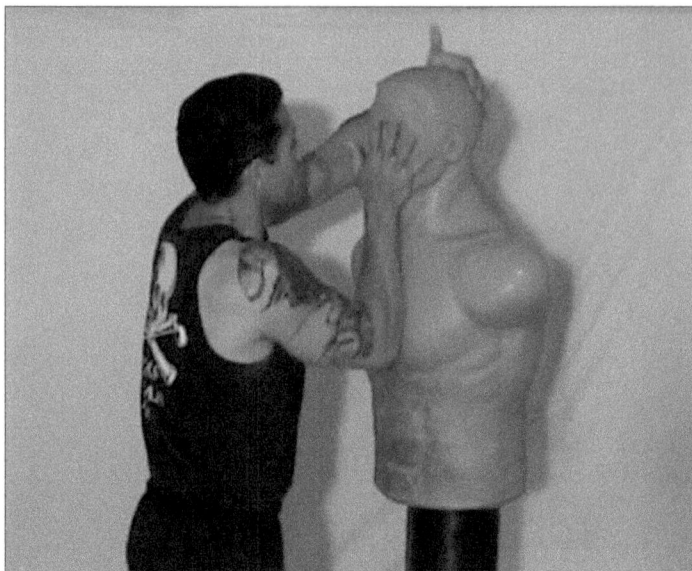

Step 11: *Franco prepares to deliver a neck crank.*

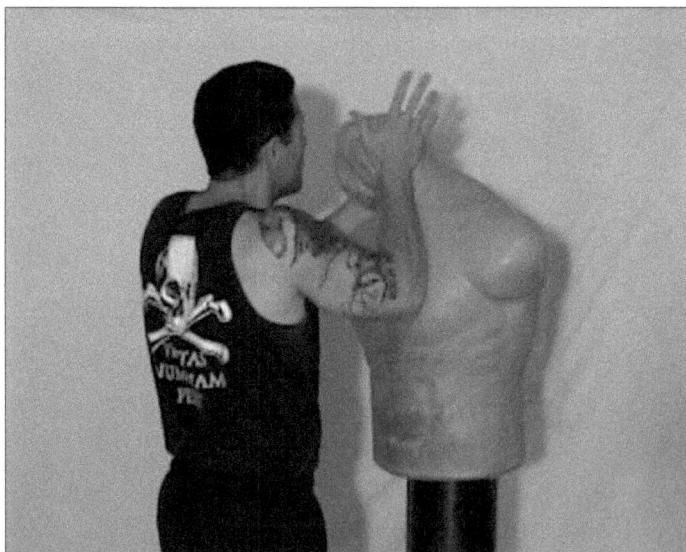

Step 12: *The razing sequence is complete with a violent neck crank.*

Looking Ahead

The Widow Maker methodology equips you with brutal, efficient techniques designed to dominate in life-threatening situations. However, in the reality of self-defense, there are rare but critical moments when even the Widow Maker may not be enough. When the threat escalates to an extreme level - where survival is the sole focus - there is one final CFA methodology that takes precedence: Savage Street Fighting.

Savage Street Fighting represents the peak of violence and force in my self-defense system. It's designed for those dire encounters where there are no second chances. This method pushes the limits of combat, combining raw aggression and tactical precision to ensure your survival against overwhelming odds.

In the next chapter, we will delve into this final stage of escalation, exploring the most extreme techniques reserved for the most dangerous situations. Prepare yourself - Savage Street Fighting is not just another tool in your arsenal, but a methodology designed for the gravest of circumstances, where only the fiercest measures will suffice.

SINISTER SELF-DEFENSE

CHAPTER FIVE

Savage Street Fighting

The Art of Tactical Savagery

Savage Street Fighting Objectives

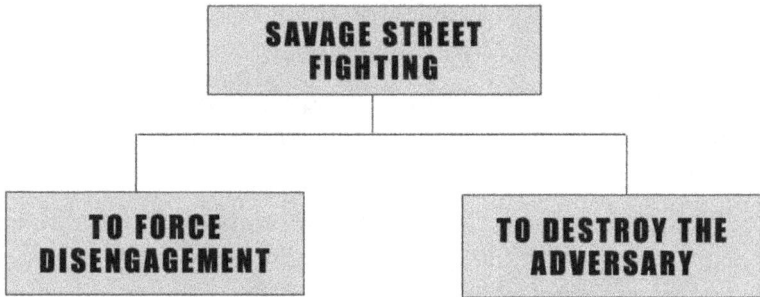

```
┌─────────────────────┐
│   SAVAGE STREET     │
│      FIGHTING       │
└─────────────────────┘
```

```
┌─────────────────────┐        ┌─────────────────────┐
│     TO FORCE        │        │  TO DESTROY THE     │
│  DISENGAGEMENT      │        │     ADVERSARY       │
└─────────────────────┘        └─────────────────────┘
```

Savage Street Fighting offers the defender two primary tactical objectives during a life-threatening self-defense situation. They are:

1.   **To compel the attacker to immediately withdraw or disengage from the figh**t. This objective is critical when faced with a larger, physically superior adversary or when confronted by multiple attackers. For instance, if a larger opponent has you in a bear hug, and you only have seconds before additional assailants join the attack, Savage Street Fighting tactics provide the necessary means to swiftly escape the situation. By employing brutal and efficient techniques focused on vital targets, these tactics enable you to create immediate openings for escape. The urgency and decisiveness embedded in Savage Street Fighting make it particularly effective in scenarios, where prolonged engagement could prove fatal.

2.   **To incapacitate a criminal adversary with speed and efficiency**. In self-defense scenarios, it's essential to employ techniques that are not only effective but also executable under the intense pressure of real-world combat. The tactics within the Savage Street Fighting system adhere to these stringent requirements. Moreover, they possess the capability to permanently disfigure, blind, maim, cripple, or fatally injure the adversary.

Savage Street Fighting Arsenal Criteria

The Savage Street Fighting program selects offensive techniques based on seven key criteria:

1. Ease of Application: Techniques must be simple and executable under combat stress, without extensive training.

2. Close-Quarter Combat Effectiveness: Must work in tight spaces, including ground fighting or when restrained by stronger and larger attackers.

3. Extreme Pain Infliction: Techniques should inflict greater pain than standard self-defense techniques, incapacitating the opponent.

4. Zero-Beat Attack: Provides continuous offensive pressure without pause.

5. Predictable Visceral Response (PVR): Consistently causes a predictable visceral reaction from the adversary.

6. Physiological Shock: Induces immediate physical shock to stop the attacker.

7. Psychological Shock: Mentally disrupts the opponent's cognitive function, mentally halting their attack.

Savage Street Fighting Beat System

Savage Street Fighting uses an unconventional offensive approach known as the *zero beat* attack. Since I covered the beat system in the previous chapter, here's a quick recap:

• **Full Beat Attack:** A strike with both an initiation and retraction phase, like a standard punch.

• **Half Beat Attack:** A strike delivered during the retraction of the preceding strike.

• **Quarter Beat Attack:** A rapid series of strikes maintaining continuous contact with the target, causing psychological trauma and panic.

• **Zero Beat Attack:** A sustained pressure technique applied until the target is completely neutralized. This involves actions such as biting, crushing, gouging, and choking, focusing on critical areas like the eyes and throat. Savage Street Fighting exclusively uses this method, making it highly effective for individuals who may lack significant strength or athleticism.

The Zero Beat Attack

The Savage Street Fighting Program centers around four brutal zero beat techniques:

• **Biting**

• **Crushing**

• **Gouging**

• **Choking**

These techniques can be executed individually or in combination. However, the real effectiveness and devastation of the Savage Street Fighting approach come from applying these techniques simultaneously against an adversary. By layering multiple attacks at once, you maximize the adversary's physical and psychological overload, disrupting their ability to defend and creating an opening for immediate incapacitation. Each technique serves a unique purpose within the methodology, targeting the most vulnerable parts of the body to induce maximum damage quickly and effectively.

With all of this in mind, let's explore each technique in detail to understand how they align with the core principles of the Savage Street Fighting methodology and why they are crucial for real-world survival in extreme situations.

Tactical Biting for Street Survival

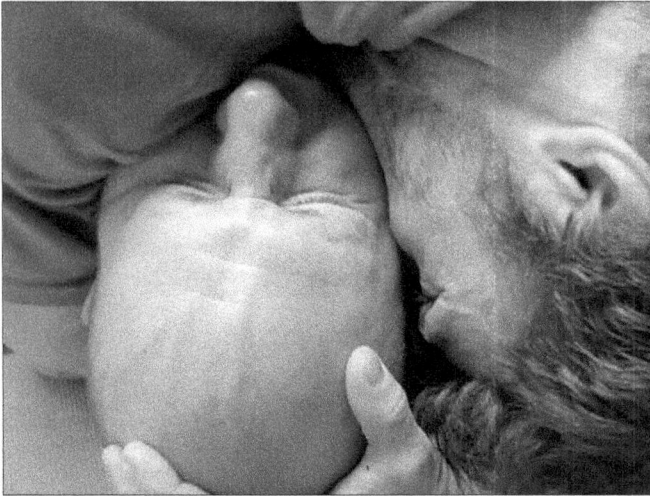

Tactical biting is a critical component of the Savage Street Fighting arsenal. While it may initially appear unremarkable or overly simplistic, in the context of this methodology, its value cannot be overstated.

Tactical biting is one of the most effective and destructive self-defense techniques available, capable of neutralizing opponents of any size. This makes it especially advantageous for individuals, regardless of their physical strength or size, when facing larger and more powerful attackers.

There is both an art and a science to biting for self-defense and self-preservation. It requires precise timing, accurate target selection, sufficient grip strength, and a clear understanding of predicable visceral responses (PVR).

In the Savage Street Fighting system, you are taught four critical aspects of tactical biting:

- **How to bite**
- **Where to bite**
- **When to bite**
- **The PVR from each bite**

A key consideration when using tactical biting is that it must be continuous and uninterrupted. This ensures that the bite achieves two essential objectives:

1. It must inflict significant damage on the intended target.

2. It must trigger an immediate and predictable visceral response, often causing the assailant to desperately attempt to disengage or push you away.

Lock and Bite: Mastering Grips

To ensure that your bite is effective, solid, and unbroken during a self-defense encounter, mastering grips is essential.

These grips provide the stability needed to maintain continuous pressure on your adversary while delivering a devastating bite. Each grip serves a specific function in helping you secure your position, control your opponent, and maximize the effectiveness of your tactical bite.

The Savage Street Fighting program emphasizes the following five grips: Indian grip, three-finger grip, edge of hand grip, wrist grip, and biceps hold.

Indian Grip

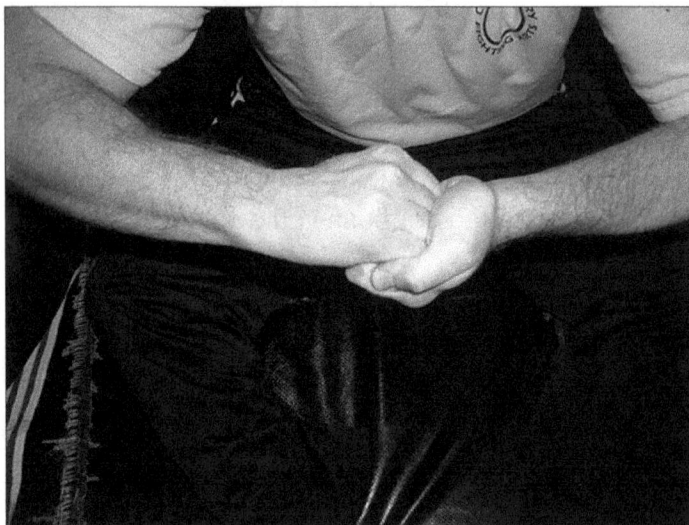

To perform the Indian grip, curl your fingers and join your hands together.

Three Finger Grip

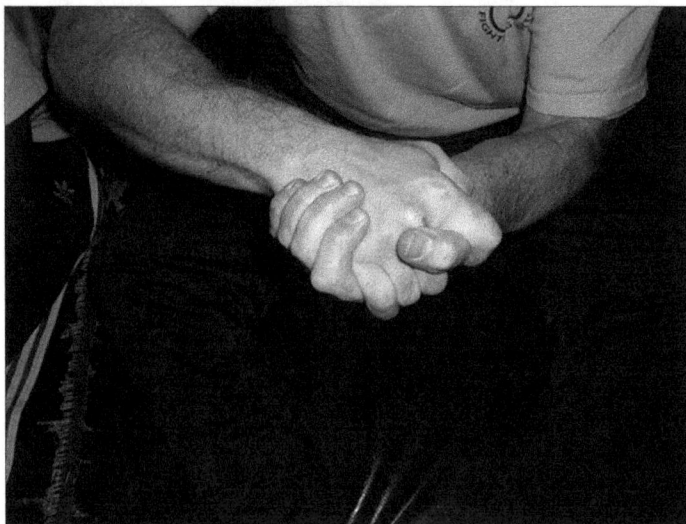

Join your hands together and place your thumb between the index and middle finger of the other hand. Now clasp your hands together.

214

Edge of Hand Grip

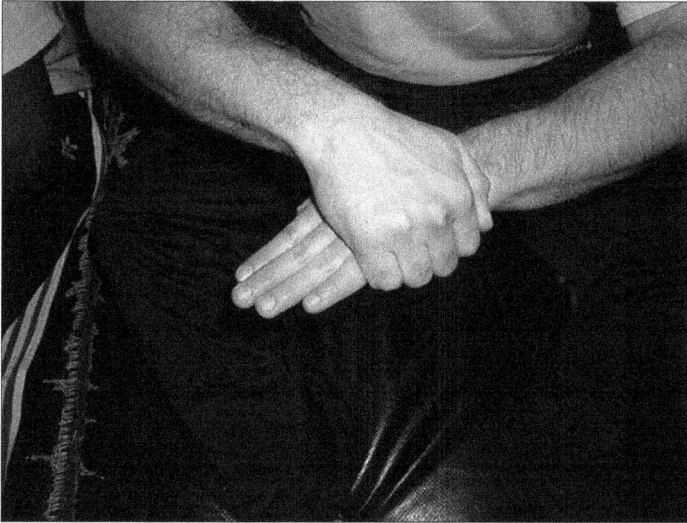

Join your hands together by grasping the knife edge of your other hand.

Wrist Grip

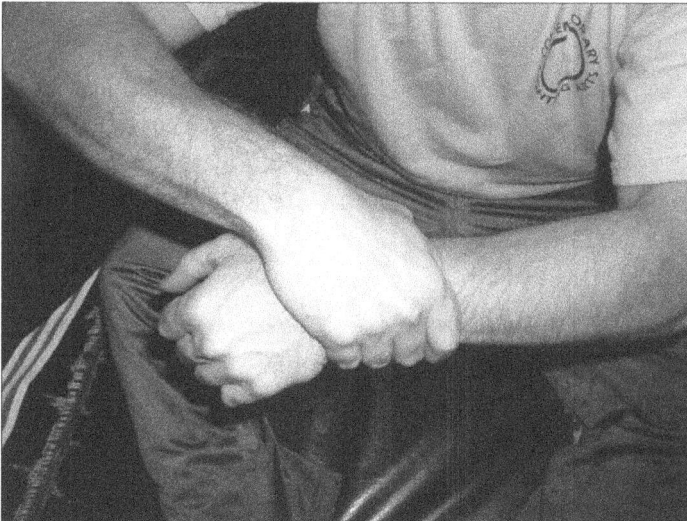

To perform the wrist grip, join your arms together by grasping the wrist of your other hand.

Biceps Hold

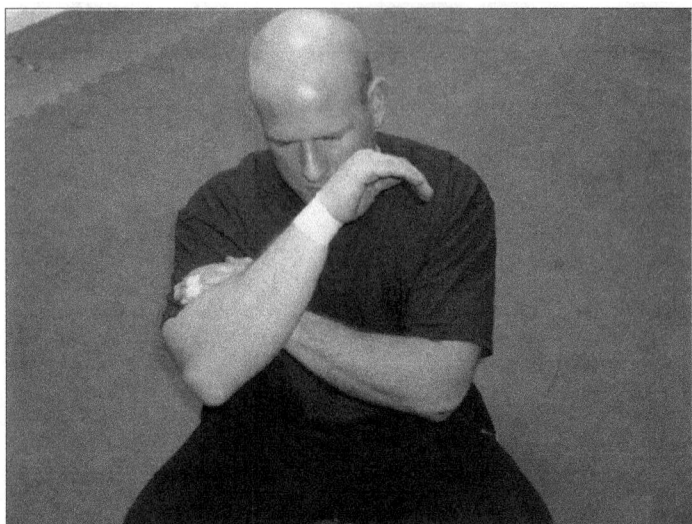

To perform the biceps hold, place your left palm on your right biceps while bending your right arm towards your face.

Strategic Bite Targets

When employing Savage Street Fighting tactics, it's crucial to target specific anatomical areas for maximum effectiveness. The suitability of a target depends on the situation, angle, and positioning. Some targets will be more advantageous than others depending on these factors. To be considered a valid bite target, the following six criteria must be met:

1. The target must ***provide a substantial amount of flesh*** to ensure an effective bite.

2. The target should be ***rich in nerve endings and highly sensitive to pain.***

3. The target must ***allow you to bite freely while preventing the adversary from retaliating with a bite of their own.***

4. The target should *not expose you to counter strikes* from the adversary.

5. The target must *enable you to maintain an uninterrupted bite for an extended period.*

6. The target should *trigger a predictable visceral response (PVR)* from the adversary.

Commonly effective bite targets include the nose, cheeks, ears, throat, neck, arms, nipples, back, groin, thighs, and fingers. These areas are selected for their sensitivity, accessibility, and potential to inflict intense pain that can disrupt the opponent's control. It's important to avoid biting random limbs, as doing so may yield poor results, wasting critical energy without delivering significant damage and leaving you vulnerable to counterattacks. Strategic targeting, therefore, is essential for ensuring that each bite serves a functional purpose within the overall assault, maximizing effectiveness and maintaining control in close-quarters situations.

How to Execute a Tactical Bite

When applying a tactical bite in self-defense, it's crucial to take a substantial portion of flesh into your mouth. Too little flesh won't trigger the desired PVR, while too much will cause jaw cramping, reducing your bite's effectiveness.

To bite effectively, clamp down forcefully with your incisors and move your head in quick, tight circles. Your bite must remain continuous and uninterrupted, so maintain a secure grip on your target to keep it in place. Continue biting for several seconds (approximately 3-5 seconds) until the adversary exhibits a predictable visceral response, then immediately capitalize on the opening.

The primary goal of the bite is to promote extreme pain and temporarily shock your opponent's nervous system, often forcing them to release their hold, giving you the opportunity to escape or secure a more advantageous position.

What is a Predictable Visceral Response?

In my book *Maximum Damage: Hidden Secrets Behind Brutal Fighting Combinations*, I emphasize the importance of understanding your opponent's Probable Reaction Dynamics (PRD) in a self-defense situation.

PRD refers to your ability to anticipate or predict how your opponent will likely react to an initial strike or action, whether in armed or unarmed combat. This foresight is invaluable, as it allows you to estimate with reasonable accuracy how your opponent will respond, giving you a strategic advantage. For example, if you strike an opponent in the groin, their probable reaction might be to bend forward - this is a predictable, response.

In the context of the Savage Street Fighting program, I use the term *Predictable Visceral Response* (PVR) to describe the instinctual, immediate reactions triggered by a tactical bite. A well-executed bite almost always provokes a primal, reflexive response. In the vast majority of cases, the adversary's instinct will be to pull away, creating distance, much like being hit with an electric shock. This predictable reaction is crucial, as it opens up opportunities to exploit your opponent's vulnerabilities in the heat of the moment.

While both PRD and PVR are crucial concepts in combat, they operate on different levels. PRD involves anticipating both reflexive and tactical movements - based on experience, pain response, or combat patterns - that allow you to predict your opponent's conscious and strategic actions. For instance, you might foresee when an adversary will block, evade, or even counterattack, enabling you to plan your next move. It requires a keen understanding of combat dynamics and helps keep you one step ahead in a fight.

PVR, by contrast, is more primal and reflexive, tapping into your opponent's automatic, instinctive responses to intense pain or trauma. It doesn't rely on tactical decision-making but instead exploits the body's immediate survival instincts. In the case of a tactical bite, the adversary's reaction is driven by overwhelming pain and panic, leaving them without the mental composure to even consider a counterattack. This forces them to disengage or retreat purely on instinct. This visceral response gives you a brief yet critical window to capitalize on their disoriented state.

In summary, PRD helps you anticipate both reflexive and strategic reactions, while PVR specifically exploits involuntary, pain-driven responses - both are essential for mastering the art of Savage Street Fighting.

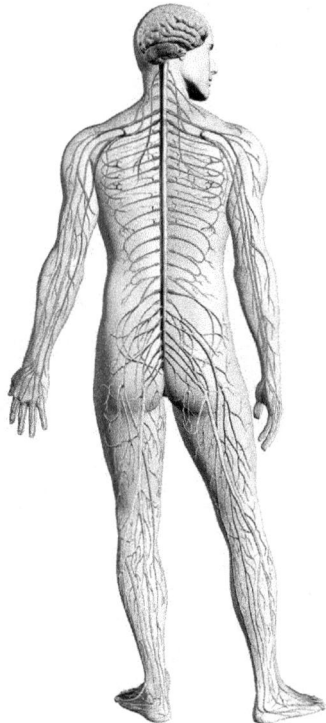

The Power of Tactical Biting

Many people, including seasoned martial artists, often underestimate the devastating power of tactical biting as a self-defense technique. In fact, recent studies have shown that, relative to our anatomy, humans have a remarkably efficient bite force, allowing us to generate significant pressure even without the larger jaw muscles seen in other primates. This efficiency makes targeted human bites surprisingly effective and damaging in close-quarters combat scenarios.

Additionally, a bite can be executed even in the tightest situations, such as when pinned or restrained, making it an invaluable weapon in real-world self-defense. To illustrate the destructiveness of tactical biting, I have provided the following sequence of photographs as a demonstration.

In the images shown, my student is equipped with two thick slabs of protective latex, strategically positioned over the throat and latissimus dorsi region - key target areas. Please note: These demonstrations are for illustrative purposes only and should not be replicated as a training drill.

Observe how the protective latex slab is securely fastened to the student's body.

Step 1: The demonstration begins with the student securing a wrist grip and biting deeply into the latissimus dorsi area of the protective latex slab.

Step 2: *The student on the left maintains their bite while vigorously shaking his head from side to side, intensifying the damage and creating a tearing effect.*

Step 3: *The man on the right attempts to break free from the hold.*

Notice how the bite target allows the practitioner to bite freely while preventing the adversary from retaliating.

In this image, the practitioner demonstrates the importance of maintaining a solid grip while the adversary tries to escape. A secure hold ensures control and keeps the tactical bite effective, preventing the adversary from breaking free or retaliating.

Shown here, the aftermath of a tactical bite on the latex slab.

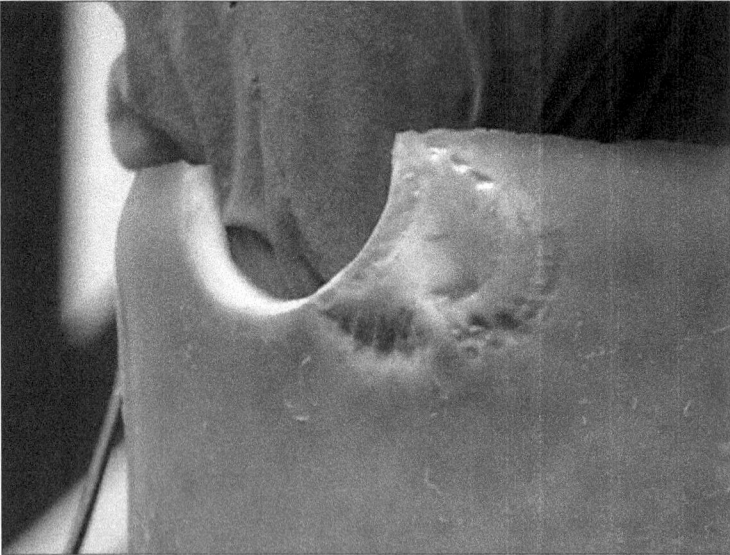

Here is a close-up view of the bite damage. Now, imagine the immense terror and destruction inflicted by just one well-executed Savage Street Fighting bite.

Neck Bite Demonstration

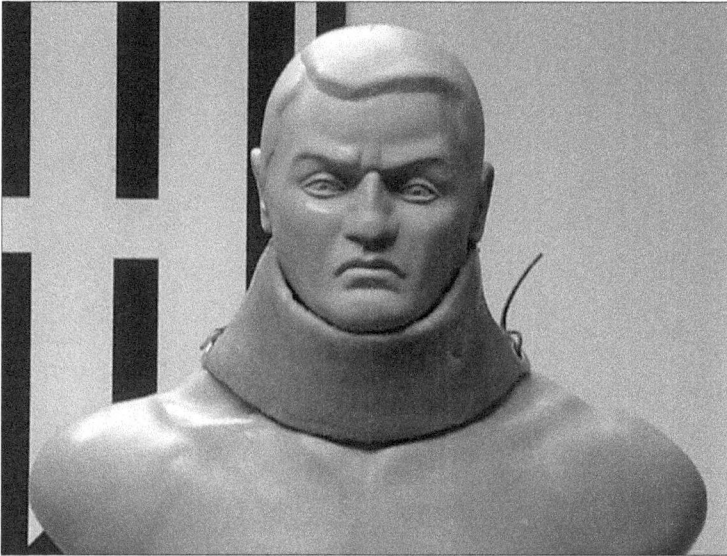

Because the neck is such a vulnerable and sensitive bite target, the latex slab demonstration is only performed when it is attached to a body opponent bag.

Step 1: *The student starts by securing the body opponent bag with a biceps hold.*

Step 2: He bites deeply into the latex slab, then vigorously shakes his head back and forth for about 5 seconds, simulating the destructive tearing action of a real tactical bite.

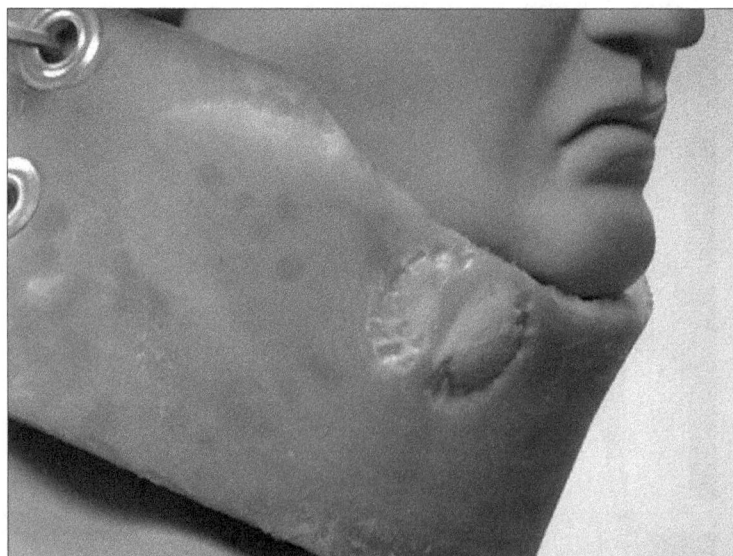

A close-up of the neck bite. A well-executed tactical bite targeting the jugular vein has the potential to be fatal for the adversary.

Growling While Biting

The importance of growling when biting into an attacker's flesh cannot be overstated. Though it may seem vile or barbaric to some, in a life-or-death encounter with a street criminal, survival must be your priority. You need to use every tool at your disposal to protect yourself and your loved ones, even if it means adopting primal methods to ensure you survive.

TWO KEY PURPOSES BEHIND GROWLING

Psychological Weapon – Growling is a primal sound that sends a powerful psychological message to your assailant. It signals that you are a ruthless, determined combatant willing to do whatever it takes to survive. This raw display of aggression can overwhelm your attacker psychologically, causing them to panic or second-guess their assault.

If you've seen my Savage Street Fighting training video, you'll immediately understand how growling amplifies the fear and terror caused by the biting technique, making it exponentially more intimidating and disruptive to your opponent's mental composure. The sound alone can make them feel as if they are facing not just an adversary but an Apex predator, pushing them into a state of fear or flight.

Pseudospeciation – Growling also helps you pseudospeciate your attacker. As I've discussed in my other books, pseudospeciation involves mentally assigning subhuman qualities to your adversary in a self-defense situation. This mindset allows you to detach from any limiting notions of combat etiquette or hesitation that might otherwise hold you back.

By viewing the attacker as an imminent threat rather than a

227

fellow human, you can access a more primal and decisive level of aggression. This mental shift is essential in high-stakes, violent encounters, as it frees you from the moral and social restrictions that can cause hesitation, empowering you to fight with raw intent, ferocity, and unwavering determination. This psychological detachment is critical for those moments when holding back is not an option, ensuring that your actions align with survival, not civility.

However, it is critical that your actions remain legally and morally justified in the eyes of the law, ensuring that your response aligns with the severity of the threat and adheres to self-defense laws.

Crushing Techniques

Crushing is another devastating weapon in the Savage Street Fighting arsenal, effective in both stand-up and ground combat. The primary targets for this technique, which I covered in detail in Chapter 1, are the assailant's throat and testicles. These vulnerable areas make crushing a highly effective tool for quickly neutralizing an opponent.

Remember that crushing techniques are particularly effective when the assailant's body is pinned against the floor or a wall. Crushing the throat is not an easy task; it demands precise finger placement, adequate leverage, and a fierce determination to neutralize the attacker. However, crushing should only be employed in life-or-death situations where deadly force is warranted and legally justified.

Gouging Techniques

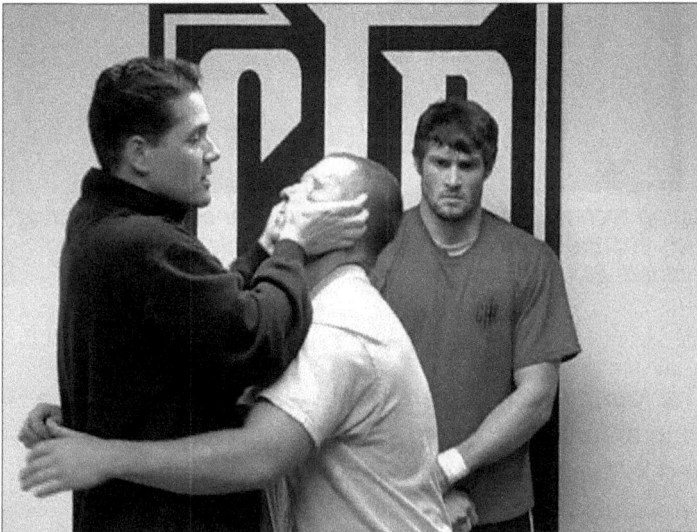

Gouging is another weapon in the Savage Street Fighting system. This technique is versatile and can be applied in both stand-up and ground combat, often in conjunction with biting for greater impact - like using two weapons at once to overwhelm your opponent.

However, be cautious - some seasoned fighters are like predators with sharp instincts, able to continue fighting even without vision. That's why it's often best to bite while gouging, applying multiple layers of pressure to overwhelm your opponent and ensure they can't fight back effectively.

Gouging techniques can be applied simultaneously with biting tactics. Pictured here is a close-up of a single thumb gouge combined with a throat bite.

Choking Techniques

The fourth and final zero beat weapon in the Savage Street Fighting arsenal is choking - a close-quarters technique applied to the assailant's throat with the intent of inducing unconsciousness.

While chokes are often executed with the arms, they can also be applied using legs, articles of clothing, truncheons, rattan sticks, belts, ropes, straps, or cords, each adding a layer of adaptability to this technique.

However, in Savage Street Fighting, we focus exclusively on arm chokes, honing in on blood restriction techniques that target the carotid arteries. By cutting off blood flow through these vital pathways, these chokes can render an opponent unconscious within seconds, delivering a decisive and efficient conclusion to the self-defense encounter.

Pictured here, a CFA student demonstrates a blood restriction choke used in the Savage Street Fighting methodology.

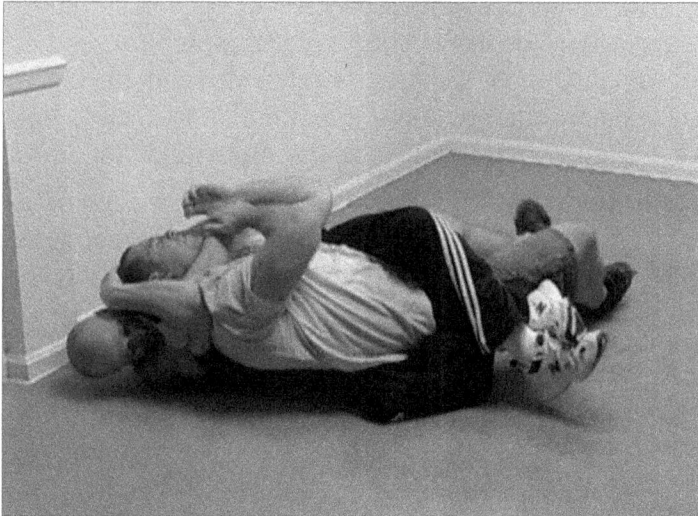

Generally, choking techniques are applied at the conclusion of the biting phase in Savage Street Fighting. Pictured here, a student demonstrates a rear naked choke from a chest-to-back position on the ground.

Savage Stand-Up Fighting

While Savage Street Fighting can be employed for both stand-up and ground fighting, I will specifically focus on using these techniques to escape and counter various stand-up street assaults. The techniques in this chapter are excruciatingly painful for the adversary and can quickly incapacitate a larger, stronger opponent. In fact, once applied, his size, strength, and motivation become irrelevant.

However, be warned - these techniques have the potential to disfigure, blind, maim, cripple, or even kill an opponent. It's crucial to ensure that your actions are both legally and morally justified in the eyes of the law. The stand-up street assaults covered in this chapter include the following:

- **Side Headlock Assault**
- **Front Bear Hug**
- **Two-Hand Lapel Grab**
- **Front Headlock Assault**
- **Waist Tackle**
- **Rear Forearm Choke**

Defending Against Stand-Up Assaults

Being caught in a throat choke, bear hug, or any stand-up restraint can catch anyone off guard. Often, it's not the choke, lock, or hold itself that defeats the victim - it's the panic. For this reason, it is crucial to stay calm so you can quickly assess the situation and respond effectively.

When placed in a hold, it's essential to react immediately, before the attacker can apply significant pressure or use leverage to their advantage. A key principle is to avoid matching strength with strength; trying to muscle your way out of a restraint will only waste time and energy, and may even help the attacker secure their hold more effectively.

Once you grasp the tactics and principles used in the assault scenarios covered here, you'll be able to adapt and apply the concepts to many other types of street attacks.

Countering a Side Headlock Assault

The first stand-up counter I'll teach you is against the side headlock - a common hold favored by street punks, barroom brawlers, and the typical street mugger. While the side headlock is an unsophisticated technique, often marking the user as a novice fighter, it is still extremely dangerous.

If not addressed immediately, this hold can quickly escalate into a life-threatening situation, leading to unconsciousness, blood drowning if pressure collapses the carotid arteries, severe hemorrhaging, restricted breathing, and even death. The headlock's grip can cut off air and blood supply within seconds, creating a critical need for fast action.

The side headlock also creates a vulnerable position where your head and neck are exposed to additional strikes, which can worsen injuries or impair your ability to respond. Despite its simplicity, this hold should never be underestimated in a real-world self-defense scenario, where even a minor lapse in response can have critical consequences.

Step 1: *When the defender is caught in a side headlock, it's crucial that they immediately turn their head inward, towards the opponent's ribs, to prevent being choked by the assailant's forearm. In this image, the author points out where the defender must turn his head to effectively avoid the choke.*

Pictured here is an example of improper head positioning. Notice how the defender is being choked by the attacker's forearm, which could have been avoided by turning the head inward.

Step 2: *Ensure your legs are spread wide apart to maintain your balance and prevent the opponent from tossing you around or taking you down. This stable stance helps you remain grounded while you work to escape the headlock.*

Step 3: *The defender must secure a firm grip around the opponent. The type of grip will depend on two key factors: the size and width of the opponent's body and the length of the defender's arms. In this photo, the defender utilizes a wrist grip to maintain control over the attacker, ensuring stability and leverage.*

Step 4: *With a solid grip secured, the defender is now ready to apply tactical biting.*

Side Headlock Counter

Step 1: *The defender is caught off guard and placed in a side headlock by the attacker, initiating the need for an immediate and strategic response.*

Step 2: *The defender quickly reacts by turning his head inward towards the attacker's ribs, widening his stance for better balance, and wraps his arms around the attacker to secure control and begin his counterattack.*

Step 3: *The defender sinks his teeth into the attacker's chest. This powerful bite inflicts excruciating pain and immediately shifts the dynamic, turning the attacker from predator to prey as he struggles to cope with the sudden counterattack.*

Step 4: *The attacker begins to panic! In a frantic attempt to escape the pain, he pulls away from the defender, losing control of the situation.*

Step 5: *The defender forces his attacker to the ground while adjusting his bite to a new location - this time, sinking his teeth into the attacker's cheek, continuing to inflict pain and maintain control.* **NOTE:** *While taking a fight to the ground is generally not recommended due to risks like multiple attackers, here it becomes necessary. The attacker's panic and attempt to escape create an opportunity for the defender to gain control on the ground, ensuring the confrontation can be ended quickly and decisively.*

Step 6: *The defender establishes a dominant top mounted position, and delivers several powerful elbow strikes to the face.*

239

Countering a Front Bear Hug

Now, I will show you how to counter a front bear hug using the Savage Street Fighting methodology. Instead of employing biting tactics, the defender will use eye gouging techniques to escape from this hold.

Many people underestimate how dangerous front bear hugs can be in a street fight. They are not limited to unskilled muggers or novice street brawlers. In fact, a moderately skilled mixed martial artist can easily convert a front bear hug into a devastating "belly-to-belly suplex" throw, which can result in serious injuries, including permanent paralysis.

If the attacker places you in a front bear hug, avoid the urge to deliver a knee strike to his groin - you won't have the necessary leverage to land a truly debilitating blow, especially if you're lifted off the ground. Instead, you'll need to use your free leg to perform the leg wrap technique described in this section, which will give you better control and increase your chances of escaping the hold effectively.

The best defense against a front bear hug is to avoid being grabbed in the first place. However, self-defense is dynamic, and even the most seasoned RBSD practitioners can be caught off guard. In this photo, the defender is grabbed and lifted off the ground, showing the importance of quick thinking in countering such attacks.

Step 1: As the attacker rushes in with a front bear hug, the defender quickly performs a leg wrap around the attacker's hamstring, a key maneuver for countering the attack and preventing control.

The leg wrap maneuver is essential for several reasons: it significantly reduces the attacker's ability to lift you off the ground, keeps you connected for a quick counterattack, and negates the leverage the assailant needs to execute a body slam or suplex.

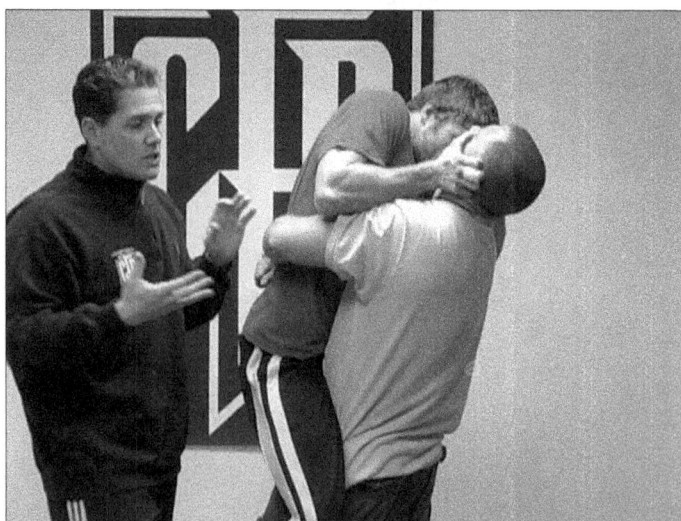

Step 2: *While maintaining the leg wrap, the defender quickly drives a double thumb gouge into the attacker's eyes. Warning: The double thumb gouge is a deadly force technique and should only be used in self-defense situations that are legally warranted and justified in the eyes of the law.*

242

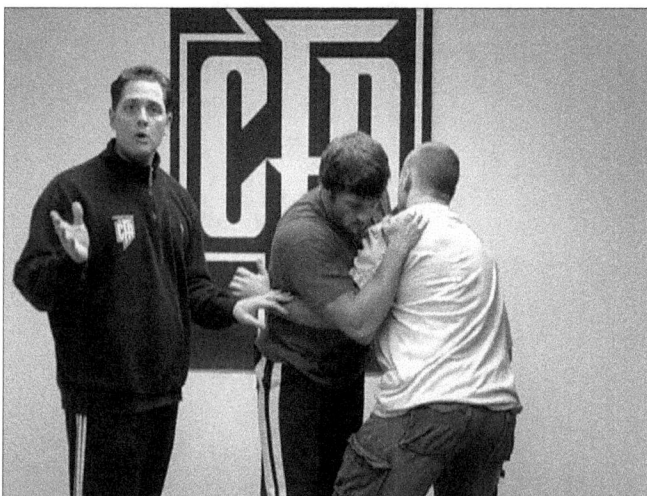

Step 3: *The intense pain from the double thumb gouge forces the attacker to immediately release his hold. With the release of the bear hug and the attacker now vulnerable, the defender follows up with powerful knee strikes to the groin, further incapacitating the opponent.*

Remember, when performing a double thumb gouge, position your thumbs into each eye socket while anchoring your other fingers behind the opponent's ears for stability. Once your grip is secure, drive your thumbs forcefully into the eye sockets.

Warning: *The double thumb gouge is a deadly force technique and should only be used in legally justified self-defense situations. Make sure that your actions are warranted and defensible in the eyes of the law.*

Front Bear Hug Counter

Step 1: The attacker (right) charges at the defender.

Step 2: The attacker attempts a front bear hug.

Step 3: *The defender quickly wraps his leg around the opponent's thigh to maintain control and immediately counterattacks with a double thumb gouge, targeting the opponent's eyes to force a release.*

Step 4: *The attacker immediately releases his hold due to the intense pain caused by the double thumb gouge.*

245

Step 5: *The defender pushes the attacker back, causing him to lose his balance and fall to the ground, further neutralizing the threat.*

Step 6: *The defender establishes a dominant top mounted position. From here, he has the option to either continue his assault to further neutralize the attacker or disengage and attempt to flee the scene, depending on the situation and the level of threat remaining.*

The Single Thumb Gouge

The single thumb gouge is a variation of the double thumb gouge that can also be effectively used when trapped in a front bear hug.

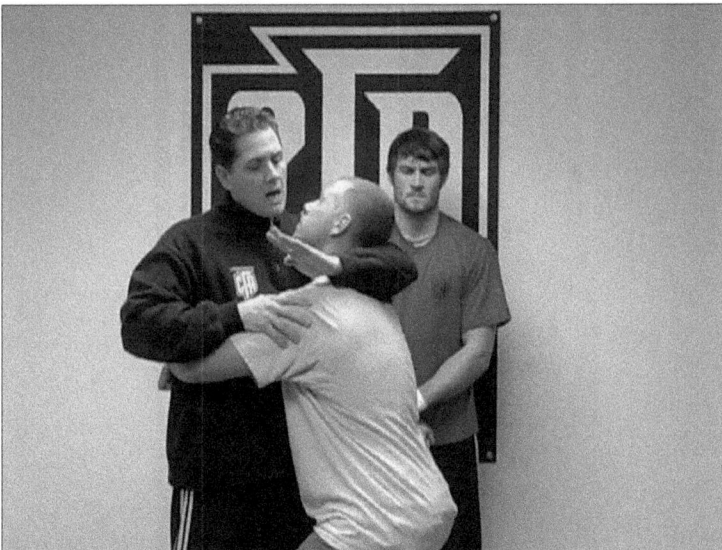

Step 1: *To perform the gouge, first wrap your left arm around the opponent's neck. This positioning helps secure the opponent and prevents them from escaping or countering easily.*

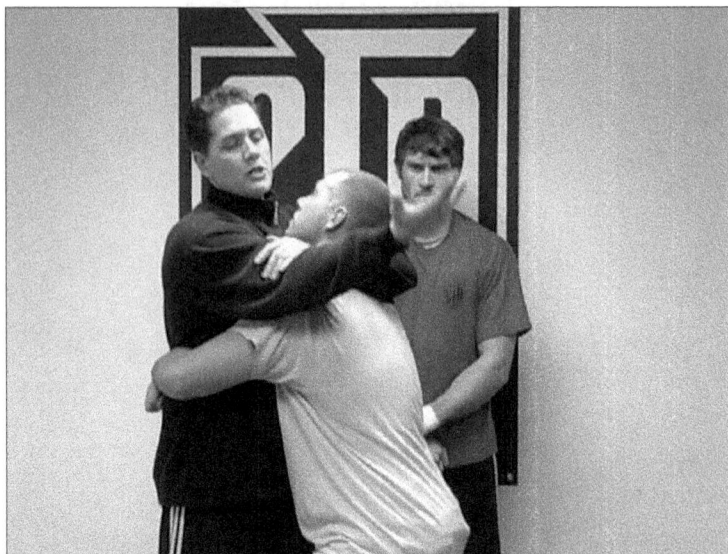

Step 2: *Bring your right arm forward and clasp your right biceps with your left hand. This creates a secure hold around the opponent's neck, giving you control while freeing your right hand to apply the single thumb gouge to the opponent's eye.*

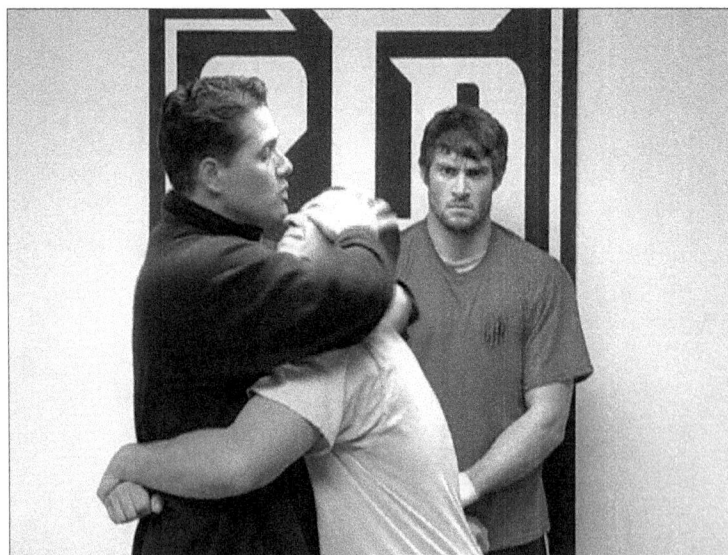

Step 3: *Squeeze your arms together tightly, applying pressure around the opponent's neck, and forcefully drive your right thumb into the opponent's eye socket.*

Escaping a Two-Hand Lapel Grab

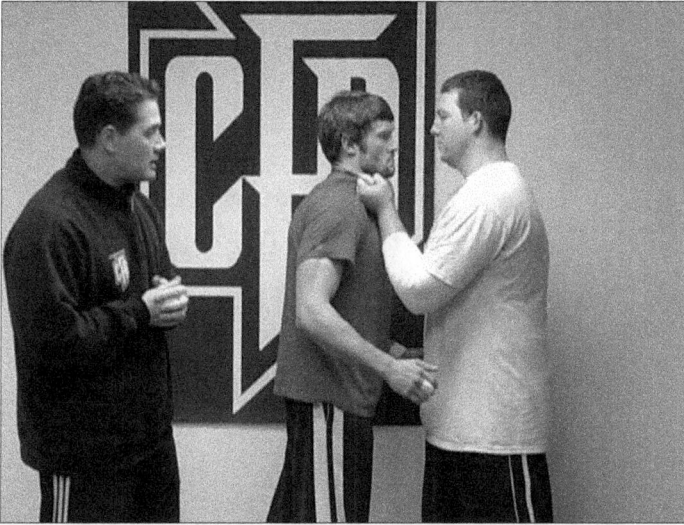

The third counter technique I am going to teach you is how to escape from a two-hand lapel grab. As a bonus, this same escape maneuver can also be used if someone attacks you with a two-hand front throat choke. In either case, the principles remain the same.

It's important to note that, while a lapel grab might not immediately seem like a life-threatening attack, any assault can escalate into a dangerous situation where deadly force might be justified. For example, a lapel grab could quickly turn into a punch, choke, or an attempt to control or throw you to the ground, potentially resulting in serious injury. Because of this, the techniques shown in this book, including the counter to a lapel grab, are designed for scenarios where the escalation justifies the use of deadly force.

In order to escape from this type of attack, you will be employing either the single or double thumb gouging techniques. Some of you may also want to incorporate biting tactics if you feel it is necessary - this is entirely up to you, depending on the severity of the threat.

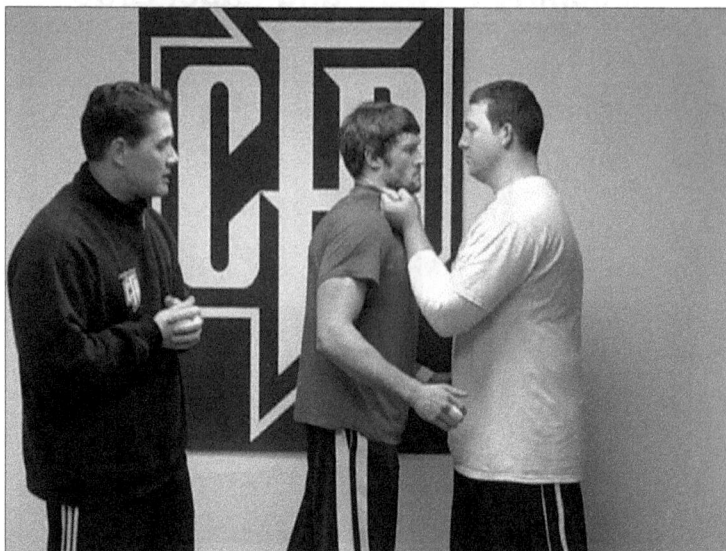

Step 1: *The defender is placed in a two-hand lapel grab, with the attacker seizing control of the front of the defender's clothing.*

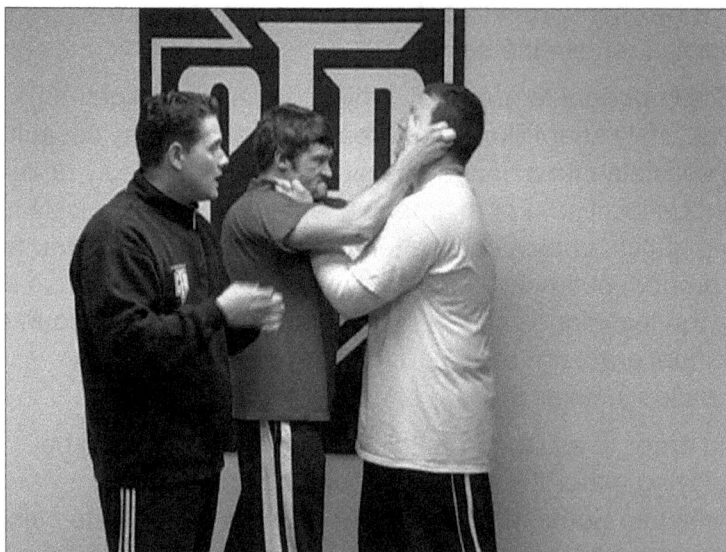

Step 2: *The defender swiftly counters by driving a double thumb gouge into the attacker's eyes, applying immediate pressure to disrupt the attacker's vision and force a release.*

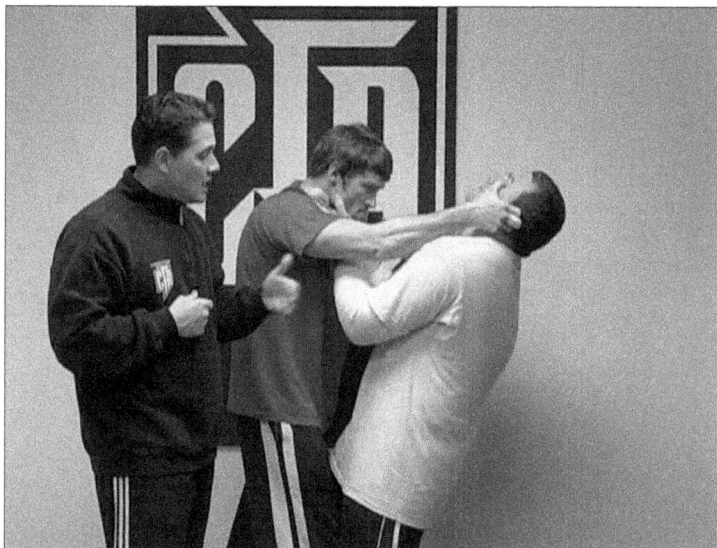

Step 3: *The intense pressure from the double thumb gouge forces the attacker to stumble backward, creating space and weakening his control over the defender.*

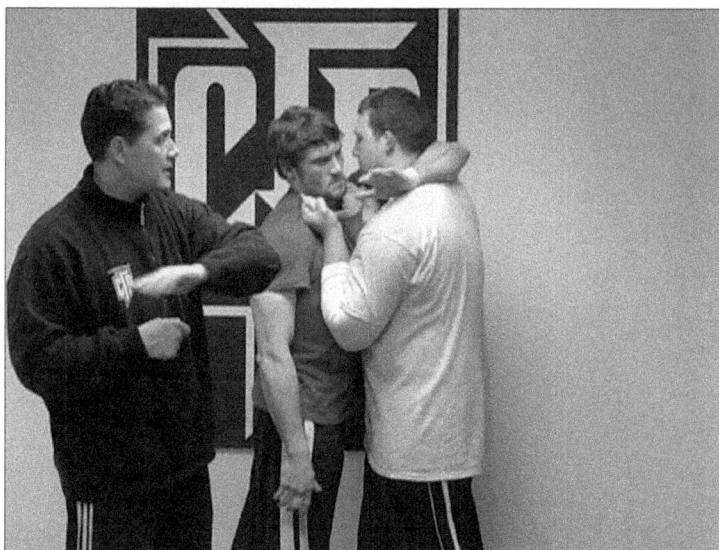

Pictured here, the defender demonstrates a variation of the lapel escape using the single eye gouge technique. **Step 1:** *To begin, wrap your left arm around the opponent's neck, establishing control and setting up the gouge.*

251

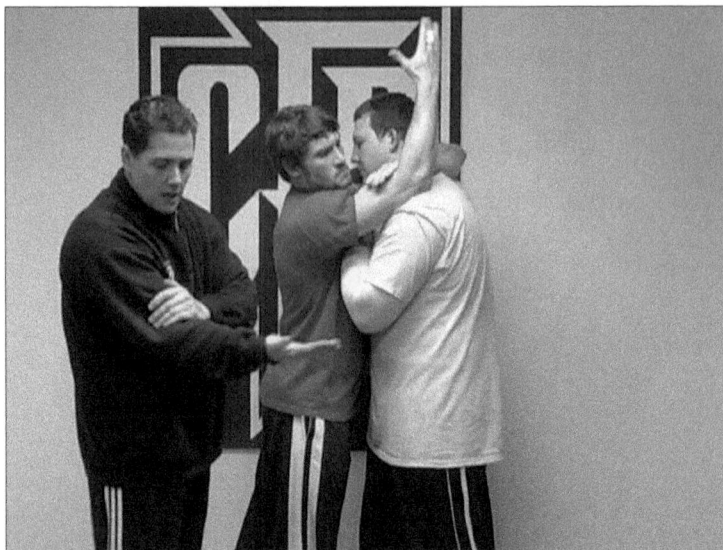

Step 2: *Bring your right arm forward and clasp your right biceps with your left hand, securing a strong hold around the opponent's neck.*

Step 3: *Squeeze your arms together tightly, applying pressure around the opponent's neck, and forcefully drive your right thumb into his eye socket. If needed, you may also bite into the assailant's neck for added control and to further incapacitate him.*

Why Take Your Attacker to the Ground?

Although I generally do not advocate initiating ground fighting in self-defense situations due to the risks posed by multiple attackers or environmental factors, there are circumstances where taking the attacker to the ground becomes a crucial and effective tactic.

You'll notice that many of the self-defense demonstrations featured in this chapter show defenders deliberately taking their attackers to the ground. This tactic significantly enhances the overall effectiveness of the Savage Street Fighting methodology.

What follows is a list of important reasons why you should know how to forcefully take your adversary to the ground during your Savage Street Fighting assault:

FALLING – The predictable visceral response from many of the Savage Street Fighting techniques often forces the opponent to retreat and fall backward to the ground. If both you and your adversary end up on the floor, you can seamlessly continue your Savage Street Fighting assault without losing momentum. This allows you to maintain constant offensive pressure, overwhelming the opponent both mentally and physically throughout the altercation.

PROVIDES A BETTER ANCHORING MECHANISM – In stand-up fighting, you may sometimes lose bite or gouge pressure, particularly when your opponent is desperately trying to pull away. This can reduce the effectiveness of your techniques. However, when the fight transitions to the ground, especially on hard surfaces, it can serve as an anchoring mechanism, helping to pin your opponent. This anchoring effect allows you to apply your Savage Street Fighting techniques - whether biting, gouging, or crushing - with maximum pressure, ensuring they are more effective.

IT'S A FREE IMPACT TOOL – The floor, particularly hard surfaces like concrete, can serve as an invaluable self-defense impact tool. Many street fight fatalities occur simply from people falling and hitting their heads on the ground. It's more common than you'd think!

When Savage Street Fighting techniques are executed correctly, your adversary will fall backwards, absorbing the full impact of the fall. This natural force significantly increases the damage inflicted on the attacker, often without requiring additional strikes.

PROVIDES A BETTER ESCAPE OPTION – Let's face it: some criminals are so determined that they won't stop at anything to murder, rape, or kidnap you. While biting and gouging will likely force them to release their hold, there's still a chance they may pursue you after letting go.

However, by taking your opponent to the ground, you gain the advantage of being able to render him unconscious, either through pummeling or choking him out. Once he's incapacitated, you'll have time to safely flee the scene without the fear of being chased down. This gives you the opportunity to escape without being pursued by a relentless attacker.

PROVIDES EXTRA FIREPOWER – In some situations, you may need additional firepower to neutralize a particularly strong or aggressive attacker. Forcing the opponent to the ground enables you to deliver a series of powerful, linear blows - known as pummeling - directly to the face with amplified force. With the assailant's head pinned against the ground, each strike becomes exponentially more devastating, as the floor stabilizes and concentrates the impact, minimizing any recoil and maximizing damage. This position not only enhances the effectiveness of each blow but also diminishes the assailant's ability to defend or evade, allowing you to maintain complete control in a high-stakes encounter.

The best strikes for this pummeling assault include tight linear punches, hammer fists, and, in certain cases, elbow strikes. With the gravitational advantage and the opponent immobilized, these strikes become highly effective and, in some cases, deadly.

Warning! Pummeling your adversary on concrete can be deadly. The hard surface amplifies the impact of each blow, especially when the opponent's head is against the ground, leaving no room for the force to dissipate. This can lead to severe head trauma, skull fractures, brain injury, or even death, as the ground concentrates the power of your strikes. It's essential to use extreme caution and ensure your actions are legally justified when applying such force in a self-defense situation.

255

Countering a Front Headlock

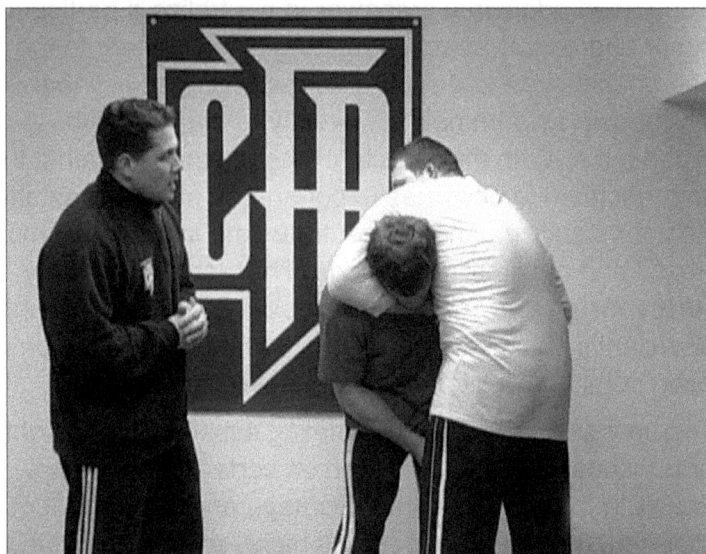

This section will focus on escaping and countering a front headlock assault.

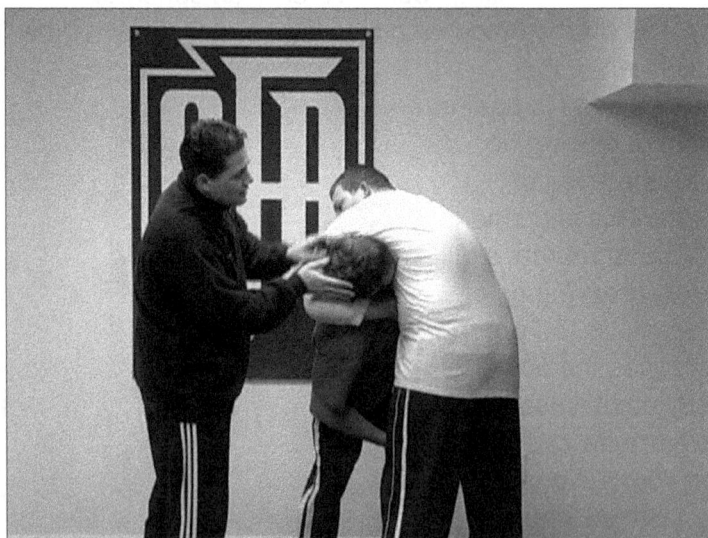

Step 1: *When the opponent places the defender in a front headlock, the defender immediately turns his head inward, towards the opponent's lats, to avoid being choked by the assailant's forearm. This position also helps the defender set up an ideal bite target.*

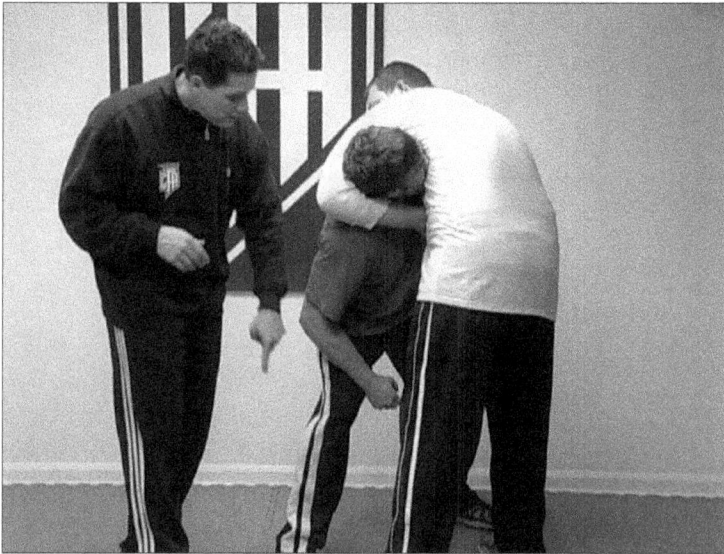

Step 2: *The defender must ensure his legs are spread wide apart to maintain balance and prevent the opponent from tossing him around or taking him down. Stability is crucial in setting up an effective counter.*

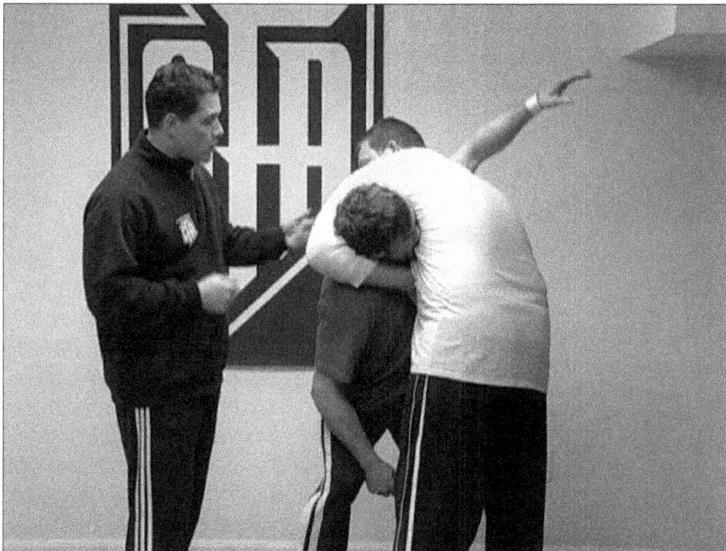

Step 3: *The defender then reaches around the opponent's shoulder with his left arm, securing a strong position to prepare for the next move.*

257

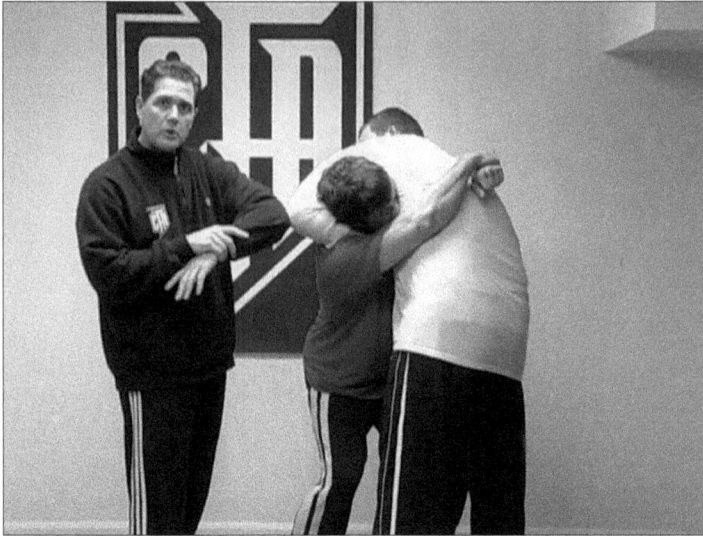

Step 4: *The defender secures a wrist grip to control his attacker. With his arms locked in place, the defender lowers his center of gravity and bites deeply into the opponent's latissimus dorsi muscle, ensuring maximum pain and leverage to break the hold.*

NOTE: *The latissimus dorsi muscle, one of the largest muscles in the back, serves as an ideal bite target due to its size and accessibility.*

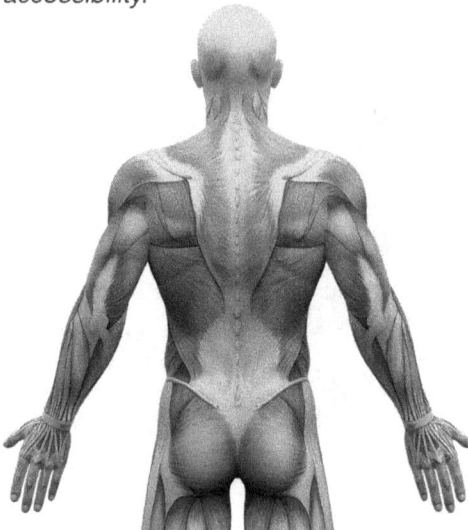

When biting this muscle, be cautious not to take in too much flesh at once. Biting too large a portion can cause your jaw to cramp, which will greatly reduce your bite pressure. The goal is to bite a reasonable amount of flesh to trigger the opponent's Predictable Visceral Response without compromising your effectiveness.

258

Countering a Tackle

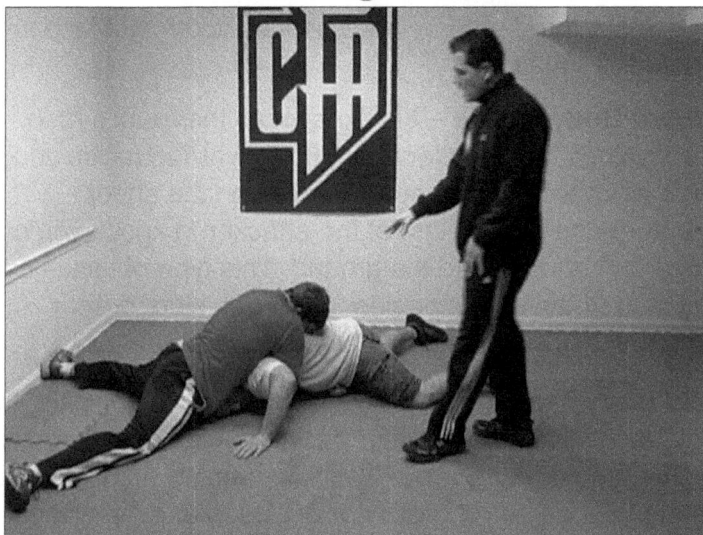

Savage Street Fighting can also be effectively used to defend against common takedown techniques. A takedown is a strategic maneuver designed to force a standing fighter to the floor immediately, compromising their mobility and often setting up the attacker for ground control. These techniques are especially popular in mixed martial arts (MMA) but are also common in street fights, where opponents may use any means necessary to bring you down.

There are various ways you can be taken down, depending on the skill and experience of your opponent. For instance, a skilled jiu-jitsu fighter might perform a precise single-leg takedown to unbalance you, while a less-trained but aggressive barroom brawler may simply attempt a rough body tackle. Each approach presents its own challenges and risks, but regardless of the style or method, Savage Street Fighting equips you with the tools to counter these attacks effectively. This approach allows you to maintain control in a confrontation, whether you manage to stay on your feet or are forced to the ground, ready to respond with powerful countermeasures.

THREE TYPES OF BODY TACKLES

There are three primary body tackles you might face in a self-defense situation:

Upper Body Tackle – Also known as the "bum's rush," this tackle involves the attacker charging forward to tackle you. While it lacks technical finesse, it relies on the sheer momentum and bodyweight of the attacker to knock you off balance and bring you to the ground. This type of tackle can be initiated from various angles - the front, side, or rear - making it especially dangerous in ambush situations.

Mid Body Tackle – Also referred to as a waist tackle, this technique involves the attacker ducking under your arms to drive their shoulder into your waistline, aiming to topple you by targeting your center of gravity. Many people, even without formal combat training, are familiar with this move from recreational sports like football, where similar techniques are used to bring opponents to the ground.

Lower Body Tackle – This tackle targets the legs and comes in two main forms: the single-leg and double-leg tackle. In the single-leg tackle, the attacker lowers his base, shoots forward toward your lead leg, and secures a grip behind your knee while driving their shoulder into your hip, using leverage and momentum to bring you down. In a double-leg tackle, the attacker targets both legs simultaneously, wrapping their arms around them and pushing forward to destabilize you entirely.

The type of takedown an opponent uses can be influenced by factors like their fighting style, experience, state of mind, and whether they are under the influence of alcohol or drugs, as well as environmental factors such as available space and proximity. Understanding these circumstances can help you anticipate and counter their moves effectively. In this section, I will focus on how Savage Street Fighting defends against the popular waist tackle.

Waist Tackle Counter

Step 1: *The attacker positions himself and prepares to launch his takedown attack, signaling the start of the assault.*

Step 2: *The attacker lunges forward, initiating his takedown attempt, using speed and momentum to close the distance.*

Step 3: *The defender immediately shoots his legs back while driving his hips into the opponent's head and shoulders. This technique, known as sprawling, effectively counters the attacker's forward momentum, preventing the takedown and putting the defender in a stronger, more controlled position.*

Step 4: *The defender secures his arms around his opponents stomach and bites forcefully into the latissimus dorsi muscle.*

Step 5: *The defender continues to bite until the opponent turns their body over, the biting tactic is used to force a reaction, causing the opponent to reposition themselves to escape the pain.*

Step 6: *After securing a new hold, the defender can continue biting to maintain control, pummel the attacker with strikes, apply a submission hold, or attempt to flee the scene if possible. The choice depends on the situation and the level of threat the defender faces.*

Countering a Rear Forearm Choke

The final stand-up counter technique I'm going to teach you is the rear forearm choke defense. Learning to defend against this assault is crucial for two key reasons:

1. It's Deadly - The rear forearm choke can kill you! Even an unskilled attacker can apply it and crush your windpipe. If you don't react immediately, the choke can cut off your air supply and cause unconsciousness or death within seconds.

2. It's Transformable - This choke can quickly evolve into a rear naked choke (RNC), one of the most dangerous choke holds. Once the RNC is locked in, it's nearly impossible to escape. This choke can compress both the carotid arteries, cutting off blood flow to the brain and rendering you unconscious within seconds. Without a timely response, the consequences could be fatal.

Immediate action and precise technique are essential to escape from this deadly hold before it tightens, limiting your chances of survival.

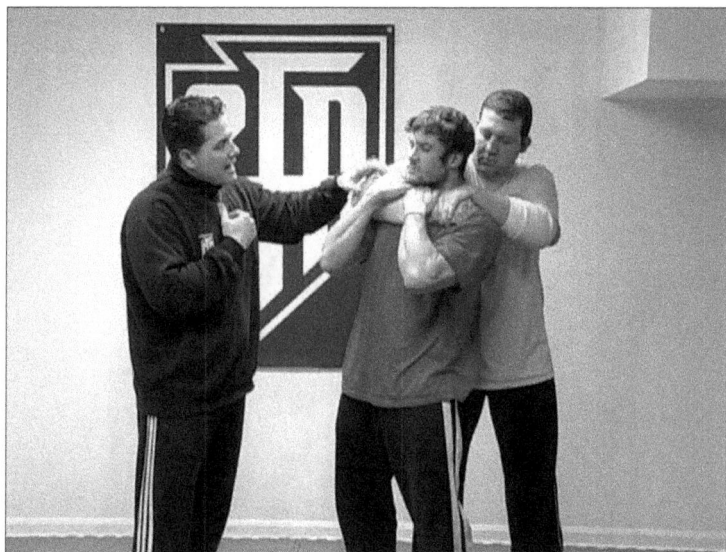

Step 1: *The attacker approaches from behind. To prevent the defender's windpipe from being damaged, he grabs the attacker's forearm and pulls it downward.*

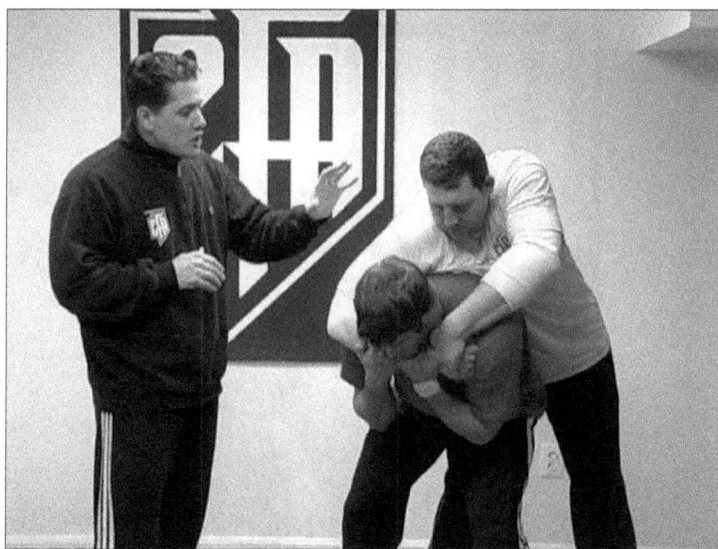

Step 2: *The defender bumps his hips back to prevent his attacker from lifting him up.*

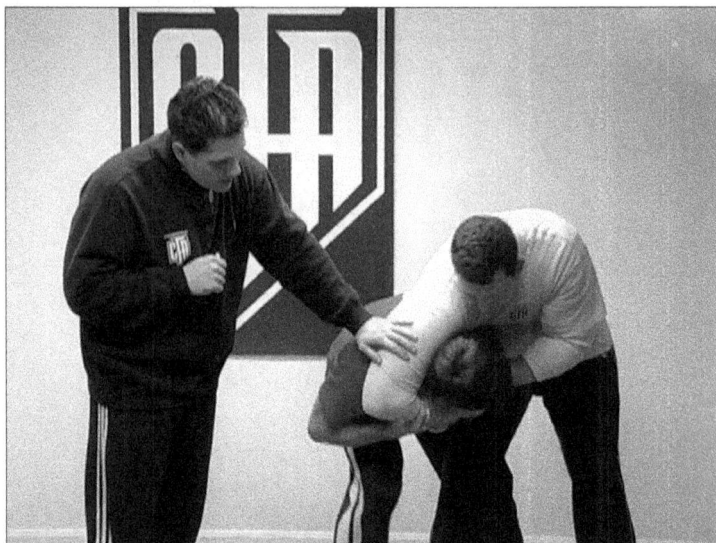

Step 3: *The defender steps behind the attacker and turns his head inward to protect his throat and to align his teeth with a flesh target.*

Step 4: *The defender widens his legs to improve his balance and stability.*

Step 5: *The defender reaches around his attackers torso and solidifies a wrist grip.*

Step 6: *The defender can now counterattack with tactical biting.*

Defending Against Multiple Attackers

Savage Street Fighting can also be applied in multiple attacker situations. However, let me be perfectly clear: successfully defending against multiple attackers is an extremely difficult and dangerous task. The odds will almost always be stacked against you, but with proper training and nerves of steel, it can be done.

This section won't dive into the science of fighting multiple attackers, but it will show you how Savage Street Fighting techniques can be highly effective when defending against more than one opponent. Understanding how to use the environment, target vital areas, and apply continuous pressure with relentless tactics is key to surviving these treacherous encounters.

To effectively apply Savage Street Fighting in a multiple attacker scenario, it is crucial to have a solid understanding of the principles of Multiple Attacker Defense. These principles provide the framework necessary to survive such dangerous encounters. Key principles include:

- **Identifying Alpha and Subordinate Opponents:** Prioritize identifying the alpha attacker, as neutralizing the leader can psychologically affect the group and reduce their morale.

- **Staggered vs. Parallel Encroachments:** Understand the difference between staggered (attackers coming one after the other) and parallel (simultaneous attacks) approaches to prepare your counter strategies accordingly.

- **Employing the Assembly Line Theory:** This theory focuses on moving through opponents one by one, delivering quick and decisive strikes to create a path to escape.

- **First Strike Techniques:** During the pre-contact stage, employ first strike methods to disrupt the attackers before they can coordinate their assault. Preemptive, well-timed strikes can disorient or incapacitate the lead attacker.

- **Environmental Makeshift Weaponry:** Use your environment to your advantage, whether it's objects around you that can be used as weapons or barriers that create obstacles for the attackers.

- **Keep Moving:** Whenever faced with multiple assailants, always maintain mobility. Constant movement makes you a difficult target to hit and prevents attackers from surrounding you. It also forces them to misjudge your range and creates opportunities to find an opening for possible escape.

By understanding these key principles, you can enhance the effectiveness of Savage Street Fighting when defending against multiple opponents. Mobility, awareness, and decisive action are essential in these high-risk situations.

Multiple Attacker Scenario

Pictured here, the defender (left) is approached by two thugs looking for trouble, setting the stage for a potential confrontation.

Step 1: *The defender initially attempts to defuse the situation by communicating with the hostile men, using verbal de-escalation techniques to avoid physical confrontation if possible. Maintaining calm and non-threatening body language can help reduce tension and potentially prevent violence from erupting.*

270

Step 2: *The man on the right (assailant #1) escalates the situation by shoving the defender's shoulder, signaling the beginning of a physical confrontation.*

Step 3: *Assailant #1 throws a punch aimed at the defender's head. Reacting quickly, the defender blocks the punch, maintaining control of the situation while preparing to counter.*

Step 4: *The defender swiftly spins the attacker around, taking control and placing him in a chest-to-back position, giving the defender the upper hand while protecting himself from further attacks.*

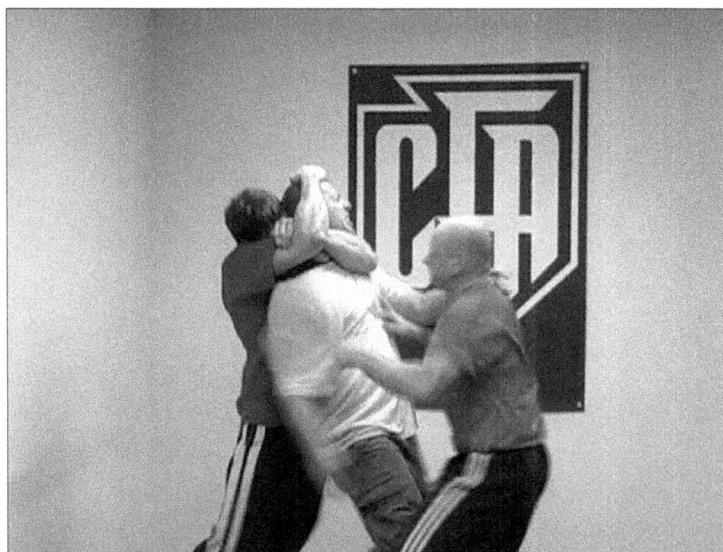

Step 5: *The defender secures a biceps hold on assailant #1 and bites into his neck, inflicting pain and confusion. Using this opportunity, the defender positions assailant #1 as a human shield, effectively protecting himself from a potential attack by assailant #2.*

Step 6: *The defender keeps moving continuously, using assailant #1 as a shield to maintain protection from assailant #2's potential attacks. This constant motion helps the defender remain a difficult target and keeps assailant #2 at a disadvantage.*

Step 7: *Assailant #2 attempts to strike the defender but, due to the defender's positioning, ends up hitting his own partner instead. This misstep further disorients the attackers and gives the defender a tactical advantage.*

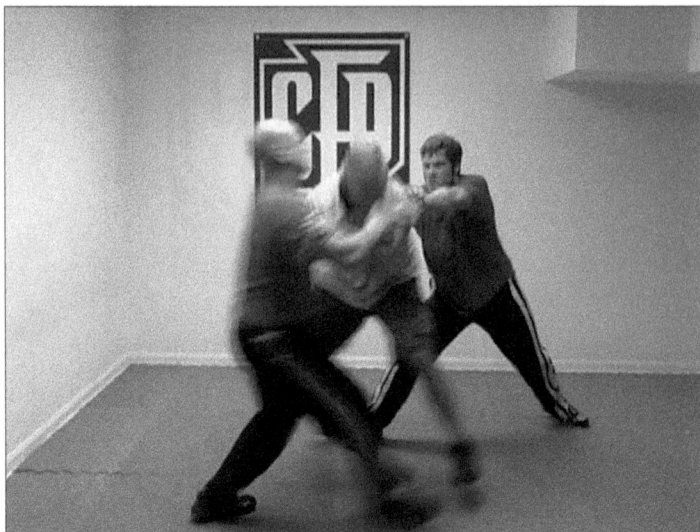

Step 8: *The defender quickly identifies an escape route. Seizing the moment, he releases his hold on assailant #1 and violently throws him into assailant #2.*

Step 9: *The two attackers collide with each other, creating confusion and further disrupting their assault, giving the defender an opportunity to flee safely.*

Final Words on Savage Street Fighting

The Savage Street Fighting chapter has provided you with a powerful and comprehensive foundation in survival-based self-defense tactics. These brutal, close-quarters techniques - focused on biting, gouging, crushing, and choking - are designed for extreme situations where your life may be on the line. While the methods in this chapter are highly effective, it's crucial to use them only when legally and morally justified. Remember, Savage Street Fighting is not about relying on extreme force but rather applying precision, control, and relentless pressure. With the right training and discipline, these techniques can help protect you and your loved ones during dangerous encounters.

Static photographs offer only a glimpse into the overwhelming and destructive nature of Savage Street Fighting. To fully understand its brutality and effectiveness, check out my free training videos on **SammyFrancoTV**, available on YouTube, where I demonstrate many of these concepts in real-time scenarios.

While this book offers a solid base, there are more advanced concepts in the Savage Street Fighting methodology, such as weapon disarming, offensive ground attacks, first-strike strategies, and adrenaline drills. Some of these topics are covered on my YouTube channel, and advanced techniques will be explored in future resources for those looking to elevate their skills.

CHAPTER SIX
Methodology Integration
The Ultimate Combat Strategy

SINISTER SELF-DEFENSE

BUILDING A UNIFIED COMBAT STRATEGY

In this chapter, we bring together the individual combat methodologies to form a unified strategy that adapts to any level of threat.

Each methodology - whether it's the preemptive power of First Strike, the precision of Combat Pressure Points, or the overwhelming force of the Widow Maker and Savage Street Fighting - has a unique role in your self-defense arsenal. Combined, they create a cohesive system that prepares you to handle any phase of a violent encounter.

THE HIERARCHY OF COMBAT METHODOLOGIES

To respond effectively to violent situations, it's essential to understand the structure of these methodologies and how to escalate their use based on the threat level. This chapter will guide you through integrating the methodologies and scaling your response accordingly, from intermediate use-of-force confrontations to life-threatening assaults.

FIRST STRIKE PRINCIPLE

The First Strike is your primary defense when you identify an imminent threat. It disrupts the attacker's plan and gives you the upper hand before the fight even begins. Preemptive action is key— targeting vulnerable areas to incapacitate the attacker quickly. This method is especially effective when danger is recognized early, allowing you to act swiftly and neutralize the threat.

Integration Strategy: During the pre-contact stage, use First Strike to stop a threat before it escalates. Position yourself in a non-threatening stance, ready to deliver a surprise blow at the first sign of aggression. Follow up with a compound attack to ensure the threat is neutralized.

COMBAT PRESSURE POINTS

When the situation demands a more destructive approach, Combat Pressure Points allow for a swift and efficient escalation without resorting to overwhelming force. By executing surgical strikes to key vulnerable areas like the eyes, throat, temple, or back of the neck, you can incapacitate an attacker with minimal effort, using their own weaknesses against them while conserving your energy.

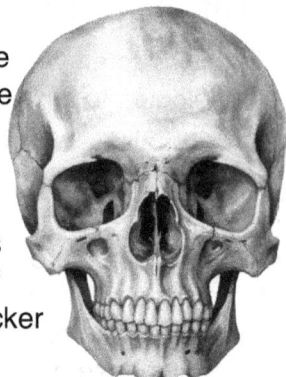

Integration Strategy: Combine Combat Pressure Points with a preemptive strike or follow up a First Strike with more destructive pressure point techniques. For example, if your initial strike doesn't neutralize the threat and the adversary escalates, targeting pressure points becomes your best option to weaken their ability to fight back effectively.

THE WIDOW MAKER

Designed for extreme situations where your life is in imminent danger, the Widow Maker uses overwhelming force to save you. This methodology attacks the adversary physically and psychologically, flipping the predator-prey dynamic in your favor.

Integration Strategy: Transition to the Widow Maker when the opponent escalates the situation beyond basic self-defense, particularly when they have a clear intent to seriously harm or kill you. Use the chaos created by a First Strike or Combat Pressure Points to blend into Widow Maker techniques, shifting into a more vicious mindset to eliminate the threat.

SAVAGE STREET FIGHTING

The ultimate no-holds-barred approach, the Savage Street Fighting methodology employs brutal tactics such as biting, gouging, crushing, and choking to neutralize overwhelming threats. It is particularly effective in situations where the attacker has you in a hold, choke, or is attempting ground control - forcing them to immediately release their hold and disengage.

Integration Strategy: If you find yourself in a life-threatening scenario where your only objective is survival, immediately shift to Savage Street Fighting techniques. These brutal methods are designed to handle extreme violence with no room for hesitation. Transition seamlessly from the calculated devastation of the Widow Maker into the raw, destructive power of Savage Street Fighting when the situation demands it.

ADAPTING TO THE SITUATION

The core of this integrated combat strategy is your ability to scale your response according to the threat level. It's crucial to assess the situation quickly, determine the appropriate use-of-force response, and transition seamlessly between methodologies as the encounter progresses. This ensures you can adapt fluidly to the evolving dynamics of a violent confrontation while staying legally and morally justified in your actions. Here's how you can apply the system in practice:

Pre-Contact Awareness: Before physical confrontation occurs, maintain situational awareness. If you sense danger, mentally prepare to act. This is where you can use the First Strike principle to preemptively neutralize the threat.

Contact Stage: Once physical contact is initiated, evaluate whether precision (Combat Pressure Points) or a more brutal response (Widow Maker or Savage Street Fighting) is necessary. Use your environment to your advantage, whether positioning yourself to limit the attacker's movement, using makeshift weapons, or finding opportunities to safely escape.

Escalation: If the opponent escalates his level of force, respond accordingly, transitioning from First Strike to Combat Pressure Points, and finally to Widow Maker or Savage Street Fighting as the threat becomes more severe.

ESCALATION OF FORCE FACTORS

When determining the appropriate level of force in a self-defense situation, several factors can rapidly shift the dynamics, requiring an escalation of your response. The fluid nature of combat means the threat level can intensify instantly, demanding decisive action to protect yourself or others. Here are critical factors that may necessitate more force:

- **The assailant reveals a weapon:** The sudden appearance of a knife, edged weapon, gun, or blunt object drastically increases the threat level, requiring immediate and severe action.

- **You are injured:** If you've been injured or your mobility is compromised, applying extreme force quickly may be necessary to neutralize the threat before your ability to defend yourself diminishes.

- **Multiple attackers:** Facing more than one assailant often forces you to escalate quickly, using brutal methods to incapacitate the first attacker and create escape routes.

- **Size or strength disparity:** When the opponent is significantly larger or stronger, more severe methods may be needed to compensate for the physical disadvantage.

- **Gender differences:** Women and young girls, who are often physically smaller, may need to escalate force more quickly to neutralize a larger assailant and protect themselves.

• **Age differences:** Seniors, who may have decreased strength and mobility, might need to escalate faster to defend against younger, stronger attackers.

• **Environmental constraints:** Being trapped in a confined or hazardous environment can limit your options, making it necessary to use more force to escape or gain control.

• **Erratic or irrational behavior:** If your attacker is under the influence of drugs, alcohol, or exhibits signs of mental instability, they may not respond to pain or de-escalation, requiring a more severe response.

• **Heightened aggression or rage:** If the attacker is exhibiting uncontrolled rage or a clear intent to cause maximum harm, you may need to escalate force quickly to end the encounter.

• **Trapped or blocked escape routes:** If you find yourself in a situation where your ability to escape is blocked, whether by physical barriers, the attacker themselves, or additional threats, escalating force becomes necessary.

• **Initial efforts are ineffective:** If your initial self-defense efforts fail to stop or slow the attacker, increasing the severity of your response may be necessary to disable them.

By understanding these factors, you can more effectively assess the situation and apply the appropriate methodology, ensuring that your response is both proportional and decisive.

MODULATING FORCE IN REAL-TIME

No two self-defense situations are the same. Combat is fluid, with variables like the environment, the attacker's behavior, and your physical condition constantly shifting. This makes it essential to adjust your use-of-force in real time as conditions evolve. Failing to modulate your response can lead to serious legal consequences for excessive force. Knowing when to escalate or de-escalate is key to staying effective while remaining within the law.

Continuously reassess the threat level and adjust your response accordingly - reduce force if the situation de-escalates, or intensify if the danger grows.

Ultimately, the responsibility for using appropriate force lies with you. Your ability to manage force in real-world self-defense determines not only your survival but also the legal and moral justification for your actions.

THE IMPORTANCE OF TRAINING

Mastering this integrated strategy requires continuous practice and a deep understanding of each methodology. Regularly revisiting the techniques in each chapter will help you respond instinctively under pressure.

One of the most effective tools to supplement physical practice is creative visualization, where you vividly imagine yourself executing various methodologies and their associated techniques in real-world scenarios. This mental training helps reinforce muscle memory, sharpen decision-making, and prepare you for high-stress encounters. By mentally rehearsing the techniques, you enhance your readiness to act decisively in self-defense situations.

BRINGING IT ALL TOGETHER

This chapter has shown how each combat methodology fits into a unified, adaptable system designed for real-world survival. Whether you face a minor confrontation or a life-threatening attack, you now have the knowledge and tools to respond appropriately at each stage of the threat. By integrating these techniques, you can confidently handle a wide range of violent encounters while staying mindful of the legal and moral implications of your actions.

Self-defense mastery requires more than just physical prowess - it demands the wisdom and mental clarity to assess threats, make quick decisions, and act decisively under pressure. Equally critical is managing your emotions, as the ability to stay composed can mean the difference between a controlled response and an unjustified overreaction.

As you continue to train, refine not only your techniques but also your ability to remain calm and strategic in the face of danger. True expertise lies in knowing not only how to fight but when to fight, ensuring that your actions are both effective and justified. Maintaining emotional control allows you to channel your skills with precision and make sound decisions, even in the most intense situations.

FINAL WORDS

The combat methodologies and techniques in *Sinister Self-Defense* are designed for one purpose: survival in the face of deadly, unlawful violence. These methods are not for sport, demonstration, or personal gratification - they are for protecting your life and the lives of those you love when all other options have failed. You now hold the power to neutralize threats with extreme force, but with that power comes an undeniable responsibility.

In the moments where your decisions can mean the difference between life and death, it is your responsibility to act decisively, justly, and within the boundaries of the law. To wield this knowledge is to accept the burden that every strike, every escalation of force, must be justified - not by ego, but by necessity.

Mastering the art of self-defense is not about becoming invincible. It's about preparing yourself to face the unpredictable, to embrace the brutal reality that violence is chaotic and merciless. But with the tools in this book, you are not defenseless. You have learned how to control chaos, how to respond with overwhelming precision and force, and how to protect what matters most.

As you continue to sharpen your skills, never forget that true mastery goes beyond physical prowess. It's about mastering the shadows - those dark moments where uncertainty and danger converge. The shadows represent the unknown, the unpredictable nature of violence, and by embracing them, you learn to thrive in the face of fear and chaos. Master the shadows both within and without, so that when violence comes, you are not caught off guard - you are the one in control.

This journey of mastery is ongoing. Train relentlessly. Sharpen your mind and body. But above all, remember this: Your greatest strength lies not in your fists, your speed, or even your knowledge - it lies in your ability to control the fight, both physically and mentally. Violence must never be sought out, but if it finds you, meet it with unflinching resolve.

- Sammy Franco

ADDITIONAL RESOURCES

Further Learning & Training

Self-defense is a lifelong journey, and as you continue to hone your skills, it's important to have access to ongoing learning and training materials. In this section, I've compiled essential resources that will expand your knowledge and complement the methodologies presented in *Sinister Self-Defense*, offering deeper insights into the combat systems discussed throughout the book. These resources - from comprehensive books on specific techniques to free video demonstrations - are designed to help you further develop your abilities and understanding.

Whether you're looking for advanced strategies, visual instruction, or tools to support your training, these materials provide valuable guidance for those serious about mastering self-defense. Each resource aligns with the principles of the Contemporary Fighting Arts system, ensuring that you can continue to train with confidence, and the proper mindset.

Stay Connected and Continue Your Training

You've built a strong foundation with the powerful techniques and strategies in *Sinister Self-Defense* - now it's time to take your training to the next level. By subscribing to **SammyFrancoTV** on YouTube, you can dive even deeper with in-depth tutorials that complement the methods covered in the book. Discover new self-defense strategies, stay up-to-date with the latest insights from the CFA system, and sharpen your fighting skills with practical demonstrations.

SammyFrancoTV also delves into fitness, strength training, and lifestyle practices that fully embody the warrior mindset— empowering you to not only fight stronger but live stronger. Plus, participate in livestream Q&A sessions with Sammy for real-time answers to your training questions, and explore online coaching opportunities to help you achieve your personal goals.

Subscribe Now!

Join our growing community of warriors and never miss out on essential content designed to enhance your training. Subscribe today at SammyFrancoTV: **https://www.youtube. com/@SammyFrancoTV**

FIRST STRIKE BOOK

Learn how to stop any attack before it starts by mastering the art of the preemptive strike. **First Strike: End a Fight in Ten Seconds or Less** gives you an easy-to-learn yet highly effective self-defense game plan for handling violent close-quarter combat encounters. First Strike will teach you instinctive, practical and realistic self-defense techniques that will drop any criminal attacker to the floor with one punishing blow. By reading this book and by practicing, you will learn the hard-hitting skills necessary to execute a punishing first strike and ultimately prevail in a self-defense situation. And that's what it is all about: winning in as little time as possible. 8.5 x 5.5, paperback, photos, illustrations, 202 pages.

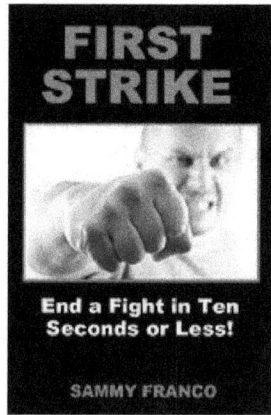

COMBAT PRESSURE POINTS

Combat Pressure Points: A No Nonsense Guide to Pressure Point Fighting is designed to teach you hard-hitting impact pressure point fighting techniques for real-world self-defense. Pressure point fighting is a fighting skill that can be performed by just about anyone, young and old, regardless of size or strength or level of experience. Best of all, you don't need martial arts training to apply these simple fighting techniques. 8.5 x 5.5, paperback, photos, illustrations, 215 pages.

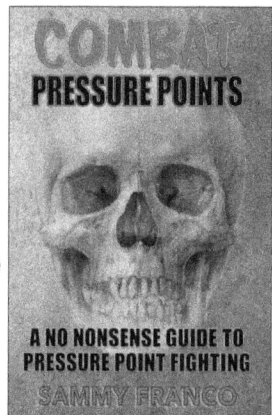

THE WIDOW MAKER COMPENDIUM

This massive book includes Sammy Franco's three best-selling Widow Maker books collected into one massive hardcover collection. This huge 500+ page book contains the complete Widow Maker Program Series (Books 1-3). With over 800 photographs and step-by-step instructions, **The Widow Maker Compendium** teaches you everything you ever wanted to know about Mr. Franco's brutal and revolutionary fighting method. The Widow Maker Compendium is a must-have for anyone interested in real world self-defense and who wants the ability to dispense extreme punishment when faced with a deadly force self-defense situation. 8.5 x 5.5, paperback, photos, illustrations, 548 pages.

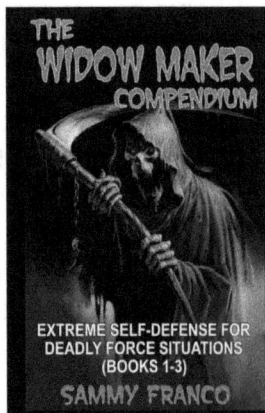

SAVAGE STREET FIGHTING

Sammy Franco reveals the science behind his most primal fighting method. **Savage Street Fighting** is a brutal self-defense system specifically designed to teach law-abiding citizens how to use tactical savagery when faced with the immediate threat of an unlawful deadly criminal attack. Savage Street Fighting is systematically engineered for the most dire circumstances - when there are no other self-defense options left! 8.5 x 5.5, paperback, photos, illustrations, 234 pages.

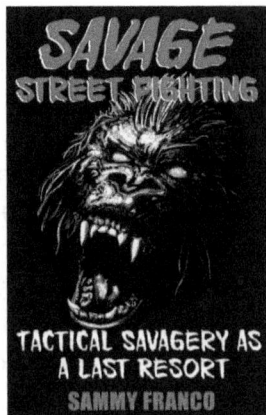

Wear the Power of the Pages!

CONTEMPORARY FIGHTING ARTS
EST. 2004
WIDOW MAKER PROGRAM

WAR MACHINE
VERITAS NUMQUAM PERIT

CONTEMPORARY FIGHTING ARTS
EST. 1989
STRIKE FIRST, SMOKE LATER

The striking imagery and bold concepts from *Sinister Self-Defense* aren't just confined to these pages—they are an integral part of the CFA system, representing the deeper ethos of embracing the warrior archetype.

Our system is more than just combat methodologies; it embodies a mindset, a lifestyle, and a way of living with purpose and power. These powerful visuals set us apart, symbolizing the full embrace of the warrior spirit. Now, you can wear the art, the energy, and the spirit of Contemporary Fighting Arts in a way that speaks to you personally.

Wear the Legacy

Featuring iconic designs like the fierce Widow Maker, the commanding War Machine and the enigmatic Wicked Jester, this clothing collection is more than just fashion - it is a bold reflection of the combat methodologies you've mastered throughout *Sinister Self-Defense*. Each design is a visual representation of the warrior ethos you've embraced, deeply connected to the core principles of Contemporary Fighting Arts (CFA).

Each image tells a story of strength, resilience, and readiness. Whether subtle or striking, these designs resonate with meaning that only those on the same path can fully appreciate. Wearing these unique symbols allows you to carry the mindset of the warrior into your everyday life, serving as a constant reminder of the power you hold and the knowledge you've gained.

From T-shirts and hoodies to hats and other apparel, these designs are not just clothing - they are a testament to the dedication and commitment you've shown in mastering self-defense. They symbolize the knowledge, confidence, and discipline that you've built through study and training. More than mere attire, they are a statement of your personal journey and a way to express the values of courage, strength, and preparedness every day.

Explore the Entire Collection:

- **Visit our official store:**
  https://sammyfranco.myspreadshop.com

- **Check out our website for exclusive offers at:**
  https://contemporaryfightingarts.com

Glossary

Many of the terms in this book may be strange to the first time reader. This is because most of the lexicon in this text are unique only to Contemporary Fighting Arts. What follows are some important terms often used in my CFA system.

A

Accuracy - The precise or exact projection of force. Accuracy is also defined as the ability to execute a combative movement with precision and exactness.

Action - A series of moving parts that permit a firearm to be loaded, unloaded and fired.

Adaptability - The ability to physically and psychologically adjust to new or different conditions or circumstances of combat.

Aerobic Exercise - "With air." Exercise that elevates the heart rate to a training level for a prolonged period of time, usually 30 minutes.

Affective Domain - This includes the attitudes, philosophies, ethics, values, discretionary use-of-force, and the spirit (killer instinct) required to use your combative tool or technique appropriately.

Affective Preparedness - Being emotionally and spiritually prepared for the demands and strains of combat.

Aggression - Hostile and injurious behavior directed toward a person.

Aggressive Hand Positioning - Placement of hands so as to imply aggressive or hostile intentions.

Aggressive Stance - (See Fighting Stance.)

Aggressor - One who commits an act of aggression.

Agility - An attribute of combat. One's ability to move his or her body quickly and gracefully.

Amalgamation - A scientific process of uniting or merging.

Ambidextrous - The ability to perform with equal facility on both the right and left sides of the body.

Ambush - To lie in wait and attack by surprise.

Ambush Zones - Strategic locations (in everyday environments) from which assailants launch surprise attacks.

American Stick Strangle - A stick strangle used with a hammer grip.

Analysis and Integration - One of the five elements of CFA's mental component. This is the painstaking process of breaking down various elements, concepts, sciences, and disciplines into their atomic parts, and then methodically and strategically analyzing, experimenting, and drastically modifying the information so that it fulfills three combative requirements: efficiency, effectiveness and safety. Only then is it finally integrated into the CFA system.

Anatomical Handles - Various body parts (i.e., appendages, joints, and in some cases, organs) that can be grabbed, held, pulled or otherwise manipulated during a ground fight.

Anatomical Power Generators - Three points on the human body that help torque your body to generate impact power. Anatomical Power Generators include: (1) Feet; (2) Hips; (3) Shoulders.

Anatomical Striking Targets - The various anatomical body targets that can be struck and which are especially vulnerable to potential harm. They include: the eyes, temple, nose, chin, back of neck, front of neck, solar plexus, ribs, groin, thighs, knees, shins, and instep.

Arm Lock - A joint lock applied to the arm.

Assailant - A person who threatens or attacks another.

Assault - The willful attempt or threat to inflict injury upon the person of another.

Assault and Battery - The unlawful touching of another person without justification.

Assert - One of the five possible tactical responses to a threatening situation. To stand up for your rights (see Comply, Escape, De-Escalate, and Fight Back).

Assessment - The process of rapidly gathering, analyzing, and accurately evaluating information in terms of threat and danger. You can assess people, places, actions, and objects.

Attachment - The touching of the arms or legs prior to executing a trapping technique.

Attack - Offensive action designed to physically control, injure, or kill another person.

Attack By Draw - One of the five conventional methods of attack. A method of attack whereby the fighter offers his assailant an intentional opening designed to lure an attack.

Attributes of Combat - The physical, mental, and spiritual qualities that enhance combat skills and tactics.

Attribute Uniformity - Various combative attributes (i.e., speed, power, accuracy, balance, etc.) which are executed the same way every time.

Autoloader - A handgun that operates by mechanical spring pressure and recoil force that ejects the spent cartridge case and automatically feeds a fresh round from the magazine. (Also known as a Semiautomatic).

Awareness - Perception or knowledge of people, places, actions, and objects. (In CFA there are three categories of tactical awareness: Criminal Awareness, Situational Awareness, and Self-Awareness.)

Axiom - A truth that is self-evident.

B

Back Position - One of the ground fighting positions. The back position is assumed when your chest is on top of your assailant's back.

Back fist - A punch made with the back of the knuckles.

Back strap - The rear, vertical portion of the pistol frame.

Balance - One's ability to maintain equilibrium while stationary or moving.

Barrier - Any large object that can be used to obstruct an attacker's path or angle of attack.

Blading the Body - Strategically positioning your body at a 45-degree angle.

Block - A defensive tool designed to intercept the assailant's attack by placing a non-vital target between the assailant's strike and your vital body target.

Bludgeon - Any club like weapon used for offensive and defensive purposes (e.g., baseball bat, club, pipe, crowbar, heavy tree branch, etc.) Bludgeons are usually heavier and thicker than sticks.

Body Composition - The ratio of fat to lean body tissue.

Body Language - Nonverbal communication through posture, gestures, and facial expressions.

Body Mechanics - Technically precise body movement during the execution of a body weapon, defensive technique, or other fighting maneuver.

Body Weapon - One of the various body parts that can be used to strike or otherwise injure or kill a criminal assailant. (Also known as Tool).

Bore - The inside of the barrel of a firearm.

Boxing - (See Western Boxing).

Break fall - A method of safely falling to the ground.

Burn Out - A negative emotional state acquired by physically over training. Some symptoms of burn-out include: physical illness, boredom, anxiety, disinterest in training, and general sluggish behavior.

C

Cadence - Coordinating tempo and rhythm to establish a timing pattern of movement.

Caliber - The diameter of a projectile.

Cardiorespiratory Conditioning - A component of physical fitness that deals with the heart, lungs, and circulatory system.

Carriage - The way you carry yourself.

Cartridge - A cylindrical case containing components of a round of ammunition: case, primer, powder charge, and bullet.

Center-Fire - A type of firearm cartridge that has its primer located in the center of the case bottom.

Centerline - An imaginary vertical line that divides your body in half and which contains many of your vital anatomical targets.

Center Mass - The center portion of the torso.

Chamber - 1) The part of a firearm in which a cartridge is contained at the instant of firing. 2) The raising of the knee to execute a kick.

Choice Words - (See Selective Semantics.)

Choke - A close quarter (grappling range) technique that requires one to apply pressure to either the trachea of carotid arteries.

Circular Movement - Movements that follow the direction of a curve.

Close Quarter Combat (CQC) - The closest range of combat, involving both armed and unarmed engagements.

Contact Shooting - Discharging a firearm with the muzzle approximately one inch distance from the target.

Cognitive Development - One of the five elements of CFA's mental component. The process of developing and enhancing your fighting skills through specific mental exercises and techniques. (see Analysis and Integration, Killer Instinct, Philosophy and Strategic/Tactical Development.)

Cognitive Domain - This encompasses the specific concepts, principles and knowledge required to use your combative tools or techniques effectively.

Cognitive Exercises - Various mental exercises used to enhance fighting skills and tactics.

Combat Arts - The various arts of war. (See Martial Arts.) Combative Attributes - (See Attributes.)

 Combative Fitness - A state characterized by cardiorespiratory and muscular/ skeletal conditioning, as well as proper body composition.

Combative Mentality - A combative state of mind necessary for fighting. Also known as the Killer Instinct. (see Killer Instinct.)

Combat Pressure Points - Techniques targeting specific head targets to neutralize threats with decisive and often maiming force. These methods go beyond conventional strikes, focusing on severely and swiftly incapacitating an attacker in extreme, life-threatening scenarios.

Combat Ranges - The various ranges of armed and unarmed combat.

Combative Power - The ability of capacity to perform or act effectively in combat.

Combative Truth - A combative element that conforms to fact or actuality and which is proven to be true.

Combative Utility - The quality of condition of being combatively useful. Combination(s) - (See Compound Attack.)

Come-Along - A series of holds or joint locks that force your adversary to move in any direction you desire.

Coming to a Base - The process of getting up to your hands and knees from the prone position.

Common Peroneal Nerve - A pressure point area located approximately four to six inches above the knee on the midline of the outside of the thigh.

Completion Phase - One of the three stages of a stick or bludgeon strike. The completion phase is the completion point of a swing.

Comply - One of the five tactical responses to a threatening situation. To obey an assailant's demands. (see Assert, De-Escalate, Escape, and Fight Back.)

Composure - A combative attribute. Composure is a quiet and focused mind set that enables you to acquire your combative agenda.

Compound Attack - One of the five conventional methods of attack. Two or more body weapons launched in strategic succession whereby the fighter overwhelms his assailant with a flurry of full speed, full force blows. (see Indirect Attack, Immobilization Attack, Attack By Draw, and Single Attack.)

Conditioning Training - A CFA training methodology requiring the practitioner to deliver a variety of offensive and defensive combinations for a four minute period (see Proficiency Training and Street Training.)

Confrontation Evasion - Strategically manipulating the distance or environment to avoid a possible confrontation.

Congruency - The state of harmoniously orchestrating the verbal and non verbal de-escalation principles.

Contact Evasion - Physically moving or manipulating your body targets to avoid being struck (i.e., slipping your head to the side or side stepping from a charging assailant).

Contact Shooting - Discharging a firearm with the muzzle touching the target.

Contemporary Fighting Arts® (CFA) - A modern martial art and self-defense system made up of three parts: physical, mental, and spiritual.

Conventional Ground Fighting Tools - Specific ground fighting techniques designed to control, restrain and temporarily incapacitate your adversary. Some conventional ground fighting tactics include: submission holds, locks, certain choking techniques, and specific striking techniques.

Cool-down - A series of light exercises and movements that immediately follow a workout. The purpose of the cool-down is to hasten the removal of metabolic wastes and gradually return the heart to its resting rate.

Coordination - A physical attribute characterized by the ability to perform a technique or movement with efficiency, balance, and accuracy.

Counterattack - Offensive action made to counter an assailant's initial attack.

Courage - A combative attribute. The state of mind and spirit that enables a fighter to face danger and vicissitudes with confidence, resolution, and bravery.

Courageousness - (See Courage).

Cover - Any object that protects you from gunfire.

Criminal Awareness - One of the three categories of CFA awareness. It involves a general understanding and knowledge of the nature and dynamics of a criminal's motivations, mentalities, methods, and capabilities to perpetrate violent crime. (see Situational Awareness and Self-Awareness.)

Criminal Justice - The study of criminal law and the procedures associated with its enforcement.

Criminology - The scientific study of crime and criminals.

Criss Cross - An entry maneuver which allows you to

travel across a threshold quickly while employing a correct ready weapon position.

Cross Stepping - The process of crossing one foot in front or behind the other when moving.

Crushing Tactics - Nuclear grappling range techniques designed to crush the assailant's anatomical targets.

Cutting Accuracy - The ability to cut your assailant with precision and exactness.

Cutting Makeshift Weapon - One of the four types of CFA makeshift weapons. Any object or implement that can be used to effectively stab or slash an assailant. (see also Distracting Makeshift Weapon, Shielding Makeshift Weapon, and Striking Makeshift Weapon.)

Cylinder - The part of a revolver that holds cartridges in individual chambers.

D

Deadly Force - Weapons or techniques that may result in imminent, unconsciousness, permanent disfigurement, or death.

Deadly Weapon - An instrument designed to inflict serious bodily injury or death (e.g., firearms, impact tools, edged weapons).

Deception - A combative attribute. A stratagem whereby you delude your assailant.

Decisiveness - A combative attribute. The ability to follow a tactical course of action that is unwavering and focused.

De-escalation - One of the five possible tactical responses to a threatening situation. The science and art of diffusing a hostile individual without resorting to physical force. (see Assert, Comply, Escape and Fight Back).

De-escalation Stance - One of the many strategic stances used in the CFA system. A strategic and non aggressive stance used when diffusing a hostile individual.

Defense - The ability to strategically thwart an assailant's attack (armed or unarmed).

Defensive Flow - A progression of continuous defensive responses. Defensive Mentality - A defensive mind-set.

Defensive Range Manipulation (DRM) - The strategic manipulation of ranges (armed or unarmed) for defensive purposes.

Defensive Reaction Time - The elapsed time between an assailant's physical attack and your defensive response to that attack (see Offensive Reaction Time).

Demeanor - One of the essential factors to consider when assessing a threatening individual. A person's outward behavior.

Dependency - The dangerous phenomenon of solely relying on a particular person, agency, instrument, device, tool, animal, or weapon for self-defense and personal protection.

Destructions - A technique that strikes the assailant's attacking limb.

Diet - A life-style of healthy eating.

Distance Gap - The spatial gap between the different ranges of armed and unarmed combat.

Distancing - The ability to quickly understand spatial relationships and how they relate to combat.

Distracting Makeshift Weapon - One of the four types of CFA makeshift weapons. An object that can be thrown into an assailant's face, body, or legs to distract him temporarily (see Cutting Makeshift Weapon, Striking Makeshift Weapon, and Shielding Makeshift Weapon.)

Distraction Tactics - Various verbal and physical tactics designed to distract your adversary.

Dojo - The Japanese term for "training hall."

Dominant Eye - The eye which is primarily used for aiming a firearm. The dominant eye is the one which is stronger and does more work.

Double-Action - A type of pistol action in which squeezing the trigger will both cock and release the hammer.

Drake Shooting - Shooting into places of likely cover.

Dry Firing - The process of shooting an unloaded firearm.

Duck - A defensive technique that permits you to evade your assailant's strike. Ducking is performed by dropping your body down and forward to avoid the assailant's blow.

E

Ectomorph - A body type classified by a high degree of slenderness, angularity, and fragility (see Endomorph and Mesomorph).

Effectiveness - One of the three criteria for a CFA body weapon, technique, tactic or maneuver. It means the ability to produce a desired effect (see Efficiency and Safety).

Efficiency - One of the three criteria for a CFA body weapon, technique, tactic or maneuver. It means the ability to reach an objective quickly and economically (see Effectiveness and Safety).

Ejector - The part of a pistol which ejects empty cartridge cases.

Embracing the Range - A ground fighting tactic whereby you pull or embrace your assailant.

Emotional Control - One of the nonverbal principles of strategic de-escalation. The ability to remain calm when faced with a hostile or threatening person.

Emotionless - A combative attribute. Being temporarily devoid of human feeling.

Endomorph - A body type classified by a high degree of

roundness, softness, and body fat (see Ectomorph and Mesomorph).

Entry Method - A method that permits you to safely enter a combat range. Entry Technique - A technique that permits you to safely enter a combat range.

Entry Tool - A tool that permits you to safely enter a combat range.

Escape - Also known as tactical retreat. One of the five possible tactical responses to a threatening situation. To flee rapidly from the threat or danger. (See Comply, De-Escalate, Assert and Fight Back).

Escape Routes - Various avenues or exits that permit you to escape from a threatening individual or situation.

Evasion - A defensive maneuver that allows you to strategically maneuver your body away from the assailant's strike.

Evasive Sidestepping - Evasive footwork where the practitioner moves to either the right or left side.

Evasiveness - A combative attribute. The ability of avoid threat or danger. Evolution - A gradual process of change.

Excessive Force - An amount of force that exceeds the need for a particular event and is unjustified in the eyes of the law.

Experimentation - The painstaking process of testing a combative hypothesis or theory.

Explosiveness - A combative attribute that is characterized by a sudden outburst of violent energy.

F

Fake - Body movements that disguise your attack. This includes movements of the eyes, head, shoulders, knees, feet and in some cases the voice.

Fatal Funnel - A danger area that is created by openings such as doorways, windows, hallways, stairwells, etc.

Feed - (See Attachment.)

Fear - A strong and unpleasant emotion caused by the anticipation or awareness of threat or danger. There are three stages of fear in order of intensity: Fright, Panic, and Terror. (see Fright, Panic, Terror).

Feeler - A tool that tests the assailant's reaction time and overall abilities.

Feint - A tool that draws an offensive reaction from the assailant, thereby opening him up for a real strike. Feints are different from fakes because they are performed through the movement of an actual limb.

Femoral Nerve - A pressure point area located approximately six inches above the knee on the inside of the thigh.

Fifth-Column Tactic: A deceptive self-defense strategy used to protect a third party by initially siding with the adversary to diffuse their aggression and lower their defenses. Through calculated verbal manipulation and non-threatening behavior, this tactic allows you to subtly position yourself for a preemptive strike while ensuring the safety of the individual you're protecting.

Fight Back - One of the five possible tactical responses to a threatening situation. To use various physical and psychological tactics to either incapacitate or terminate a criminal assailant. (See Comply, Escape, Assert and De-Escalate.)

Fighting Stance - One of the different types of stances used in CFA's system. A strategic posture you can assume when face-to-face with an unarmed assailant (s). (See De-escalation Stance, Knife Defense Stance, Knife Fighting Stance, Firearms Stance, Natural Stance, Stick Fighting Stance).

Fight-or-Flight Syndrome - A response of the sympathetic nervous system to a fearful and threatening situation, during which it prepares your body to either fight or flee from the perceived danger.

Finesse - A combative attribute. The ability to skillfully execute a movement or a series of movements with grace and refinement.

Firearm Follow Through - Continuing to employ the shooting fundaments throughout the delivery of your shot.

First Strike Principle (FSP) - A CFA principle which states that when physical danger is imminent and you have no other tactical option but to fight back, you should strike first, strike fast, strike with authority, and keep the pressure on.

Follow - A defensive technique used in the mid to long range of knife combat.

Formlessness - A principle that rejects the essence of structure or system.

Footwork - Quick, economical steps performed on the balls of the feet while you are relaxed, alert, and balanced. Footwork is structured around four general movements: forward, backward, right, and left.

Fractal Cognizance -Being knowledgeable and aware of the fractal ranges and tools of combat.

Fright - The first stage of fear; quick and sudden fear (see Panic and Terror).

G

Gemini Principle: A tactical approach in self-defense that utilizes strategic deception through verbal and nonverbal cues to manipulate an opponent's perception and lower their defenses. This method involves adopting a calm, non-threatening demeanor to distract the adversary, creating an optimal moment to execute a preemptive strike.

GLOSSARY

Grappling Range - One of the three ranges of unarmed combat. Grappling range is the closest distance of unarmed combat from which you can employ a wide variety of close-quarter tools and techniques. The grappling range of unarmed combat is also divided into two different planes: vertical (standing) and horizontal (ground fighting). (see Kicking Range and Punching Range).

Grappling Range Tools - The various body tools and techniques that are employed in the grappling range of unarmed combat, including head butts; biting, tearing, clawing, crushing, and gouging tactics; foot stomps, horizontal, vertical, and diagonal elbow strikes, vertical and diagonal knee strikes, chokes, strangles, joint locks, and holds. (see and Kicking Range Tools).

Grapevine - A stabilizing technique used during a ground fight. The grapevine can be applied when you have either one (single leg grapevine) or both (double leg grapevine) of your feet hooked around the assailant's legs.

Ground Fighting - Fighting that takes place on the ground. (Also known as horizontal grappling plane).

Guard - 1) A fighter's hand positioning. 2) One of the positions used in ground fighting. The guard is a scissors hold applied with the legs.

H

Hammer - The moving part of a gun causes the firing pin to strike the cartridge primer.

Hammer Grip - A hand grip used to hold an edged weapon, bludgeon and some makeshift weapons; assumed when the top of the bludgeon or the tip of the edged weapon is pointing upwards.

Handgun - A firearm that can be held and discharged with one hand. Hand Positioning - (See Guard.)

Hang fire - A perceptible delay in the ignition of a cartridge after the primer has been struck.

Head-Hunter - A fighter who focuses predominantly on targeting and attacking the opponent's head to incapacitate or gain a tactical advantage.

High-Line Kick - One of the two different classifications of a kick. A kick that is directed to targets above an assailant's waist level. (See Low-Line Kick)

Histrionics - The use of theatrics or exaggerated acting in self-defense to deceive, distract, or manipulate an opponent, enhancing one's strategic advantage in combat situations.

Homicide - The death of another person without legal justification of excuse.

Hook Kick - A circular kick that can be delivered in both kicking and punching ranges.

Hook Punch - A circular punch that can be delivered in both the punching and grappling ranges.

Hold - A specific manner of grasping or holding an assailant.

Human Shield - Using your assailant's body as a shield or obstacle in combat.

I

Ice Pick Grip - A hand grip used to hold an edged weapon, bludgeon and some makeshift weapons; assumed when the tip of the edged weapon or the top of the bludgeon is pointing downward.

Ice Pick Stick Strangle - A stick strangle used with an ice pick grip.

Immobilization Attack - One of the five conventional methods of attack. A highly complex system of moves and countermoves that allows you to temporarily control and manipulate the assailant's limbs (usually his arms and hands) in order to create an opening of attack.

Impact Power - The destructive force produced by the combination of mass and velocity, crucial for delivering powerful and effective strikes in combat

Impact Training - A training exercise that develops pain tolerance.

Incapacitate - To disable an assailant by rendering him unconscious or damaging his bones, joints or organs.

Indirect Attack - One of the five conventional methods of attack. A progressive method of attack whereby the initial tool or technique is designed to set the assailant up for follow-up blows.

Initiation Phase - One of the three stages of a stick or bludgeon strike. The initiation phase is initiation point of a swing.

Insertion Points - Specific anatomical targets you can stab with a knife and some makeshift weapons.

Inside Position - The area between both of your assailant's arms where he has the greatest amount of control.

Intent - One of the essential factors to consider when assessing a threatening individual. The assailant's purpose or motive (see Demeanor, Positioning, Range, and Weapon Capability).

Intuition - The innate ability to know or sense something without the use of rational thought.

Intuitive Tool Response (ITR) - Spontaneously reacting with the appropriate combative tool.

J

Jab - A quick, probing punch designed to create openings in the assailant's defense.

Joint Lock - A grappling range technique that immobilizes the assailant's joint.

Judo - "Gentle Way." A Japanese grappling art (founded by Jigoro Kano in 1882) which is used as a sport. Judo utilizes shoulder and hip throws, foot sweeps, chokes, and pins.

Jujitsu - "Gentleness" or "suppleness." A system of self-defense that is the parent of both Judo and Aikido. Jujitsu specializes in grappling range but is known to employ a few striking techniques.

K

Karate - "Empty hand" or "China hand," a traditional martial art that originated in Okinawa and later spread to Japan and Korea (see Kung-Fu).

Kata - "Pattern" or "Form". A traditional training methodology whereby the practitioner practices a series of prearranged movements.

Kick - 1) A sudden, forceful strike with the foot (see High-Line Kick and Low- Line Kick); 2) The recoil of a firearm.

Kick boxing - A popular combat sport that employs full-contact tools.

Kicking Range - One of the three ranges of unarmed combat. Kicking range is the furthest distance of unarmed combat wherein you use your legs to strike an assailant. (see Grappling Range and Punching Range).

Kicking Range Tools - The various body weapons employed in the kicking range of unarmed combat, including side kicks, push kicks, hook kicks, and vertical kicks.

Killer Instinct - A cold, primal mentality that surges to your consciousness and turns you into a vicious fighter.

Kinesics - The study of nonlinguistic body movement communications (i.e., eye movement, shrugs, facial gestures, etc.).

Kinesiology - The study of principles and mechanics of human movement.

Kinesthetic Perception - The ability to accurately feel your body during the execution of a particular movement.

Kneeling Firearm Stance - A strategic stance you assume when kneeling down with a handgun.

Knife-Defense Stance - One of the many stances used in CFA's system. A strategic stance you assume when face-to-face with an knife or edged weapon attacker. (See De-escalation Stance, Fighting Stance, Knife Fighting Stance, Firearms Stance, Natural Stance, Stick Fighting Stance).

Kung-Fu - "Accomplished task or effort," a term used erroneously to identify the traditional Chinese martial arts (see Karate).

L

Lead Side -The side of the body that faces an assailant.

Leg Block - A blocking technique used with the legs. The leg block can be angled in three different directions: forward, right and left.

Limited Penetration - The (LP) is a corner clearing movement performed by positioning your firearm and one eye around the corner.

Linear Movement - Movements that follow the path of a straight line.

Long Range Combat - The furthest distance of knife and bludgeon combat. At this distance you can only strike or slash your assailant's hand.

Low Maintenance Tool - Offensive and defensive tools that require the least amount of training and practice to maintain proficiency. Low maintenance tools generally don't require preliminary stretching.

Low-Line Kick - One of the two different classifications of a kick. A kick that is directed to targets below the assailant's waist level. (See High-Line Kick.)

Lock - (see Joint Lock).

Loyalty - The state of being faithful to a person, cause, or ideal.

M

Makeshift Weapon - A common everyday object that can be converted into either an offensive or defensive weapon. There are four Makeshift Weapon classifications in the CFA system: Cutting Makeshift Weapons, Shielding Makeshift Weapons, Distracting Makeshift Weapons, and Striking Makeshift Weapons.

Maneuver - To manipulate into a strategically desired position.

Manipulation Accuracy - The ability to manipulate your assailant's limbs and joints with precision and exactness.

Martial Artist - One who studies and practices the martial arts.

Martial Arts - The traditional "arts of war" (see Karate and Kung-Fu).

Martial Truth - (See Combative Truth.)

Mechanics - (See Body Mechanics.)

Meet - A defensive technique that intercepts your assailant's line of attack with a slash.

Mental Attributes - The various cognitive qualities that enhance your fighting skills.

Mental Component - One of the three vital components of the CFA system. The mental component includes the cerebral aspects of fighting including the Killer Instinct, Strategic & Tactical Development, Analysis & Integration, Philosophy and

Cognitive Development (see Physical Component and Spiritual Component).

Mesomorph - A body type classified by a high degree of muscularity and strength. (see Endomorph and Ectomorph).

Methods of Attack - The five conventionally recognized methods of attacking. They include: single attack, indirect attack, attack by draw, immobilization attack, and compound attack.

Mexican Standoff - A precarious situation where both you and your adversary have the drop on one another.

Mid Phase - One of the three stages of a stick swing. The mid phase is the contact or impact point of the swing.

Mid Range Combat - One of the three ranges of knife and bludgeon combat. At this distance you can strike, slash or stab your assailant's head, arms and body with your weapon.

Misfire - A failure of a cartridge to fire after the primer has been struck.

Mixed Martial Arts (MMA) - A full-contact combat sport that incorporates techniques from various martial arts disciplines, including striking, grappling, and submissions, allowing fighters to compete across multiple ranges of combat. While effective in controlled environments, MMA is not related to reality-based self-defense (RBSD), as it operates within a sport-based framework with rules and limitations not present in real-world combat.

Mobility - A combative attribute. The ability to move your body quickly and freely while balanced. (see Footwork).

Modern Martial Art - A pragmatic combat art that has evolved to meet the demands and characteristics of the present time.

Modification - To make fundamental changes to serve a new end.

Mounted Position - One of the five general ground fighting positions. The mounted position is where the practitioner sits on top of his assailant's torso or chest.

Muscular Endurance - The muscles' ability to perform the same motion or task repeatedly for a prolonged period of time.

Muscular Flexibility - The muscles' ability to move through maximum natural ranges.

Muscular Strength - The maximum force that can be exerted by a particular muscle or muscle group against resistance.

Muscular/Skeletal Conditioning - An element of physical fitness that entails muscular strength, endurance, and flexibility.

Muzzle - The front end of the barrel.

Muzzle Flash - An incandescent burst of light which is emitted from the muzzle and cylinder of a handgun.

N

Natural Stance - One of the many stances used in CFA's system. A strategic stance you assume when approached by a suspicious person who appears non threatening. (See De-escalation Stance, Fighting Stance, Knife Fighting Stance, Firearms Stance, Knife-Defense Stance, and Stick Fighting Stance).

Neutralize - (See Incapacitate.)

Neutral Zone - The distance outside of the kicking range from which neither the practitioner nor the assailant can touch the other.

Nomenclature Awareness - The ability to understand and recognize the system of names used in combat.

Non aggressive Physiology - Strategic body language used to de-escalate a potentially violent individual.

Non telegraphic Movement - Body mechanics or movements that do not inform an assailant of your intentions.

Nuclear Ground Fighting Tools - Specific grappling range tools designed to inflict immediate and irreversible damage. Some nuclear tools and tactics include: (1) Biting tactics; (2) Tearing tactics; (3) Crushing tactics; (4) Continuous Choking tactics; (5) Gouging techniques; (6) Raking tactics; (7) And all striking techniques.

O

OC (Oleoresin Capsicum, also known as pepper gas) - A natural mixture of oil and cayenne pepper used as a self-defense spray. OC is an inflammatory agent that affects the assailant's mucus membranes (i.e. eyes, nose, throat, lungs).

Offense - The armed and unarmed means and methods of attacking a criminal assailant.

Offensive Flow - A progression of continuous offensive movements or actions designed to neutralize or terminate your adversary. (see Compound Attack).

Offensive Range Manipulation (ORM) - The strategic manipulation of ranges (armed or unarmed) for offensive purposes.

Offensive Reaction Time (ORT) - The elapsed time between target selection and target impaction.

One-Hand Reloading - The process of reloading a firearm with only one hand.

One-Mindedness - A state of deep concentration wherein you are free from all distractions (internal and external).

Opposite Poles - One of the ground fighting positions. The opposite pole position is assumed when both you and your assailant are facing opposite directions. This often occurs when sprawling against your adversary.

Ornamental Techniques - Techniques that are

characterized as complex, inefficient, and or impractical for real combat situations.

P

Pain Tolerance - Your ability to physically and psychologically withstand pain.

Palming - The strategic concealment of a knife or edged weapon behind the forearm. Also known as Knife Palming.

Panic - The second stage of fear; overpowering fear (see Fright and Terror).

Parry - A defensive technique; a quick, forceful slap that redirects an assailant's linear attack.

Pass - A defensive technique used in knife fighting.

Patience - A combative attribute. The ability to endure and tolerate difficulty.

Perception - Interpretation of vital information acquired from your senses when faced with a potentially threatening situation.

Perpendicular Mount - One of the five general ground fighting positions. The perpendicular mount is established when you are lying on top of your adversary and both of your legs are on one side of his body.

Philosophical Resolution - The act of analyzing and answering various questions concerning the use of violence in defense of yourself and others.

Philosophy - One of the five aspects of CFA's mental component. A deep state of introspection whereby you methodically resolve critical questions concerning the use of force in defense of yourself or others.

Physical Attributes - The numerous physical qualities that enhance your combative skills and abilities.

Physical Component - One of the three vital components

of the CFA system. The physical component includes the physical aspects of fighting including Physical Fitness, Weapon/Technique Mastery, and Combative Attributes (see Mental Component and Spiritual Component).

Physical Conditioning - (See Combative Fitness).

Pistol - A gun with a short barrel that can be held, aimed, and fired with one hand.

Power - A physical attribute of armed and unarmed combat. The amount of force you can generate when striking an anatomical target.

Pitch - One of the four components of the human voice. The relative highness or lowness of the voice.

Poker Face - A neutral and attentive facial expression that is used when de- escalating a hostile individual. The poker face prevents a hostile person from reading your intentions or feelings.

Positioning - The spatial relationship of the assailant to the assailed person in terms of target exposure, escape, angle of attack, and various other strategic considerations.

Positions of Concealment - Various objects or locations that permit you to temporarily hide from your adversary. Positions of Concealment are most commonly used to evade engagement with your assailant(s) and they permit you to attack with the element of surprise. Positions of Concealment include: trees, shrubbery, behind doors, the dark, walls, stairwells, under cars, large and tall objects, etc.

Positions of Cover - Any object or location that temporarily protects you from the assailant's gun fire. Some Positions of Cover include: large concrete utility poles, large rocks, thick trees, an engine block, corner of a building, concrete steps, etc.

Post Traumatic Syndrome (PTS) - A group of symptoms that may occur in the aftermath of a violent confrontation with a criminal assailant. Common symptoms of Post Traumatic Syndrome include denial, shock, fear, anger, severe depression, sleeping and eating disorders, societal withdrawal, and paranoia.

Power Generator - (See Anatomical Power Generators)

Predictable Visceral Response (PVR) - describes the instinctual, immediate reactions triggered by a tactical bite.

Premise - An axiom, concept, rule or any other valid reason to modify or go beyond that which has been established.

Pressure Point - A specific area on the body where a nerve lies near the surface, often supported by bone or muscle, that can be targeted to cause pain, incapacitation, or disruption of bodily function.

Probable Reaction Dynamics (PRD) - The anticipated or predicted movements and responses of an opponent immediately after being struck, helping fighters exploit these reactions to maintain control and effectively neutralize the threat.

Probe -A offensive tool that tests the assailant's combative abilities.

Proficiency Training - A CFA training methodology requiring the practitioner to execute a specific body weapon, technique, maneuver or tactic over and over for a prescribed number or repetitions (see Conditioning Training and Street Training).

Progressive Indirect Attack -(see Indirect Attack).

Proxemics - The study of the nature and effect of man's personal space.

Proximity - The ability to maintain a strategically safe distance from a threatening individual.

Pseudospeciation - A combative attribute. The tendency to assign subhuman and inferior qualities to a threatening assailant.

Psychological Conditioning - The process of conditioning the mind for the horrors and rigors of real combat.

Psycho/Emotional Training - Combative training conducted when you're experiencing different types of emotional states.

Psychomotor Domain - This includes the physical skills and attributes necessary to execute a combative tool, technique or maneuver.

Psychopath - A person with an antisocial personality disorder, especially one manifested in aggressive, perverted, criminal, or amoral behavior.

Pummel - A flurry of full-speed, full-force strikes delivered from the top mounted position.

Punch - A quick, forceful strike of the fists.

Punching Range - One of the three ranges of unarmed combat. Punching range is the mid range of unarmed combat from which the fighter uses his hands to strike his assailant. (see Kicking Range and Grappling Range)

Punching Range Tools - The various body weapons that are employed in the punching range of unarmed combat, including finger jabs, palm heel strikes, rear cross, knife hand strikes, horizontal and shovel hooks, uppercuts, and hammer fist strikes. (see Grappling Range Tools and Kicking Range Tools)

Q

Qualities of Combat - (see Attributes of Combat).

Quick Peek - A technique which is executed from a position of cover by rapidly darting out a small portion of your head and one eye to quickly observe.

R

Range - The spatial relationship between a fighter and a threatening assailant.

Range Deficiency - The inability to effectively fight and defend in all ranges (armed and unarmed) of combat.

Range Manipulation - A combative attribute. The strategic manipulation of combat ranges.

Range Proficiency - A combative attribute. The ability to effectively fight and defend in all ranges (armed and unarmed) of combat.

Ranges of Armed Combat - The various distances a fighter might physically engage with an assailant while involved in armed combat: including knives, bludgeons, projectiles, make-shift weapons, and firearms.)

Ranges of Engagement - (See Combat Ranges).

Ranges of Unarmed Combat - The three distances a fighter might physically engage with an assailant while involved in unarmed combat: kicking range, punching range, and grappling range.

Reaction Dynamics - The assailant's physical response to a specific tool, technique, or weapon after initial contact is made, which can be analyzed to anticipate and exploit subsequent movements.

Reaction Time - The elapsed time between a stimulus and the response to that particular stimulus (see Offensive Reaction Time and Defensive Reaction Time).

Reality Based Self-Defense (RBSD) - A generic term that describes practical methods focused on real-world self-defense scenarios, emphasizing survival in violent, unpredictable encounters. While RBSD defines the overall approach, specific systems like Contemporary Fighting Arts (CFA) embody and implement its principles as both an art and a science of combat, offering a comprehensive and structured method for real-world self-defense.

Rear Cross - A straight punch delivered from the rear hand that crosses from right to left (if in a left stance) or left to right (if in a right stance).

Rear Side - The side of the body furthest from the assailant (see Lead Side).

Reasonable Force - That degree of force which is not excessive for a particular event and which is appropriate in protecting yourself or others.

Refinement - The strategic and methodical process of improving or perfecting.

Repetition - Performing a single movement, exercise, strike or action continuously for a specific period.

Research - A scientific investigation or inquiry.

Rest Position - A relaxed posture you assume (when holding a stick or bludgeon) during idle periods in class (i.e., talking to another students, receiving instructions, etc.).

Reverberation Path - The path at which your stick or bludgeon can bounce back at you.

Revolver - A handgun consisting of a cylinder that brings several chambers successively into line with the barrel of the gun.

Rhythm - Movements characterized by the natural ebb and flow of related elements.

Right to Bear Arms - A provision of the Second Amendment to the United States Constitution that protects the individual's right to possess and carry weapons for personal defense, prohibiting government interference with the people's ability to arm themselves.

Rimfire - A firearm cartridge which has its primer located around the rim of the case bottom.

S

Safe Room - A strategic location in your residence where you and family members can escape from an intruder who has entered your home.

Safety - One of the three criteria for a CFA body weapon, technique, maneuver or tactic. It means the that the tool, technique, maneuver or tactic provides the least amount of danger and risk for the practitioner (see Efficiency and Effectiveness).

Savage Street Fighting - A radical self-defense system designed to teach law-abiding citizens how to apply "tactical savagery" in response to imminent deadly criminal attacks. The program centers around four vicious zero-beat techniques, enabling swift and brutal counterattacks to neutralize threats with uncompromising efficiency.

Scissors Hold - (see Guard).

Secondary Hand - A close quarter technique used in both knife and bludgeon fighting whereby you temporarily hold your assailant's weapon hand in place after you have employed a defensive maneuver.

Secondary Weapons - Various natural body weapons that are applied during armed combat.

Selective Semantics - The selection and utilization of strategic words to de-escalate a hostile person. Also known as Choice Words.

Self-Awareness - One of the three categories of CFA awareness. Knowing and understanding yourself. This includes aspects of yourself which may provoke criminal violence and which will promote a proper and strong reaction to an attack. (see Criminal Awareness and Situational Awareness.)

Self-Confidence - Having trust and faith in yourself.

Self-Defense - The act of defending yourself or one's family (also called Personal Protection or Self-Protection).

Self-Enlightenment - The state of knowing your capabilities, limitations, character traits, feelings, general attributes, and motivations (see Self- Awareness.)

Semiautomatic Handgun - (see Autoloader).

Set - A term used to describe a grouping of repetitions.

Setup Tool - A tool used to throw the assailant off balance and/or open his defenses.

Shadow Fighting - A CFA training exercise used to develop and refine your tools, techniques, and attributes of armed and unarmed combat.

Shielding Makeshift Weapon - One of the four types of CFA makeshift weapons. Any object that can be used to effectively shield oneself from an assailant's attack (see also Distracting Makeshift Weapon, Cutting Makeshift Weapon, and Striking Makeshift Weapon.)

Shooting Accuracy - The ability to shoot a firearm with precision and exactness.

Shot - A package or wad of metal balls that vary in size and spread out as they travel away from the muzzle of a shot gun.

Shotgun - A single-or double-barreled, smooth-bore firearm used for firing shot or slugs at a relatively close distance.

Shoulder Roll - A defensive technique that rocks your body away from a punch in order to nullify its force.

Side Fall - A firearm engagement technique which is executed from a kneeling position behind cover.

Sight Alignment - A component of marksmanship whereby you correctly align your dominant eye with both the front and rear sights of your firearm.

Sights - Various electronic, optical, and mechanical

devices used to aim a firearm.

Single Action - A type of pistol action in which pulling the trigger will release the hammer.

Single Attack - One of the five conventional methods of attack. A method of attack whereby you deliver a solitary offensive strike. It may involve a series of discreet probes or one swift, powerful strike aimed at terminating the encounter. (See Compound Attack, Indirect Attack, Immobilization Attack, and Attack By Draw).

Situational Awareness - One of the three categories of CFA awareness. A state of being totally alert to your immediate surroundings, including people, places, objects, and actions. (see Criminal Awareness and Self-Awareness.)

Skeletal Alignment - The proper alignment or arrangement of your body. Skeletal Alignment maximizes the structural integrity of striking tools.

Slash - One of the two ways to cut someone with a knife or edged weapon. A quick, sweeping stroke of a knife (see Stab.)

Slipping - A defensive maneuver that permits you to avoid an assailant's linear blow without stepping out of range. Slipping can be accomplished by quickly snapping the head and upper torso sideways (right or left) to avoid the blow.

Snap Back - A defensive maneuver that permits you to avoid an assailant's linear and circular blow without stepping out of range. The snap back can be accomplished by quickly snapping the head backwards to avoid the assailant's blow.

Somatotyping - A method of classifying human body types or builds into three different categories: ectomorph, mesomorph, and endomorph.

Speed - A physical attribute of armed and unarmed combat. The rate or a measure of the rapid rate of motion.

Spiritual Component - One of the three vital components of the CFA system. The spiritual component includes the metaphysical issues and aspects of existence (see Physical Component and Mental Component).

Sprawling - A defensive technique in grappling range. The sprawl technique is accomplished by lowering your hips to the ground while simultaneously shooting both of your legs back.

Square-Off - The act of facing a hostile or threatening assailant directly, often preceding an imminent attack or confrontation.

Squib Load - A cartridge which develops less than normal velocity after the ignition of a cartridge.

Stab - One of the two ways to cut someone with a knife or edged weapon. A quick thrust made with a pointed weapon or implement, usually a knife. (see Slash.)

Stable Terrain - Terrain which is principally characterized as stationary, compact, dense, hard, flat, dry, or solid.

Stance - One of the many strategic postures that you assume prior to or during armed or unarmed combat.

Stance Selection - A combative attribute involving the ability to instinctively choose the most effective stance for a given combat situation, ensuring optimal balance, mobility, and readiness.

Standing Firearm Stance - A strategic stance you assume when standing with a handgun.

Step and Drag - Strategic footwork used when standing on unstable terrain. Stick Block - A defensive technique that stops your assailant's stick strike.

Stick Deflection - A defensive technique that deflects and redirects your assailant's stick strike.

Stopping Power - A firearm's ability to stop the assailant from continuing any further action.

Strategic Leaning - A defensive maneuver which permits you to evade a knife slash while remaining in range to counter.

Strategic Positioning - Tactically positioning yourself to either escape, move behind a barrier, or use a makeshift weapon.

Strategy - A carefully planned method of achieving your goal of engaging an assailant under advantageous conditions.

Street Fight - A spontaneous, violent confrontation between two or more individuals where no rules or regulations apply, often occurring in uncontrolled environments with unpredictable outcomes.

Street Fighter - An unorthodox combatant lacking formal training, whose combative skills and tactics are typically developed through real-life encounters and a process of trial and error in street environments.

Street Smarts - Having the knowledge, skills and attitude necessary to avoid, defuse, confront, and neutralize both armed and unarmed assailants.

Street Training - A CFA training methodology requiring the practitioner to deliver explosive compound attacks for ten to twenty seconds (see Conditioning Training and Proficiency Training).

Strength Training - The process of developing muscular strength through systematic application of progressive resistance.

Striking Accuracy - The ability to strike your assailant with precision and exactness (this includes natural body weapons, bludgeons and some makeshift weapons).

Striking Art - A combat art that relies predominantly on striking techniques to neutralize or terminate a criminal attacker.

Striking Tool - 1) A natural body weapon that impacts with the assailant's anatomical target. 2) A hand-held implement that impacts with the assailant's anatomical target.

Striking Makeshift Weapon - One of the four types of CFA makeshift weapons. Any object that can be used to effectively strike a criminal assailant (see also Distracting Makeshift Weapon, Cutting Makeshift Weapon, and Shielding Makeshift Weapon.)

Strong Side - The strongest and most coordinated side of your body. Structure - A definite and organized pattern.

Style - The distinct manner in which a fighter executes or performs his combat skills.

Stylistic Integration - The purposeful and scientific collection of tools and techniques from various disciplines, which are strategically integrated and dramatically altered to meet three essential criteria: efficiency, effectiveness, and combative safety.

System - The unification of principles, philosophies, rules, strategies, methodologies, tools, and techniques or a particular method of combat.

T

Tactical Calming - (See De-Escalation.)

Tactic - The skill of using the available means to achieve an end.

Tactical Option Selection - A combative attribute. The ability to select the appropriate tactical option for any particular self-defense situation.

Tactile Sight - A combative attribute. The ability to "see" through tactile contact with your assailant.

Takedowns -Various grappling maneuvers designed to take your assailant down to the ground.

Target Exploitation - A combative attribute. The strategic maximization of your assailant's reaction dynamics during a fight. Target Exploitation can be applied in both armed and unarmed encounters.

Target Impaction - The successful striking of the appropriate anatomical target.

Target Orientation - A combative attribute. Having a workable knowledge of the assailant's anatomical targets. Target orientation is divided into five different categories: (1) Impact Targets - anatomical targets that can be struck with your natural body weapons; (2) Non-Impact Targets - anatomical targets that can be strangled, twisted, torn, crushed, clawed, gouged, broken, dislocated, or strategically manipulated; (3) Edged Weapon Targets - anatomical targets that can be punctured or slashed with a knife or edged weapon; (4) Bludgeon Targets - anatomical targets that can be struck with a stick or bludgeon; (5) Ballistic Targets - anatomical targets that can be shot by a firearm.

Target Recognition - The ability to immediately recognize appropriate anatomical targets during an emergency self-defense situation.

Target Selection - The process of mentally selecting the appropriate anatomical target for your self-defense situation. This is predicated on certain factors, including proper force response, assailant's positioning and range.

Target Stare - A form of telegraphing whereby you stare at the anatomical target you intend to strike.

Target Zones - The three areas which an assailant's anatomical targets are located. (See Zone One, Zone Two and Zone Three)

Technique - A systematic procedure by which a task is accomplished.

Telegraphic Cognizance - A combative attribute. The ability to recognize both verbal and non-verbal signs of aggression or assault.

Telegraphing - Unintentionally making your intentions known to your adversary. Tempo - The speed or rate at which you speak.

Terrain - The type of surface that you are standing on. There are two classifications of terrain: stable and unstable. (See Stable Terrain and Unstable Terrain)

Terrain Orientation - A combative attribute. Having a working knowledge of the various types of environmental terrains and their advantages, dangers, and strategic limitations.

Terror - The third stage of fear; defined as overpowering fear. (see Fright and Panic)

Throw - Grappling techniques designed to unbalance your assailant and lift him off the floor.

Timing - A physical and mental attribute or armed and unarmed combat. Your ability to execute a movement at the optimum moment.

Tone - The overall quality or character of your voice.

Tool - (See Body Weapon.)

Traditional Style/System - (See Traditional Martial Art.)

Traditionalism - The beliefs and principles of a traditional or classical martial art.

Traditionalist - One who subscribes to the principles and practices of traditional martial arts.

Traditional Martial Arts - Any martial art that fails to evolve and meet the demands and characteristics of the present time. (see Karate and Kung-Fu)

Training Drills - The various exercises and drills aimed at perfecting combat skills, attributes, and tactics.

Training Methodologies - Training procedures utilized in the CFA system.

Training Zone - The training zone (or target heart rate) is a safe and effective level of physical activity that produces cardiorespiratory fitness.

Trapping - Momentarily immobilizing or manipulating the

assailant's limb or limbs in order to create an opening to attack.

Trapping Range - The distance between punching and grappling range in which trapping techniques are attempted.

Traversing Skills - Pivoting and twisting laterally. Traversing skills can be used for both armed and unarmed combat.

Trigger Squeeze - A component of marksmanship. Trigger Squeeze is achieved by squeezing the trigger of your firearm straight to the rear in a smooth and fluid manner without disturbing the sight alignment.

Trouble Shooting Skills - A combative attribute. The ability to immediately diagnose and solve problems when engaged with the adversary.

U

Unified Mind - A mind which is free and clear of distractions and focused on the combative situation.

Unstable Terrain - Terrain which is characterized as mobile, uneven, flexible, slippery, wet, or rocky. (See Stable Terrain)

Unstructured Modernist - A martial artist who adheres to the abstract principles of combative formlessness.

Use of Force Response - A combative attribute. Selecting the appropriate level of force for a particular emergency self-defense situation.

V

V-Grip - A strategically defensive grip used to defend against an edged weapon attack.

Vertical Trapping - Trapping techniques that are applied while standing face to face with your adversary. (See Immobilization Attack)

Viciousness - A combative attribute. Dangerously aggressive behavior. Victim - Any person who is the object of a particular crime.

Visualization - The purposeful formation of mental images and scenarios in the mind's eye.

Visual Monitoring Points - Specific points or locations on your assailant that you should look at during an emergency self-defense situation.

W

Warm-up - A series of mild exercises, stretches, and movement designed to prepare you for more intense exercise.

Weak Side - The weakest and most uncoordinated side of your body.

Weapon and Technique Mastery - A component of CFA's physical component. The kinesthetic and psychomotor development of a weapon or combative technique.

Weapon Capability - An assailant's ability to use and attack with a particular weapon.

Weapon Hierarchy Mastery - Possessing the knowledge, skills and attitude necessary to master the complete hierarchy of combat weapons.

Weapon Uniformity - Gripping and/or drawing your hand-held weapon the same way every time.

Webbing - The first phase of the Widow Maker Program. Webbing is a two hand strike delivered to the assailant's chin. It is called Webbing because your hands resemble a large web that wraps around the enemy's face.

Wicked Jester: A symbolic figure within the Contemporary Fighting Arts (CFA) system, representing the duality of chaos and control in combat. The Wicked Jester embodies cunning, unpredictability, and psychological manipulation, traits that align with CFA's unconventional self-defense tactics. It serves as a reminder that in the face of violent encounters, mastery of deception, strategy, and controlled aggression can turn the tables on an opponent, much like the jester's calculated mischief in court.

Widow Maker Program – A specialized CFA program designed to equip law-abiding citizens with the skills to apply extreme force in response to imminent, unlawful deadly attacks. The program is structured in two distinct phases: Webbing and Razing.

Y

Yell - A loud and aggressive scream or shout used for various strategic reasons.

Z

Zero Beat – One of the four beat classifications of the Widow Maker, Feral Fighting and Savage Street Fighting Programs. Zero beat strikes are full pressure techniques applied to a specific target until ruptures. They include gouging, crushing, biting, and choking techniques.

Zone One - Anatomical targets related to your senses, including the eyes, temple, nose, chin, and back of neck.

Zone Three - Anatomical targets related to your mobility, including thighs, knees, shins, and instep.

Zone Two - Anatomical targets related to your breathing, including front of neck, solar plexus, ribs, and groin.

Zoning - A defensive maneuver designed to negate your assailant's stick strike through strategic movement and precise timing. Zoning can be accomplished by either moving into the direction of your assailant's strike (before it generates significant force) or by moving completely out of his stick's arc.

About Sammy Franco

With over three and a half decades of experience, Sammy Franco is widely recognized as one of the preeminent global authorities in both armed and unarmed self-defense. Esteemed as a leading innovator within the field of combat sciences, Mr. Franco stands as a pioneer in the development of reality-based self-defense (RBSD) methodologies and martial arts pedagogy.

Mr. Franco is most notably acknowledged as the architect and founder of Contemporary Fighting Arts (CFA), an advanced, offensive-based combat system meticulously engineered for real-world self-defense applications. The CFA system is a sophisticated and pragmatic framework designed to equip practitioners with the tactical knowledge and physical skills required to avert, de-escalate, engage, and neutralize a range of adversaries—both armed and unarmed.

Throughout his distinguished career, Mr. Franco has been featured prominently in various martial arts publications, newspapers, and has appeared on numerous radio and television broadcasts. In addition to his media presence, Mr. Franco has authored over 60 books, numerous magazine articles, and editorials, alongside developing a comprehensive library of instructional videos.

Sammy Franco's authority within the combat sciences is unparalleled. Among his many notable achievements, he holds the prestigious designation of Law Enforcement Master Instructor, having developed and delivered officer survival training programs to the United States Border Patrol (USBP). He has also instructed members of the U.S. Secret Service,

Military Special Forces, the Washington D.C. Police Department, Montgomery County Deputy Sheriffs, and the U.S. Library of Congress Police. Furthermore, Mr. Franco has been a respected member of the International Law Enforcement Educators and Trainers Association (ILEETA) and the American Society of Law Enforcement Trainers (ASLET), and is listed in the "Who's Who Directory of Law Enforcement Instructors."

In addition to his law enforcement contributions, Mr. Franco holds national certification as a Law Enforcement Instructor in several specialized areas, including the PR-24 Side-Handle Baton, Police Arrest and Control Procedures, Police Personal Weapons Tactics, Police Power Handcuffing Methods, Oleoresin Capsicum Aerosol Training (OCAT), Weapon Retention and Disarming Methods, Edged Weapon Countermeasures, and Use of Force Assessment and Response Strategies.

Mr. Franco's academic credentials include a Bachelor of Arts degree in Criminal Justice from the University of Maryland. He is also a regularly invited speaker at prominent professional conferences and delivers compelling, informative seminars on various dimensions of self-defense and combat training.

Beyond his professional accomplishments, Mr. Franco is deeply committed to animal welfare, often taking extraordinary measures to assist and rescue animals in need. His personal efforts have involved the rescue of a diverse range of species, from turkey vultures to goats.

For further information about Mr. Franco and his contributions to the field of self-defense, please visit his official website at: https://ContemporaryFightingArts.com

www.ingramcontent.com/pod-product-compliance
Lightning Source LLC
Chambersburg PA
CBHW071405090426
42737CB00011B/1354